CEAWLIN

CEAWLIN

The Man Who Created England

by

Rupert Matthews

Pen & Sword
MILITARY

First published in Great Britain in 2012 by
Pen & Sword Military
an imprint of
Pen & Sword Books Ltd
47 Church Street
Barnsley
South Yorkshire
S70 2AS

ISBN 978 1 84884 676 0

A CIP catalogue record for this book is available from the British Library

Typeset in Sabon by
Phoenix Typesetting, Auldgirth, Dumfriesshire

Printed and bound in England by
CPI Group (UK) Ltd, Croydon, CR0 4YY

Pen & Sword Books Ltd incorporates the Imprints of Pen & Sword Aviation, Pen & Sword Family History, Pen & Sword Maritime, Pen & Sword Military, Pen & Sword Discovery, Wharncliffe Local History, Wharncliffe True Crime, Wharncliffe Transport, Pen & Sword Select, Pen & Sword Military Classics, Leo Cooper, The Praetorian Press, Remember When, Seaforth Publishing and Frontline Publishing

For a complete list of Pen & Sword titles please contact
PEN & SWORD BOOKS LIMITED
47 Church Street, Barnsley, South Yorkshire, S70 2AS, England
E-mail: enquiries@pen-and-sword.co.uk
Website: www.pen-and-sword.co.uk

Contents

Part III: England and the English

I would like to dedicate this book
to my daughter Boadicea.

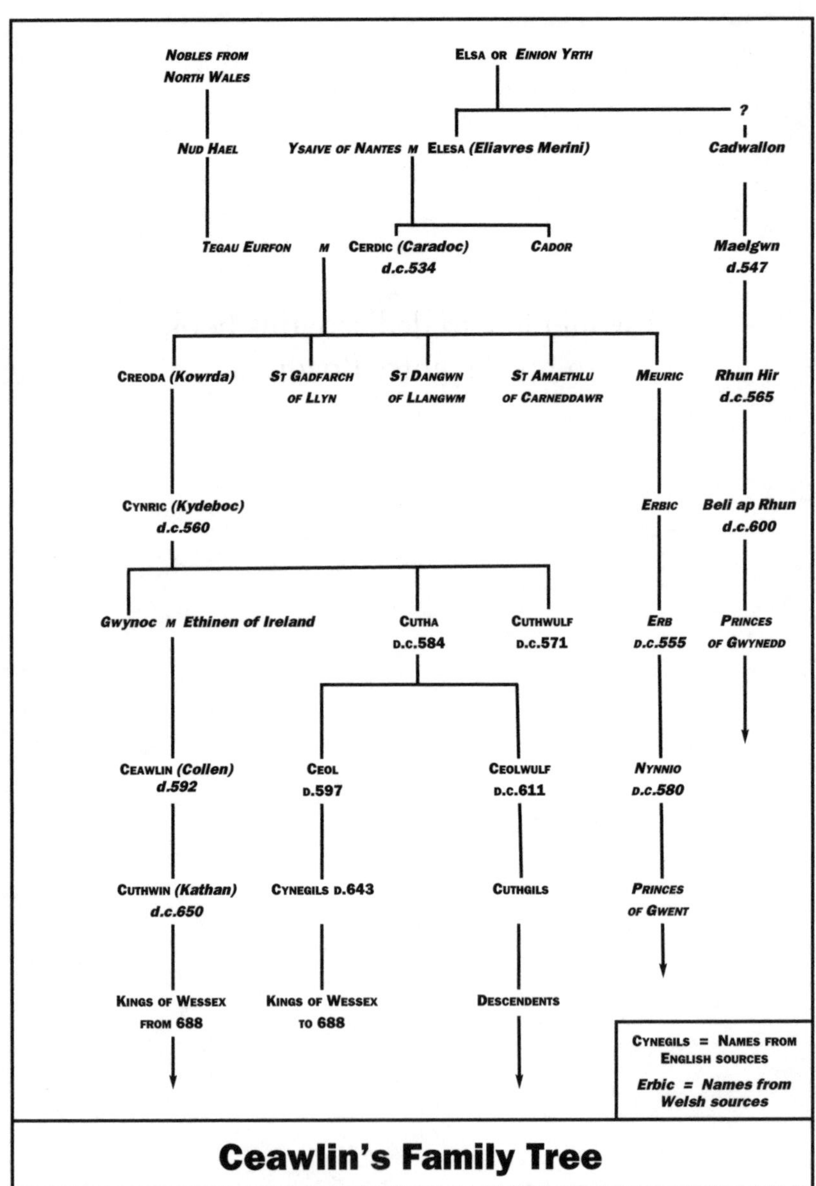

Ceawlin's Family Tree

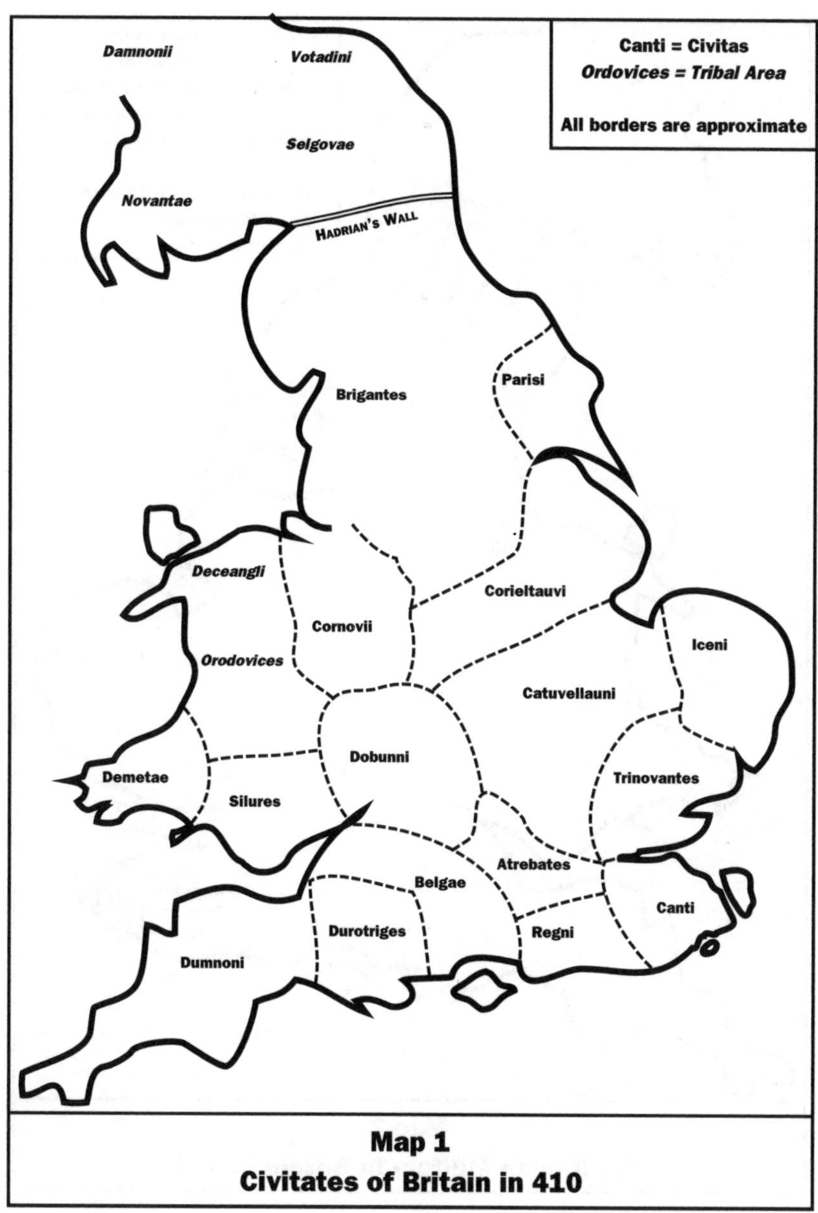

Map 1
Civitates of Britain in 410

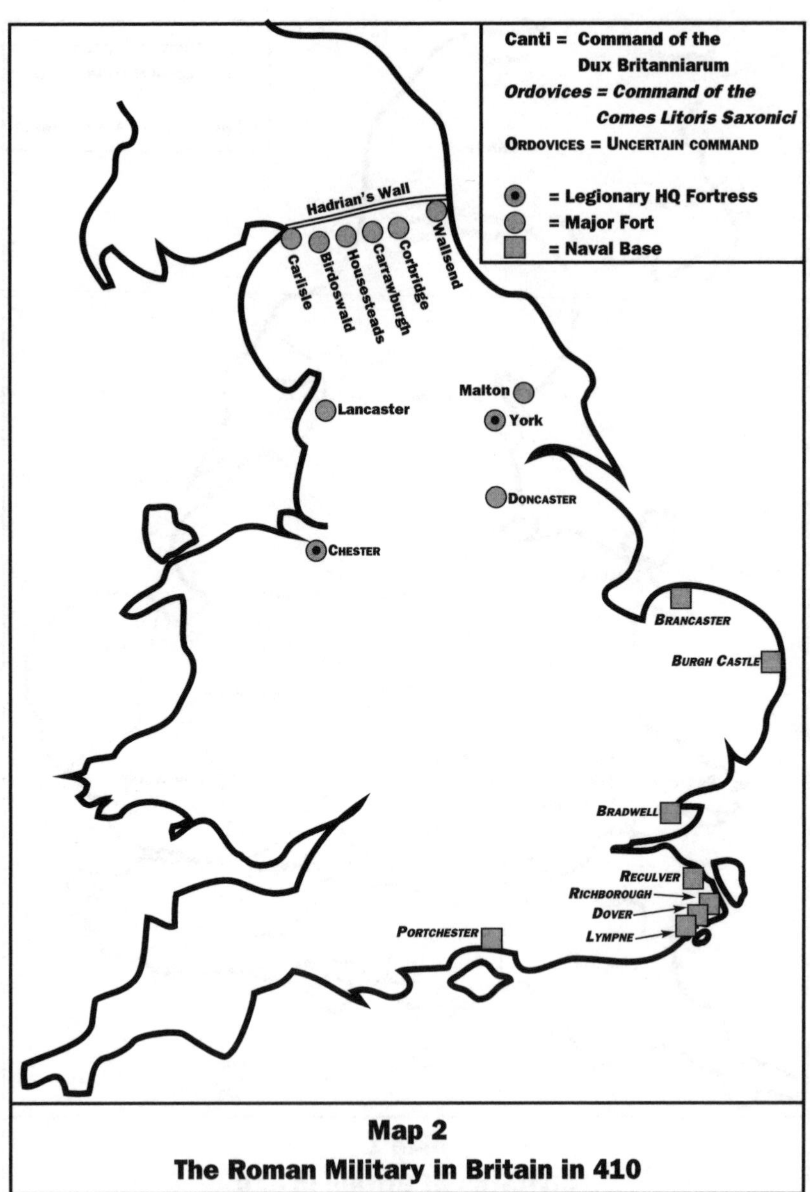

Map 2
The Roman Military in Britain in 410

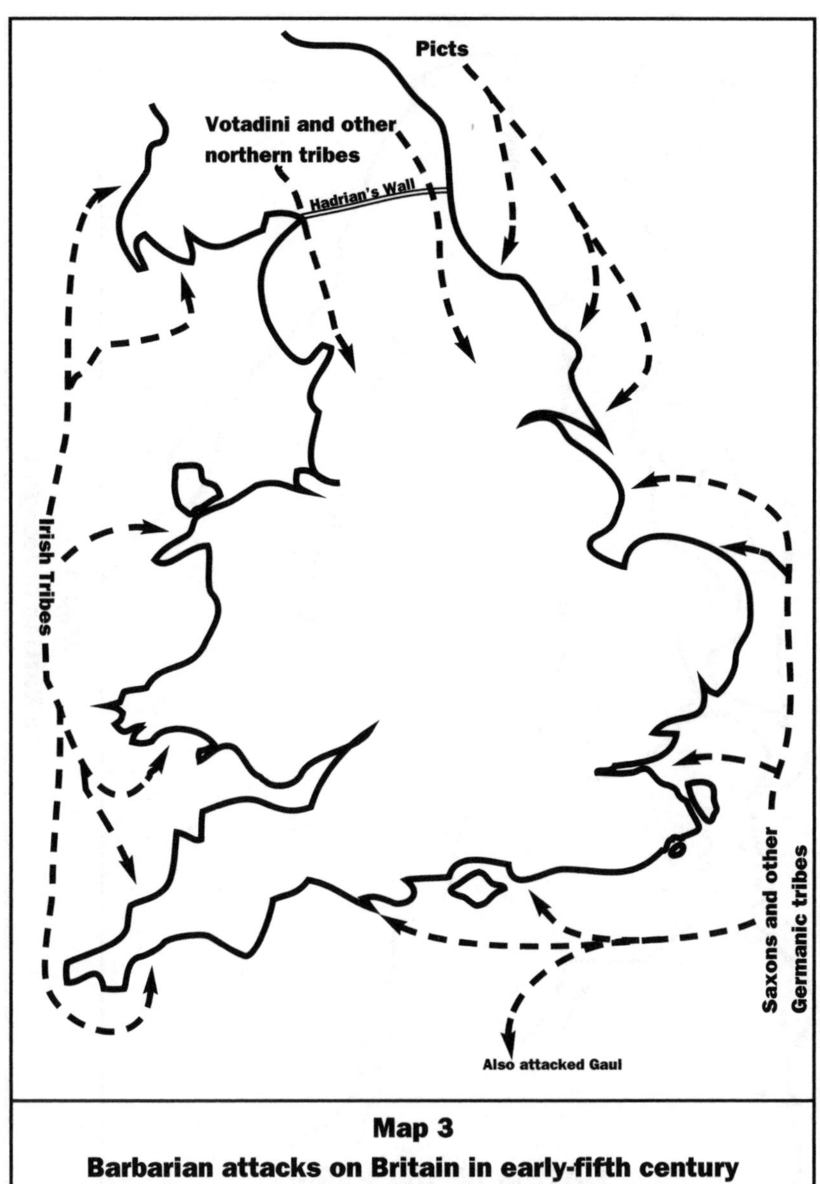

Map 3
Barbarian attacks on Britain in early-fifth century

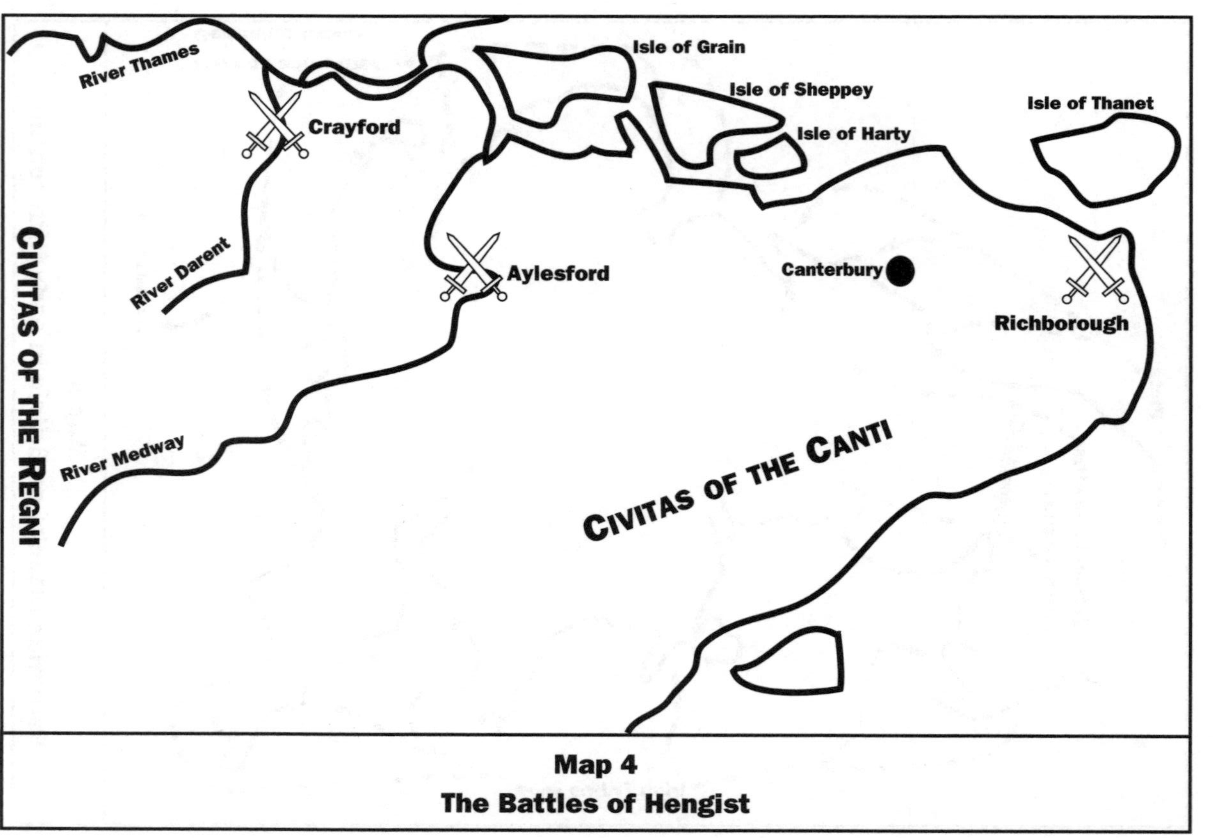

Map 4
The Battles of Hengist

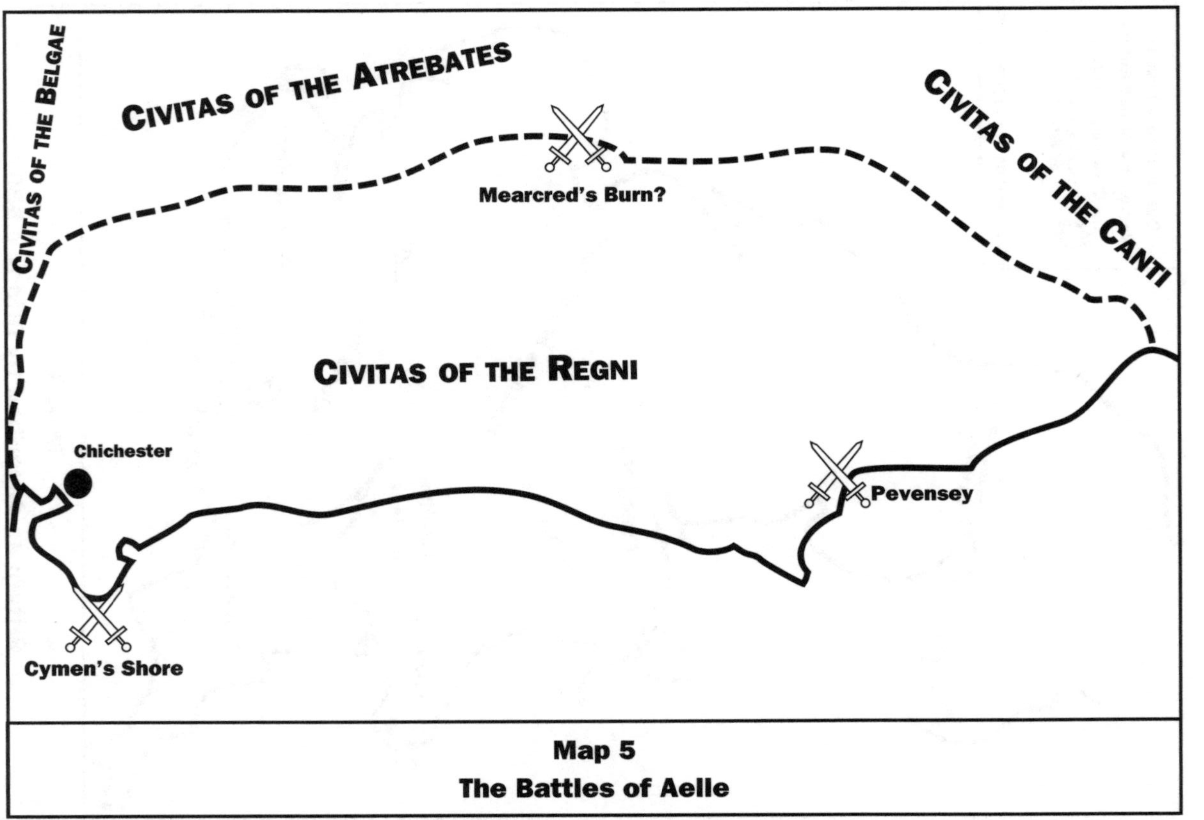

Map 5
The Battles of Aelle

Map 6
Britain as described by Gildas c.530

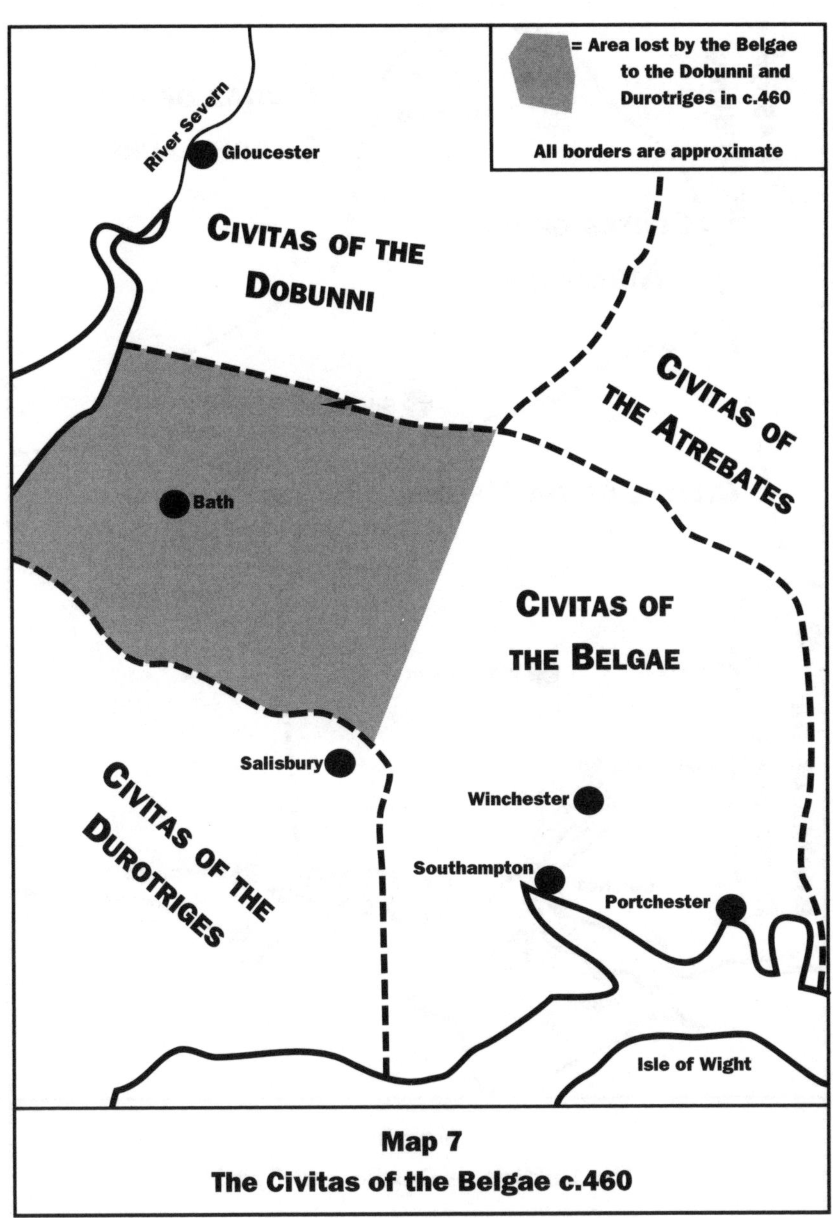

Map 7
The Civitas of the Belgae c.460

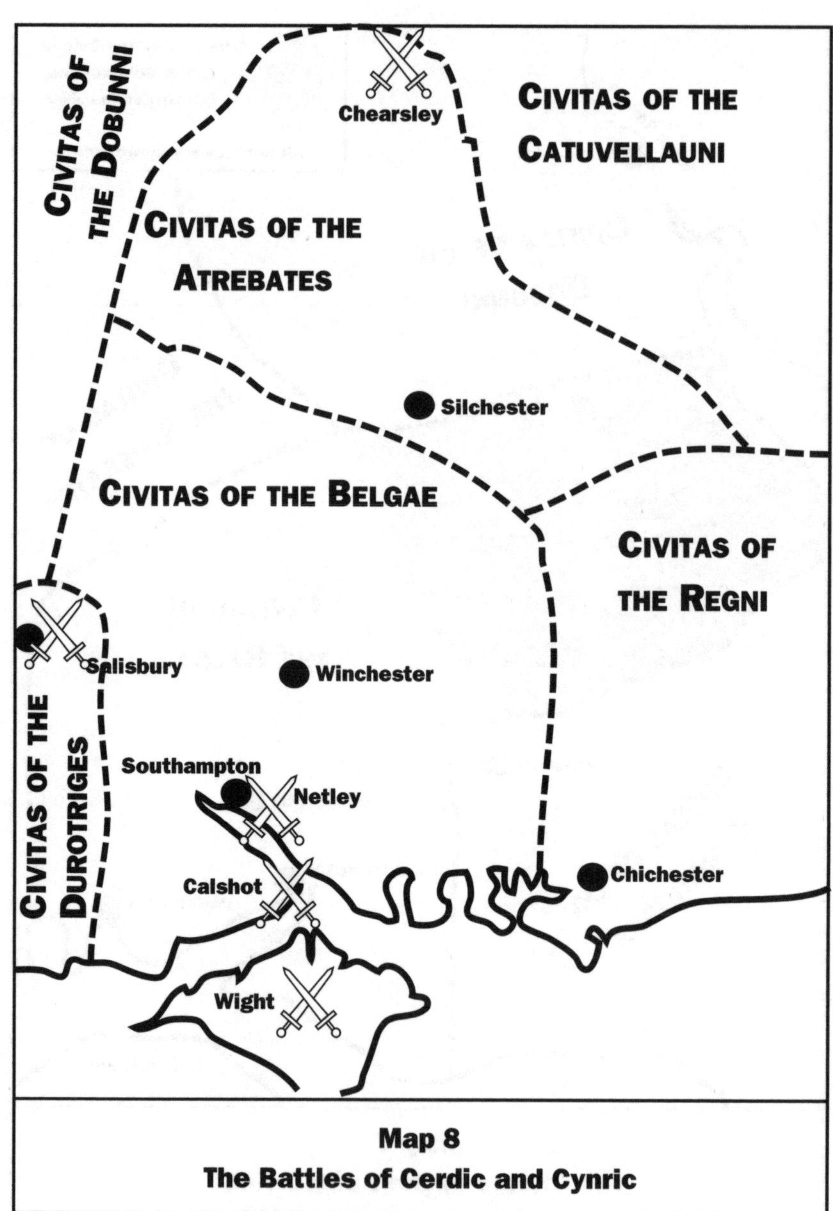

Map 8
The Battles of Cerdic and Cynric

Map 9
The Battles of Ceawlin

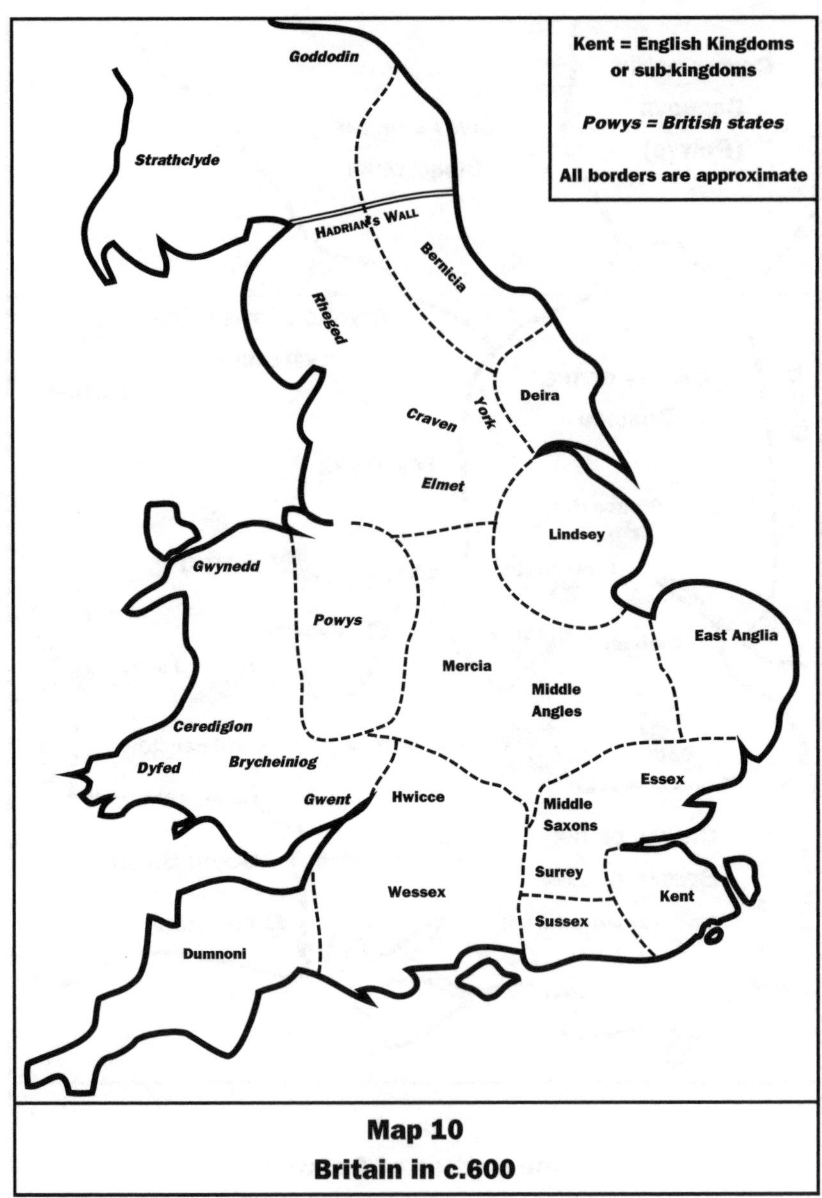

Map 10
Britain in c.600

Preface

When I was about nine years old we went down to Somerset to stay with relatives who had a place in Bath. I suppose that they had to think of something to entertain a boy with lots of energy, so we went out and climbed Solsbury Hill to explore the ancient hillfort up there.

I loved it.

I can't recall the order we did things in, but I know we went up to look at Wansdyke on the hills just south of Bath, then to the north to wander over the battlefield of Lansdown. I did not really appreciate it then, but I was wandering over some two millennia of British history. On subsequent visits to Bath we roamed farther afield – to Uffington, Bratton, Barbury, Sarum and other places.

It was not until some years later that I learned how all these different monuments, ruins and fortresses fitted together into our island story. And by then I was totally hooked on history. I read voraciously about Celts, Romans, Saxons, Vikings and Normans. Later I learned the more subtle distinctions between the ages of our history, the continuities as well as the changes.

But there was one period that fascinated me. As an Englishman I always wondered where the English had come from. So far as conventional wisdom had it, the Celts had always been here, the Romans came from Rome, the Vikings from Denmark and Norway and the Normans from Normandy. But the English? Nobody really knew. There were Angles and Saxons and Jutes from assorted places in northern Europe, but how they had become English was obscure.

And there was another puzzle. Across all the Roman Empire the people today speak languages descended from Latin or their own native language. But in Britain people speak neither a Latin- nor a Celtic-based language. They speak English.

I wondered over the puzzle. Clearly something had happened here that did not happen in France, Spain or Italy. It must have been something dramatic and sweeping, but what it was had been hidden by the destruction of written records wrought at the time – perhaps by the very event that had created the English.

Over the years I have picked up clues here and there. I have come up with a theory as to what happened, why it happened and how it came to have such a profound effect. This book is the result.

No doubt many will disagree with me, but that is their privilege. Hopefully it will spark debate and we will start to get closer to what went on in those lost centuries when the English came into existence.

Rupert Matthews

CEAWLIN

Introduction

Something happened in Britain in the third quarter of the sixth century. That event moulded the nations of Great Britain that we know today: the English, Welsh and the Cornish, and to a lesser extent the Scots. What that event was has always been something of a mystery. The political turmoil, economic collapse and bloody violence that followed was so severe that very little written evidence has survived, and what there is remains controversial.

This book seeks to uncover what it was that happened in Britain to destroy the old order and to create new nations. Many historians have preferred not to delve too deeply into this period of our island history on the grounds that so little is known for certain, and so little ever will be known, that to speculate is fruitless. In the past I have at times taken this attitude myself. But there comes a time when simply avoiding the issue is no longer acceptable. I have reached that point myself. For me, it is time to speculate.

I must say straight off that what follows in this book is not going to be accepted by all historians; in fact I expect the vast majority to stick to the view that there is too little evidence to be certain of what really happened. And they are correct. What follows is what I consider to be the most likely course of events based on the evidence. I think that I am probably right, though obviously I may not be.

What is certain is that something very dramatic indeed did happen. On that everyone is agreed. Old political entities were destroyed and new ones created. Old nations were exterminated and new ones arose. And what took place in Britain was unique.

Across the entire Western Roman Empire the old imperial administration was replaced during the fifth century by kingdoms ruled by monarchs who were very often barbarians. In all those provinces — Gaul, Spain, Italy, Libya and others — there was some form of continuity from the age of late antiquity to the early medieval period. Most noticeably the peoples of those areas continued to speak languages based either on Latin or on the languages spoken there before the Romans invaded. As Gaul became France they adopted a Latin-based language, as did Hispania as it became Spain, Lusitania as it became Portugal and Italia as it became Italy. Only in the lightly-Romanized German provinces did the native language reassert itself. Moreover, all these old Roman provinces remained Christian in religion. Even if the barbarian rulers were pagan, the people were Christian and the rulers converted within a generation or two. The continuity is as noticeable as the changes.

In Britain the picture was very different indeed. In 410 Britain was a fully functioning part of the Roman Empire like anywhere else. But by the mid-seventh century nobody in Britain spoke a Latin-based language, and the pre-Roman Celtic languages were confined to a western fringe. Christianity had also vanished across vast swathes of the country. The pagan religion of the barbarian rulers had taken over among the people. The old churches were in ruins or were being used as houses and workshops. Britain had been utterly transformed in a way that other Roman provinces had not.

From what evidence remains to us, the change seems to have happened in the late-sixth century. But why then, and what form did the change take? To answer those questions we will have to delve far back into our history, and that means looking at the evidence.

The first thing to realize is that the evidence for what happened in Britain during these years is very sparse indeed. The ability to read and write was exterminated across most of Britain. Nobody wrote down what was happening for the simple reason that they could not write, and if they had been able to write there was nobody able to read what they had written.

The Romans had used writing to organize their empire — to calculate and exact taxation, to account for the payments made for building roads and bridges, to ensure provincial governors were not cheating the central state authorities, to keep all the bureaucratic records needed by an empire covering thousands of square miles and ruling over tens of millions of people. The new rulers in Britain, controlling what are collectively termed the 'successor states' did not need writing. Their kingdoms were small and the bureaucratic needs of their governments paltry. A ruler could ride to any part of his kingdom in a few days and knew all his nobles personally. He could see for himself if a nobleman was not keeping law and order, or not passing on tax revenues, and so written records were not needed.

Nor was writing needed for history or geography. The new rulers and nobles had more limited horizons than had the Romans. They had poets and bards who memorized and recounted great events and the deeds of famous men. History was for entertainment on a dark winter's evening, it was a way in which a ruler could emphasize his importance by extolling the mighty deeds of his ancestors. Songs and tales were told by firelight, so again writing was not needed.

And crucially, writing was not needed for religion. Christianity is a written religion, its teachings being based on the book known as the Bible. The gods of the pagan English did not inhabit pages of books: they stalked the forests, bathed in pools and rode the thunderclouds. They were powerful, passionate and dynamic beings who did not need the written word to show how great they were.

And so the skills of writing and reading died across most of Britain. Only in a few places where Christianity survived did the knowledge of writing likewise persist. And in those places the key need was to preserve, maintain and copy sacred works. Bibles and theological commentaries were patched up or copied anew, but histories and the old records of Roman Britain mouldered and were lost.

But for us looking back to those years from the twenty-first century, writing is essential. It is only by reading the few written records of those years that we can hope to know what happened. There are very few of them to rely on, and none of them is comprehensive in any meaningful way. The problem is that most of those records were written long after the event. They were written by men looking back at events that had happened some 300 years earlier, and they were using sources and records at which we can only guess. How accurate those sources were, we do not know. Nor can we be certain that the men turning them into a history repeated them faithfully. And finally, we do not actually have any of those original histories written so long after the event. What we have are copies of them made some centuries later as the original manuscripts got tatty and began to fall to pieces. Again, we do not know if the medieval copyist copied accurately what was in front of him.

So with all those caveats in mind, it is time to look at the written sources that have survived.

The only contemporary work among these is a book written in Latin by a British monk named Gildas entitled *De Excidio et Conquestu Britanniae*, or *On the Ruin and Conquest of Britain.* This book is usually referred to either as *Gildas* or as *DEB*. Gildas wrote his book in the first half of the sixth century, though its precise date is disputed. In it he gives a brief historical overview of Britain from the time the Romans first arrived down to his own date. The emphasis is on the later decades after Britain separated from the Roman Empire and fell prey to Germanic invaders from across the North Sea – the peoples who would become the English. Gildas was not writing a history, he was writing a sermon as befitted his station in life as a highly-respected monk and holy man.

The facts of history and geography that Gildas includes are mentioned only in so far as they support the message of his sermon. This message is that the people of Britain are a crowd of miserable sinners who are being punished by God for their sins, that God's instruments are the pagan invaders and that if the people of Britain do not stop their sinful ways soon they will be utterly destroyed – and quite right too. So Gildas includes some information, but misses out much more. Reading Gildas is very frustrating for a modern historian.

We shall be looking at what Gildas has to tell us about Britain both in his own time and in his recent past in later chapters, but here we need to decide just how reliable Gildas is. To a large extent that depends on where and when he was writing. When Gildas says 'in our own time' to what time does he refer? After all, nowhere in his book does Gildas say where or when he composed his book. We know that Gildas died in or after AD 569, but he was very old at that date and could conceivably have written his book any time in the previous fifty years or so.

The traditional method to date Gildas is to cross reference events that he describes to other sources. The key dating point is that Gildas says that the great warrior king Maelgwn was alive and well (though deeply sinful) as he wrote. So if we can know when Maelgwn lived, we will have an approximate date for when Gildas wrote his book.

Maelgwn is well known in later writings as a great early monarch of the royal dynasty that later ruled Gwynedd in northern Wales. His name features in many lists of ancestors, or genealogies, attached to princes and nobles who lived much later. It is generally reckoned that on average a son during the early medieval period would be thirty years younger than his father. Clearly this was not always the case, some sons would be born when their father was eighteen, others when he was fifty-five. The figure is only an average, but it does allow us to count back through the generations to get an approximate date for an ancestor. If the ancestor is ten generations before the known prince, for example, he will have lived about 300 years earlier. We know when the later princes and nobles lived, so by counting back generations of their ancestors to get to Maelgwn we can get a rough date for his lifetime. The genealogies are each different in detail, but they generally agree that Maelgwn lived somewhere between AD 490 and 550.

Potentially more decisive is the chronicle known as the *Annales Cambriae*, or *Welsh Annals*. This gives the date of Maelgwyn's death as being 547. As we shall see, however, there are a few problems with the earlier stages of the *Annales Cambriae* and, as a result, this date cannot be taken as being precise. It is probably no more than twenty years out, but that is all that can be said.

The other events or people in Gildas's work are even more obscure. He names four other sinful rulers: Constantine, Aurelius Caninus, Vortiporius and Cuneglasus. All these men are known from later genealogies. Counting back the generations from men whose dates are known gives a range of dates for these four rulers that varies from about 490 through to around 560. Gildas also says that the Battle of Badon Hill (which we will be looking at later) took place when he was born, apparently forty-four years before he was writing. That battle can be dated from other sources to anywhere between 480 and 516.

As for his geographical location, Gildas makes some elementary mistakes about the geography of northern Britain, so it is generally assumed that he did not live there. He is also astonishingly rude about the rulers of western Britain, so it must be assumed he did not live there either. Gildas is just as clearly not in English-held territory, for if anything he is more caustic about them than about the western rulers. By contrast he is well informed about southern Britain and the trade links to Gaul, now slowly becoming France.

All things considered, it would seem that Gildas wrote his book somewhere around 520 to 540, possibly toward the latter end of that range of dates. He probably lived and worked in a non-English part of southern Britain, near to both the coast and to a major port, perhaps Portsmouth. It is not possible to be more precise. So the Britain that he describes was in existence at about that date.

Another early source is the *Annales Cambriae* referred to briefly above. This document was compiled in the early-tenth century at the monastery of St David's in southern Wales. It purports to be a compilation of earlier annals copied from documents that were falling to pieces and thus all brought together into a single new document. If this were the case it would be valuable indeed, but there are problems.

The first issue is that the *Annales Cambriae* takes the form of a long list of years, each of which is indicated by the letters 'an', for 'annus' the Latin for year, but none of which actually has a date attached to it. Every tenth year there is an extra mark giving the number of years that have elapsed since the *Annales* began. Many, but not all, of those years is then followed by a short entry that records any event of importance that happened that year.

In its later sections the *Annales Cambriae* includes events the dates of which are known precisely from other sources. It should, therefore, be possible to count back the years from those known dates to ascribe dates to the undated earlier entries. Doing this gives a date for the very first entry of 444 and a date for the death of Maelgwn of 547, as noted above.

Unfortunately the *Annales Cambriae* as we have them are

clearly not correct. Some periods marked as comprising ten years actually comprise nine or eleven years instead. Not only that but we have no way of knowing how accurately the tenth century monks of St David's copied the older annals into the new annal that they were compiling. It is generally thought that the compilers will have got events in the correct chronological order, but that their actual dating is suspect. The further back the *Annales Cambriae* go the less reliable their dating is thought to be. By the time of Gildas and Maelgwn they might be anything up to twenty years adrift.

Like the *Annales Cambriae*, the document known as the *Historia Brittonum*, or *History of Britain*, was written some centuries after our period, but claims to contain copies of documents dating back to the period we are studying. This document is generally thought to have been written in Wales, probably in the north, around the year 810. It is a compilation of other histories, chronicles and assorted sources. Whoever wrote the *Historia Brittonum* wove these sources together to give a coherent chronological walk through of British history between the years 55 BC to AD 640. The result is patchy, with detailed accounts of some events, sketchy references to others and huge gaps elsewhere. It really does read as if a selection of different documents has been simply stuck together without much effort at editing. Added to the end is a list of the most important cities in Britain and a list of natural wonders, such as the hot springs of Bath.

Some copies of the book have a prologue written by a Welsh monk named Nennius, who claims to be the author of the book and to have compiled it from a large number of older books and sources. Opinion is divided as to whether the prologue was part of the original, but was lost from those versions that do not have it, or whether it was not part of the original and was added to those that do have it. Certainly none of the copies that survive are originals, all of them being later copies. It is not considered proper these days to refer to the author as Nennius, since he may not have actually written the book. It is, however, a convenient shorthand and so I intend to use that name when referring to this source.

Debate over whether or not the prologue is original and whether or not Nennius was the author has been long and fierce. For our purposes, however, it is irrelevant. What is important is whether or not the *Historia Brittonum* is accurate. Much depends on whether the ninth century author (whoever he was) accurately copied his sources. It is generally thought that he did, but that he probably added in some explanations and descriptions to help his ninth century readership understand references and comments that would otherwise have been obscure to them.

The next question is how reliable were the documents he was copying. Some of them read like sober historical accounts, others include tales of dragons and magic. Much ink has been spilt over which parts of the *Historia Brittonum* can be accepted as fact and which cannot. In the final analysis it is pretty much a matter of opinion. Certainly what the book contains is what an educated and widely-travelled Welsh monk living in about 820 believed to be true.

The northern English monk, the Venerable Bede, wrote a history of Britain that he completed in AD 731. The book is called the *Historia Ecclesiastica Gentis Anglorum*, or *Ecclesiastical History of the English People*. As its title suggests it is primarily a history of Christianity and the Church in which kings, nobles and other people get mentioned only in so far as their actions affected the Church.

Bede was a great scholar, was widely read and took great pains to ensure accuracy in all his written works — most of which are theological. For events close to his own time, Bede is invaluable and accurate. For events further back in history, and in particular for the period in which we are interested, Bede is less reliable. He was relying on older works, some of which no longer survive, and he himself was uncertain how accurate some of these works were. Nevertheless he is our sole source for many events.

Where Bede made an invaluable contribution to early British history was in his adoption of our modern system of dating years. Bede, like us, used the anno domini (AD) system that counts years forward and back from what was considered to be the birth date of Jesus Christ. Earlier systems of designating years had mostly relied on reference to political rulers. The Romans had dated years by whomever held the government post of Consul that year and the English before Bede had referred to how many years a particular king had been on the throne. This inevitably made for a confusing mass of different dating systems. It is to Bede's credit that he went to extraordinary lengths to work out in which year AD any particular event had taken place. He did not always get it right, but he did at least try which is more than can be said for Gildas or Nennius.

While on the subject of ecclesiastical writings, we should mention the hagiographies of various saints. These books were enormously popular among monks and have survived in relatively large numbers. Each recounts the life story of a particular saint, with special emphasis on his or her holy works, learning, theological insights and general worthiness to be a saint. Many of them do, in passing, refer to secular figures and historic events contemporary to the saint under discussion.

In theory they could be used to establish the dates of otherwise undateable events and establish the reality of shadowy figures. Unfortunately most hagiographies date to after 900 and were written by a person who quite obviously felt no qualms about inventing stories to make the subjects appear even more holy than they already were. Most historians dismiss hagiographies as being worthless and unreliable as historic documents. When it comes to detail this is fair enough, but the men writing the hagiographies were closer to their subjects than are we. At worst a hagiography represents what a well-read monk of about 900 believed was likely to have been true some centuries earlier.

Generally considered to be almost as unreliable as the hagiographies are the ancient poems that take as their subject the events of these years. These poems are written mostly in an early form of Welsh that would date them to around 850 to 950. This would make them much later than the events they describe and it is for this reason that they have not been well regarded. However, it is undoubtedly true that the bards who recited these poems did so from memory. This means that the versions written down around 850 might simply be versions of the originals in which the language was updated as language changed, but that the actual contents remained unchanged. If this were the case then the old poems might actually date back to the events they describe and so be valuable sources of historic information.

The key poems here are those that have been ascribed to the poets Taliesin and Aneirin. Taliesin is known to have died around the year 594 and to have lived at least the later part of his life in

Rheged, a state that covered what is now northwestern England in the years before the English took it over. In the poems Taliesin gives accounts of battles, wars and dynastic marriages that are unknown from any other source. Scholarly opinion is divided as to how reliable the poems are, but is generally moving to a more favourable opinion. Aneirin lived a little later in what is now southern Scotland.

A final and invaluable work is the *Anglo-Saxon Chronicle*. This is a history of Britain and its peoples that was composed on the orders of King Alfred the Great of Wessex in about 890. England had by this date suffered extensive damage during the Viking wars and many monastic libraries had gone up in flames. The *Chronicle* was a deliberate attempt by Alfred to collect together everything that had survived and put it together into a single, new history of his people. It takes the form of a long list of dates, next to each of which is recorded an important event that took place that year. In the earlier sections there are large gaps, but as the *Chronicle* gets closer to its year of composition the entries become more frequent, longer and more detailed.

Alfred was a powerful and highly respected monarch. His clerks had the time and influence to get hold of copies of almost any document that they wanted and they were conscientious in their work. They gathered histories, chronicles, land deeds, courtly records, historic poetry and genealogies from across England and the different English kingdoms that then existed. It is a comprehensive work, but not without its problems especially in the earlier sections.

The work was composed for Alfred, King of Wessex. As a result it frequently gives the Wessex version of events and portrays the enemies of Wessex to be in the wrong or ascribes to them underhand motives. They sought also to glorify the royal house of Wessex. In the terms of the later-ninth century this meant establishing a clear and legitimate line of succession from an heroic founder of the dynasty down to the current monarch. There was no time for usurpations or regicides, nor for succession between remote cousins. Undoubtedly the *Chronicle* glossed over some such incidents in the early years of the Wessex dynasty.

Certainly, the *Chronicle* sought to extend the ancestry of Alfred back beyond what was known. They could trace his ancestors back to around 470, but that was not good enough as other royal families were older. They therefore grafted on to the list of ancestors some Germanic heroes known from old legends and a couple of pagan gods which together made Alfred's pedigree longer than that of anyone else in England.

The writers of the *Chronicle* also sought to make things clear to their own audience. They therefore explained events in terms that an English person living in 890 would understand. The Roman Empire is, for instance, called a kingdom and its rulers are named as kings. As with other records written later, but referring to earlier events there are inconsistencies over dates that become more serious the further back in time the *Chronicle* goes.

Before leaving the written sources mention needs to be made of the controversial Geoffrey of Monmouth. Geoffrey was a twelfth-century Welsh monk who was intent on making a career in the church for himself; indeed he went on to become Bishop of Asaph, and it was with this in mind that he began writing. He produced a number of books, each dedicated to a high-ranking ecclesiastic who might be able to do his career some good. In 1139 he changed tack and dedicated a book to Robert, Earl of Gloucester, who was interested in history and literature and who was himself influential in Church circles. This book was a *History of the Kings of Britain*, and it is with this book that most historians associated Geoffrey of Monmouth.

The book starts with the entirely legendary Brutus who, Geoffrey says, led a group of survivors from Troy to the Atlantic to seek safety from the vengeful Greeks led by Achilles. After assorted adventures, Brutus arrived in Britain (which is named after him) and founded a dynasty of rulers which Geoffrey then traces down to Gruffydd ap Cynan, Prince of Gwynedd, who had died in 1137.

Geoffrey claimed that his book, in Latin, is a translation of an ancient book in Welsh given to him by Walter, Archdeacon of Oxford. However, it is quite clear that this is not the case. Sections of Geoffrey's book can be seen to have been lifted from Gildas, from the *Historia Brittonum* or from Bede. Other sections seem to come from other history books, since lost, and parts read very like folk tales or legends that Geoffrey may have picked up on his many travels. Other parts are almost certainly invented by

Geoffrey himself. The difficulty lies in trying to disentangle the various elements. Undoubtedly there are sections in the book that pass on historical facts not recorded elsewhere. Equally clearly some of it is pure invention.

In large measure, the reputation of the work was boosted at the time and then undermined more recently because of the large section that occupies the central third of the book. These chapters deal with the reign of King Arthur. At the time stories about Arthur were hugely popular, and Geoffrey managed to squeeze most of them into his work. Where he scored over other writers was that he seemed to have put Arthur into a secure historic setting, establishing when and where he lived. This made his book immensely popular while he was alive, but in more recent times has served to discredit it.

The figure of Arthur looms over all the sources we have mentioned, except for the *Anglo Saxon Chronicle* which does not mention him at all. Academic opinion is as prone to fashion as any area of human endeavour. In recent decades there has been a growing fashion among historians to declare that Arthur did not exist, and therefore to treat sources that mention him as being suspect. The scholarly research underpinning this view is impressive, but not altogether convincing. In some cases it would seem that Arthur is being singled out for special treatment. In some sources the section talking about Arthur is denounced as being a later addition, while all the rest of the source is accepted as genuine. There is a danger of circular logic here. Arthur did not exist and so a document that mentions him must be suspect, and because the document is suspect Arthur did not exist.

Fortunately the Arthurian period took place before the key events that we will be looking at in this book, but they do form a critical background and so we will be looking at it in outline.

Leaving behind the written sources, we should turn to the archaeological sources. These have come on in leaps and bounds in recent years, and each year brings fresh evidence. There used to be a view that the archaeological record showed a total collapse of British society within a generation of the end of Roman rule in 410. It is now recognized that although there was a clear and dramatic change, it was not a collapse as such. The Romans built in brick, stone and concrete which has survived well. The generations that followed built in wood, which rots away and is more difficult to identify in excavations.

The tricky subject of dating finds has also been improved. Roman coins made Roman sites relatively easy to date, but post-Roman sites lacked such easy markers. Recently it has become easier to assign dates to different styles of pottery and jewellery, thus making the dating of sites easier and more accurate.

By contrast some older certainties have vanished. It used to be thought that the presence of a Roman brooch on a site meant that the people who used it were Roman, while the presence of a German brooch meant the people were German. We now recognize that this was not necessarily the case. To take an obvious modern example, McDonald's burgers are an American invention and a key indicator of American culture. But this does not mean that the presence of a McDonald's restaurant in a town means that the town has been overrun by immigrants from America. It means only that the people there like eating hamburgers. Thus a change in objects on an archaeological site from Roman to Germanic might mean that the English had moved in and taken over, but it might also mean that the existing population had ditched their Roman culture and adopted a Germanic one.

Nor is it possible to infer from archaeological finds the aims or motivations of people identified from buried finds. It was formerly thought that Germanic warriors resident in Britain before 410 were mercenaries hired by the Roman government, but that Germanic warriors resident in Britain after 410 were invaders seeking to establish English kingdoms. The picture is now known not to be so clear. The later warriors might well have been mercenaries as well.

The centuries after the end of Roman control of Britain are obscure to say the least. We know what Britain was like in 410, and we know what Britain was like by 650. What happened in between is the story of this book. And the figure of Ceawlin dominates all. It is he, I believe, who holds the key to what happened, when it happened and why it happened.

PART I

Cometh the Hour

Chapter 1

Late Roman Britain

From the point of view of written history, and to a lesser extent from archaeology, we lose clear sight of conditions in Britain between about AD 410 and AD 440. At that time Britain separated from the Roman Empire as a political unit, but it remained tied to the empire by economic links, personal visits and culture. For the people at the time the political split from Rome was expected to be only temporary. Such divisions had happened before and had always ended within a few years. It is only with hindsight that we know that the Roman Empire was doomed.

The people of Britain did not know the split from Rome would become permanent. They would have behaved as if they were still Roman and would soon again be part of the Empire. If we are to understand what followed and why people behaved as they did we need to appreciate this simple fact. And that means understanding what late Roman Britain was like and how it functioned.

Britain had been invaded by the Roman army in AD 43 and over the following half century the legions had spread out to conquer all of Great Britain, the largest of the British Isles, as far north as the River Tyne in the east and the River Solway in the west. The northern boundary would vary over the years, moving north to the Clyde and the Forth for a while before moving back south again. The Tyne-Solway line would be formalized by the elaborate system of wall, turrets, forts and roads that is today known as Hadrian's Wall.

The Romans, meanwhile, set about exploiting the wealth of their new acquisition. The economic wealth of Britain appears to have been slow to be fully exploited. As late as AD 150 the Roman government seems to have been making a loss in Britain – it was spending more on the army and construction works in the island than it was raising in taxation. That position seems to have been reversed by around AD 200 and a century later Britain was one of the most profitable areas of the Empire.

Gold was mined in Wales, though in fairly small quantities. Much more productive were the great lead mines of the Mendips, Pennines, the Peak District and the Tyne Valley. Until the conquest of Britain, the Romans had been able to mine lead only in Spain. The new British mines proved to be richer and more productive than those in Spain and, as a bonus, they yielded small quantities of silver as well. Tin was mined in Cornwall, producing more tin than the rest of the Empire put together. There are signs of extensive transport engineering works in Cornwall, linking the mines to ports from where the metal could be exported. Clearly the profits were great enough for the mine owners to be able to afford such costs. Iron was mined and worked in quantity in the Weald and the lower Severn Valley. There seems to have been some small-scale copper mining in Wales.

Impressive as the list of minerals being exploited in Britain might be, it is dwarfed by the scale and variety of agricultural products. The chalk uplands of southern Britain were home to vast flocks of sheep, which were sheared for their wool. This wool was processed locally – we know of one very large blanket workshop in Winchester – and the products exported. British cloaks, known as *tossia*, were famous for their warmth and durability, and commanded high prices as far away as Greece.

The lowlands were home to large herds of cattle and pigs that were raised both for leather and for meat. To the west the Cotswolds and Mendips seem to have been used for breeding horses. At first the horses in Britain were native ponies of about 11 hands in height, not too dissimilar to the New Forest or Dartmoor ponies of today. By about AD 200, however, finds show that the horses in Britain were getting bigger and stronger. They were now averaging some 14.2 hands tall and had broader chests.

But it was grain that had first attracted the Romans to Britain. Long before Julius Caesar launched his raid into Britain in 55 BC, Roman merchants had been buying British grain in large quantities. That export market grew greatly during the long years of Roman rule. Areas of the Fens around the Wash were expertly drained to produce more grainfields. Elsewhere there seems to have been a gradual, but unstoppable felling of forests to open up more and more fields to agriculture. The scale of the British grain export market can be glimpsed in AD 359 when the Emperor Julian was inspecting army positions along the Rhine. In passing the account of his visit mentions that the cities and army posts bought most of their grain from Britain, and that some 800 ships were engaged in the trade.

One fact that would later prove to be crucial and is not always appreciated in surveys of the economic wealth of Roman Britain is that, to a large extent, this prosperity relied upon the Roman army. If large amounts of British grain went to feed the legions on the Rhine, almost as much went to feed the soldiers stationed on Hadrian's Wall. The meat and leather from pigs and cattle likewise found a ready market among the soldiers who not only ate the meat, but also used the leather to make tents, sandals, belts, straps and shields. It should not be thought that the economy of Britain at this time was entirely dependent on the army, which may have bought only around twenty per cent of British output, but Britain was much more dependent on the army than were other parts of the empire. And some industries relied very heavily indeed on the legions. Pig farmers may have sold up to eighty per cent of their products to the armed forces and government.

In addition to these industries that are mentioned by contemporaries, archaeology has shown a vast number of local craft industries. These served the British population itself. For instance we know of nine fairly large pottery factories, each of which supplied towns and villages within about fifty miles of its base. No doubt there were similar leather, blacksmith and textile works but their products do not survive so well in Britain's damp soils.

There was another benefit in addition to taxing the wealthy industries and trades that acquiring Britain brought to the Roman government, and to the Roman army in particular – men. As early as AD 96 there were 4,500 men recruited from Britain serving on the Rhine frontier. By AD 200 there were some 12,000 Britons under arms on the Rhine or the Danube borders. By this date many Britons had joined local *cohortes*, army units which seem to have carried out duties akin to those of modern police, as well as army units. By AD 300 Britons were joining the legions and there is evidence that by AD 350 the Roman army units stationed in Britain were composed mostly of British men.

In the economic sphere Britain had done well out of the Roman Empire, and the empire did well out of Britain. Taxes and men were extracted from Britain for the use of the empire as a whole. It is now time to turn to the Roman governmental structure in Britain toward the end of Roman rule for it was on that basis that the post-Roman government was to be built.

By the later-fourth century, Britain formed a *diocese* within the empire. This designation had nothing to do with Christian bishops, the word was merely to be adopted later by the Catholic church, instead it designated the top level of government administration. There were twelve dioceses in all, of which Britain was but one. The head of the diocese administration was the *Vicarius* who was appointed directly by the emperor. The word vicarius means deputy, and its use here meant that the vicarius of a diocese was acting as the deputy for the emperor. Indeed, within his diocese, a vicarius had almost the same powers as the emperor.

The most important of these powers was that he acted as a form of court of appeal from the lower levels of administration and justice within the diocese. From the very earliest days of the Roman Empire one of the key benefits of being a citizen of Rome was that you could appeal to the Emperor to overturn a decision made by a provincial court or official. In the early days of the empire this had been a little used privilege for the simple reason that only a small minority of the inhabitants of the empire were citizens of Rome. The rest of the population were either citizens of their local city, were slaves or were women. However, by the time the Romans arrived in Britain the granting of citizenship was being used as an important tool of Romanization. Those who cooperated with the Roman government were made citizens of Rome, giving them enhanced prestige and a wide array of improved civil rights. In AD 212 the Emperor Caracalla announced that all free men in the empire were now citizens of Rome.

The number of citizens who could, and did, appeal to the Emperor rose dramatically. The institution of the position of vicarius at a diocesan level was brought in partly to deal with these appeals. The position was a lucrative one. Bribery – both open and clandestine – was a part of Roman life. A vicarius of a wealthy diocese such as Britain could expect to rake in a lot of money during his time in office. Increasingly the emperors used the granting of the post of vicarius as a way to reward political allies or to get potential troublemakers away from the centre of power in Italy.

It was important, however, to ensure that the scale of corruption did not get too out of hand. If the locals lost faith in Roman justice and Roman administration there would be trouble. Each diocese therefore had a second official appointed by the emperor. This was the *Prefectus*. Officially he commanded the bodyguard of the vicarius, but in practice he was the senior military officer in the diocese. He also had the task of writing reports back to Rome on the activities of the vicarius. It was intended that the prefectus would act as a corrective to the vicarius. To ensure that the two did not get too close and start to collude, it was usual for terms of office to last no more than two years, and sometimes men were changed annually.

The bureaucrats who toiled in the diocesan offices were more long-term appointments, often serving for many years. It was usual for there to be a chief of staff, two chief accountants, a secretary of correspondence, a record keeper and a law officer. Each of these officials had a staff of varying size, so the office of a vicarius might easily run to a hundred men or so. In Britain the office of the vicarius was in London, though a more active vicarius would travel around the diocese from time to time.

Beneath the diocese came the provinces. In Britain there were four provinces. Britannia Prima covered what is now Wales and the southwest of England. Britannia Secunda covered the area from Hadrian's Wall south to a line drawn from the Humber to the Mersey. Flavia Caesariensis covered the area from the Mersey-Humber line south to a line drawn roughly from Ipswich through Cambridge to Northampton and on to Redditch. The south-eastern area fell under the province of Maxima Caesariensis.

Within each province the bureaucracy mirrored that of the diocese. In place of a vicarius there was a *consularis* (a term usually translated as governor) appointed by the emperor and a military officer, often termed a *Comes* or *Dux*. There were also accountants, law officers and masters of works. In theory it was at the provincial level that the vast majority of the hard work of governing the empire took place. In practice it was here that the official business that affected the Roman state took place. Taxation, army recruitment, justice and other formal affairs were conducted at provincial level.

The majority of government tasks that actually affected the daily life of ordinary folk took place at the next level down, the *civitates*. Throughout the Mediterranean, these civitates were based on the old city states that had preceded the empire. Rome itself had begun as a city state like Athens, Sparta, Corinth or Carthage. In those areas the civitates was effectively the old city state using the old boundaries and old governmental systems, but with matters such as taxation and justice removed and elevated to the provincial level where an official appointed by Rome was in charge.

In Britain there had been no city states before Rome came. Instead there had been a number of tribes and tribal alliances ruled by monarchs and hereditary nobles. The civitates system was imposed on Britain by Rome, but in highly modified form. Each civitates was based on the territory of a pre-Roman tribe. The administration of the civitates was run on quasi-democratic lines in which voting rights were restricted to those whom the Roman provincial governor decided could be trusted to toe the Roman line and were rich enough to devote the time to the business of government. In practice these men were generally the former tribal nobles, who were thus brought into the Roman system.

This civitates citizenship was later superseded when all non-slave adult males became citizens of Rome. By the later fourth century, all citizens in a civitas could vote in the internal elections. These citizens elected a council, or *curia*, generally of 100 men. There were strict qualifications imposed on candidates for the council, which were generally to do with wealth but occasionally on family membership or property ownership. In effect, the voters had a very limited pool of candidates from which to choose. Men elected to the curia were called *decuriones* and by the end of the fourth century there seem to have been about 2,000 of them across Britain as a whole.

The curia then elected two senior officials to oversee the day-to-day administration of the civitas. There was also a varying number of junior officials to take care of the specific tasks that needed to be done. These at first included road repairs, emptying rubbish tips, ensuring a flow of fresh water to towns, patrolling roads to deter bandits and so forth. These officials were not paid a salary, but were expected to cream off a percentage of the money allocated to them to hire men or contractors to do the various jobs. The officials elected by the decuriones in the curia were known as *rectores*.

Each civitas was based on a town. Roman provincial officials expected the decuriones to live in the main town of the civitas. This was largely because the Romans came from an urban culture in which cities were the natural residence of educated and wealthy men. The Britons, however, came from a very different and more rural society. In practice most of the decuriones maintained a town house, but lived out in the countryside. These rural residences were often built in the style of a Roman villa, but the people who lived there were British.

In northern and western Wales the civitates system was not imposed. Details are scarce, but it would seem that the Romans were content to allow the traditional tribal system to continue there. Roman garrisons were stationed among the tribes, but so long as the locals paid tribute and caused no trouble they were left to themselves.

The Roman administration in a frontier province such as Britain was complicated by a large army presence. In addition to the armed security forces of the civitates and the (sometimes very large) bodyguards of the governors and the vicarius, there was also the formal Roman army. There was a tendency elsewhere in the empire for the local armed police and bodyguards to adopt military-style equipment and weaponry. It has been suggested that the steady increase in the number and distribution of military belt buckles found in archaeological sites from fourth-century Britain shows that this process was happening in Britain.

In late-fourth-century Britain the army was divided into three commands, each headed by a senior army officer appointed by the emperor. The *Dux Britanniarum* (Duke of Britain) commanded the forces on and around Hadrian's Wall. The *Comes Litoris Saxonici* (Count of the Saxon Shore) commanded the naval and military forces based on both sides of the English Channel. The

Comes Britanniae (Count of Britain) was based at some unknown location with what seems to have been a mobile striking force. We do not know how large any of these army commands were, and in any case they probably varied in size over time, but the *Comes Britanniae* clearly had a smaller force than did his colleagues.

It is reasonable to assume that the Duke of Britain was tasked with fending off raids from the Picts of the north and, increasingly, from the Irish. The Count of the Saxon Shore would have been tasked with beating off the seaborne raids coming over the North Sea from the Germans beyond the empire's frontier. It is worth noting that the bases of the Count of the Saxon Shore were partly in the Diocese of Britain and partly in the Diocese of Gaul. The role of the Count of Britain is less clear. He may have faced the Irish, or he may have been expected to rush to the aid of whichever of his colleagues was most hard pressed.

For most of its time in Britain, the Roman army was composed of men recruited within the Roman Empire. As we have seen, as time passed there was an increasing proportion of men recruited from Britain itself. However, from about AD 300 onward a new element began to emerge. Increasingly the emperors preferred to recruit men from the fringes of the empire and then from outside the empire itself. The vast majority of these men were of Germanic origins. The motivation may have been that such men were more likely to be loyal to their imperial paymaster than were local recruits who may have had attachments to local cities and nobles. No doubt there was also a financial side since a poor German would join up for lower pay than would a prosperous British farmer.

By the mid-fourth century some of these men were the sons of Germans recruited from outside the empire. They had been born in the empire, brought up to the military life and probably considered themselves as much Roman as German. Some rose to very high office in both the military and the bureaucratic hierarchies of the empire. The influx did, however, have the unfortunate effect of causing the army men to consider themselves somehow separate from and superior to the Roman civilians they were supposed to serve.

Around AD 350 a new element arrived, the *foederati*. The word means 'those bound by treaty' and referred to units of men recruited from outside the empire and who served under their own commanders. Typically a noted warrior leader would recruit a band of young men, then hire himself and his men to the Roman government for a set period of time under terms of pay and conditions agreed in a treaty. By the 380s it was becoming increasingly common for the foederati to be paid as much in land as in cash. They would be given land on which to settle with their families, and in return would agree to serve as fighting men for a set number of days each year. This type of land-for-warriors deal made the foederati even cheaper than the Germans recruited into the formal army. They became increasingly numerous, especially around the frontiers.

Another parallel system of governance that was of increasing importance as the fourth century progressed was the Christian network of bishops and priests. The peoples of Britain seem to have long clung to their pre-Roman pagan deities, sometimes dressed up as Roman gods to please the new occupying power. Christianity was certainly slow to come to Britain. The first sign of any formal Christian hierarchy in Britain comes in AD 314 when three bishops from Britain attend a Church council in Arles. These men were the bishops of London, York and Lincoln (or Colchester in one version). In AD 359 a much larger number (sadly we do not know how many) travelled to a council in Rimini. Some of these bishops of 359 paid their own expenses, but a few took money from the emperor. This has been interpreted in different ways. It may mean that some of the bishops were wealthy men, or it might mean that some had so few followers that they could not collect enough cash to pay the bills.

Either way, it would seem that Christianity was more of an urban religion in Britain than a rural one. From AD 312 when the Christian emperor Constantine the Great won the Battle of the Milvian Bridge to become sole ruler of the empire, all ambitious men would have been wise to have adopted Christianity as their religion. It is impossible for us to know how widespread Christianity was in Britain by AD 400. Probably it was followed by the majority of town dwellers, and by nearly all government officials and educated people, but was a minority among the rural folk and particularly the poorer farm workers. As a consequence the religion and its officials probably had an importance and an influence much greater than the numbers of its adherents in Britain would suggest.

The later-fourth century was a period of great change and crisis in Britain. In the early spring of AD 367 there had been a massive and well-orchestrated raid on Britain by the combined forces of the Picts, Irish and Saxons. The event was dubbed The Great Barbarian Conspiracy by Roman writers who were appalled by both the scale of the co-operation among their enemies and by the damage inflicted. Hadrian's Wall was overwhelmed, the Duke of Britain captured and his garrisons butchered. The Count of the Saxon Shore, a man named Nectarides, was killed but his men did rather better than those further north and staved off the worst of the Germanic onslaught. The fate of the Count of Britain is not known, but the Irish overran large areas of western Britain, so he may not have fared too well.

The towns and cities which were barricaded closed their gates and prepared to hold out until help came. The barbarians were not equipped for siege warfare and most towns held out successfully, but large areas of countryside were pillaged. The invaders were joined by some army units, probably Germans, who mutinied and joined the looting. After roaming about for some weeks the barbarians went home, no doubt chased on their way by the men of the Count of the Saxon Shore and the Count of Britain.

In the spring of AD 368 the Emperor Valentinian I arrived in Britain with a large army. He executed some mutineers and the few barbarians who had been captured, then launched punitive raids against the Picts, and probably against the Irish as well. The defences of Britain were rebuilt or strengthened and new army units moved into the diocese.

The years that followed saw sporadic raids by Picts, Irish and Saxons, but they did not again come in the numbers that had been seen in AD 367. The real problems for Roman Britain came from within. Since about AD 300 there had been a general decline in the economic wealth of the Roman Empire. In the 260s Europe had been hit by a devastating plague, that returned at intervals over the following years. Ancient accounts of the symptoms indicate that this disease may have been smallpox, and the high death rate indicates that it was the first time the disease had swept the continent. The depopulation that followed meant that much farmland went untended.

This blow was followed from about AD 320 by a change in the climate that grew increasingly severe. Since about 200 BC Europe, and perhaps the world, had been basking in a climate rather warmer than ours today. Crop yields had been high, and crops such as grapes and olives had been able to grow farther north than they can today. But as the climate grew cooler, crop yields fell and with them prosperity. The picture of a declining economy is not even or consistent. The great farming estates of the western Midlands seem to have been prospering at this time. The overall picture is, however, one of decreasing trade and wealth.

It was in this condition that Britain found itself centre stage in a great imperial crisis in AD 406. The winter of 406/7 was astonishingly cold and the slow-flowing lower reaches of the Rhine froze over. On the last day of 406 a vast horde of Germanic barbarians came pouring over the ice – Suebi, Vandals and Alans are mentioned, but there were no doubt others as well. The Roman frontier defences were annihilated and the horde swept south and west into Gaul.

At about the same time, and perhaps caused by the invasion, the army in Britain rose in revolt against the Emperor Honorius, who ruled the Western Empire as his brother Arcadius ruled the Eastern Empire. The reasons for the uprising are unknown, but they may have been influenced by the fact that Honorius and his military commander Stilicho had been concentrating all their attention on the Danube frontier. Perhaps the British army blamed Stilicho and Honorius for leaving the Rhine comparatively unguarded.

Whatever the cause, the uprising was led by a soldier named Marcus. Within a few weeks Marcus was murdered and the leadership of the uprising taken over by a British nobleman and senior government official named Gratian. This move may have been due to a power struggle between the civilian and military hierarchies in the diocese for, in the early summer of AD 307, Gratian stood down to make way for a senior general named Flavius Claudius Constantinus, who promptly declared himself to be Emperor and took the name of Constantine III.

Constantine III sent a small force of men led by an officer

named Justinianus over to Gaul to announce the start of his reign and summon the army units in Gaul to recognize him as their ruler. Justinanus was met by a large force of Gothic foederati led by their chief Sarus. Sarus and his men proved to be loyal to their paymaster Stilicho and killed Justinianus out of hand. Constantine III then sent a larger force under his British general Gerontius, who chased Sarus out of Gaul and over the mountains into Italy. The Roman troops stationed in Gaul then declared for Constantine and threw off their allegiance to Honorius.

Constantine himself then crossed to Gaul. He spent the summer repairing and remanning the Rhine defences, then set to work tracking down the bands of barbarians still roaming and looting across Gaul. It has long been a matter of dispute how many men Constantine took to Gaul as part of his bid for power. The ancient sources give no clue, nor do they state if those soldiers returned to Britain or not once the Gallic garrisons had declared for Constantine. All that can be said with certainty is that Britain suffered no immediate invasions from Pict, Irish or Saxon, so there must have been a functioning defence left in place.

Constantine's work of exterminating the barbarians was still incomplete when he heard that Honorius was planning to invade Gaul from Italy, while a second army would invade from Spain led by Didymus, a cousin of Honorius. In the spring of AD 308, Constantine brought his son Constans out of the monastery to which he had retired with his wife and children some years earlier – monastic life did not then include celibacy – and made him a junior emperor with the title of Caesar. Constans and Gerontius were then sent to Spain where they defeated and captured Didymus.

At this point the army of Honorius in northern Italy rebelled for reasons that are not entirely clear and Stilicho was murdered. Sarus and his Goths at once fled north back to the Gothic homelands. This left Honorius without an army. He might have expected help from his brother in the East, but Arcadius had recently died, leaving the title of Emperor in the East to his seven-year-old son Theodosius and a power struggle to control the boy emperor was paralysing the East. Honorius sent a messenger to Constantine III recognizing him as joint emperor of the Western Empire and allotting him control over the dioceses of Spain, Gaul and Britain.

By September AD 409 Constans was back with his father, who had established a capital at Arles. For some reason Constans had taken against Gerontius and, rightly or wrongly, accused him of plotting to overthrow and kill Constantine. Rather than await orders for his execution, Gerontius now rebelled and rallied the garrisons in Spain to his cause. That same year a vast army of Goths under their ruler Alaric invaded Italy, bypassed Honorius holed up in the fortress of Ravenna and moved south.

Meanwhile, events in Britain had been moving fast. Some time early in 410 there was a new coup, apparently led by the civilian bureaucracy against the military men installed in power by Constantine. Whether Gratian was involved in the coup is unknown, but it seems likely. Certainly the move seems to have been prompted by the declining fortunes of Constantine III in Gaul. It is not clear exactly what happened, but almost certainly the officials appointed by Constantine III were ousted from office and either executed, imprisoned or sent over to Gaul to join their master. These would have been the Vicarius of the Diocese of Britain, the Governors of the four provinces, the Count of Britain, the Duke of Britain and the Count of the Saxon Shore.

That left in Britain the only officials holding legitimate office those at civitates level. These decuriones and rectores had clearly acted together in ousting the imperial officers appointed by Constantine III. Still working together, they sent an urgent message to Honorius that reached him sometime in the summer of AD 410. In the message the assembled rectores asked Honorius to appoint new imperial officials to take over the offices that could be filled only by appointment by an emperor.

But with the Goths rampaging through Italy, Constantine III threatening to invade Italy and his own army in open revolt, Honorius was far too busy to appoint anyone to any sort of position in a distant province. Moreover, Britain was on the far side of territory held by Constantine III and it seemed unlikely that the rival emperor would allow hostile officials through to take up their positions. In the circumstances Honorius did the only thing he could do. He sent a message back to Britain telling the civitates officials to choose whoever they thought fit for the time being and that he would send properly-appointed officials as soon as he could do so.

This message was intended only as a temporary stopgap measure and may have been dashed off by Honorius under great pressure. With hindsight it assumed great significance and has become known as the Rescript of Honorius.

That summer of AD 410 saw the cataclysmic sacking of Rome by Alaric and his Goths. The entire world was stunned. The city of Rome had remained inviolable for seven centuries. Nobody believed it could ever be defeated, and yet now German barbarian warriors were swaggering through the streets, looting at will. Theodosius in the Eastern Empire sent six legions to help his uncle Honorius, and Honorius found a new and talented commander in the shape of Flavius Constantius. Alaric then died of a fever, and his brother Ataulf contented himself with settling down in southern Italy to live off the fruits of the land and try to negotiate an advantageous peace treaty with Honorius. He would later marry Honorius' sister and declare peace with Rome.

Meanwhile, in the spring of AD 411 Constantius led Honorius' army over the Alps to attack Constantine III. He was beaten to it by Gerontius who invaded Gaul from Spain, defeating and killing Constans on the way. Gerontius and Constantius converged on Arles, where Constantine III was put under siege. After a stand off lasting some weeks, Constantine III surrendered on condition that he would be allowed to retire to live out his life in a monastery. Constantinus gave the defeated emperor a military escort to take him to a famously learned monastery in northern Italy, but they had secret orders to kill him and did so by the roadside. Constantinus then turned on Gerontius, bribing his men to abandon him. Gerontius fled, but was tracked down and killed.

While the three Roman armies had been tearing each other to pieces around Arles, fresh waves of Germanic tribes had surged over the Rhine. The Alemanni set themselves up to rule the area now known as Alsace, the Franks overran the areas around le Mans, Cambrai and Tournai, the Burgundians established a kingdom on the middle Rhine and a branch of the Goths established themselves in control of southern Gaul. Even more dramatic were the wanderings of the Vandals, Suebi and Alans who wandered south, crossed the Pyrenees and set about looting their way across Spain.

Honorius saw his rule now restricted to Italy and the wealthy north African provinces. Even that seemed under threat when the governor of Carthage rose in revolt. Honorius allied himself to the Goths, put down the African revolt, then turned on the Goths. That war ended in AD 418 with a treaty which granted the various Germanic peoples inhabiting what had been the Diocese of Gaul effective independence in return for a formal but vague acknowledgement of Roman sovereignty. In AD 423 Honorius died to be replaced by his nephew Valentinian III who came with legions from the east to impose his rule on Italy, North Africa and – with less success – Spain. No sooner had Valentinian secured himself in power than the terrible Attila the Hun led his savage warriors over the Danube to invade the Eastern Empire.

Amid all this chaos, bloodshed and warfare everyone seems to have forgotten all about Britain. But Britain was still there. It was still keeping the barbarians at bay. And the officials of the civitates were still waiting for an emperor to send them officials.

Chapter 2

The Wide Ruler

With the Romans out of touch with their former province of Britain our contemporary written sources for British history effectively end. No word seems to have got through to either Rome or Constantinople about what was taking place in Britain, or if it did it nobody thought it important enough to write down. We are reliant on documents written in Britain much later, and on archaeology.

Of the written sources, Gildas was the closest in time. Looking back from around AD 530 or so, he did not spend much ink on these years. Writing of the British political and Church leaders after the break with Rome, he wrote:

> they did all things that were contrary to salvation, as if there were no remedy to be supplied for the world by the true Healer of all men. It was not only men of the world who did this, but the Lord's flock itself also and its pastors, who ought to have been an example to the whole people; they, in great numbers, as if soaked in wine through drunkenness, became stupefied and enervated, and by the swelling of animosities, by the jar of strifes, by the grasping talons of envy, by confused judgement of good and evil, were so enfeebled that it was plainly seen, as in the present case, that contempt was being poured out upon princes, and that they were led astray by their vanities and error in a trackless place, and not on the way.

It is what Gildas does not say that is as interesting as what he does say. The main theme of Gildas is that the British are sinners, and that their political leaders in particular sin by arrogant pride, ignoring the teachings of Christ and by fighting against each other. If he had known of any specific examples of civil war or sacrilege during these years he would undoubtedly have said so. The fact that he makes only vague accusations would imply that he had no such records. If documents from the years AD 410 to 440 had survived to be read by Gildas they clearly did not fit his theme and presumably showed the British leaders to have been doing a competent job. Alternatively, such records may not have survived, leaving Gildas with nothing to go on. Given the society that Gildas describes in his own time of c.530 it seems unlikely that nothing survived so it is, perhaps, more likely that Britain in these years was well run.

The *Anglo-Saxon Chronicle* looks at things from the point of view of the Saxons and supplies only one entry for these years:

> 418: The Romans gathered all the gold there was in Britain. Some they hid in the earth so that nobody could find it and some they took to Gaul.

This sounds rather like the disappointed grumblings of a raider who had returned home to Germany from an attack on Britain without any loot worth mentioning.

Nennius, or whoever wrote the *Historia Britonnum*, gives a bit more information. He starts by recounting the ousting of the officials appointed by Constantine III:

> The British overthrew the rule of the Romans, and paid them no taxes and did not accept their kings to reign over them, and the Romans did not dare to come to Britain to rule anymore for the British had killed their generals. And after the end of the Roman Empire in Britain the British went in fear for forty years.

The only writer to give any detail of what happened during those forty years of fear was the unreliable Geoffrey of Monmouth. But before looking at what he has to say, it is worth looking at things from the point of view of the British rectores who governed and represented the various civitates. They had been told by the Emperor Honorius to appoint whoever they saw fit to the official positions that were in the gift of the emperor. To the British, this would have seemed to be a mere temporary state of affairs to last a few years, but no more. The safest and wisest course for them to follow would have been to do what Honorius said. After all, if they disobeyed him they expected to find themselves in the awkward position of explaining their actions a short while later.

The military positions would have been the easiest to fill. The officer who was second in command could be made the acting officer in command pending word from Honorius. The civilian appointments would have been more difficult. It was usual practice for the vicarius and governors to come from outside of Britain so that they would not be influenced in their work by local loyalties or contacts.

It is with this in mind that it is worth turning to what Geoffrey of Monmouth has to say. According to him the 'princes of Britain' (presumably he was using a word familiar to his twelfth century audience to describe the rectores) met in a great council held in London. After much talk they completely failed to fill any of the positions left vacant by the withdrawal of the Romans. Geoffrey says that the most important of these was the post of 'King of the Britons', but again he is using a twelfth-century term and must be presumed to mean the post of Vicarius of Britain. Apparently the rectores failed to agree on who should take this post because nobody wanted the job. They therefore turned to Vitalinus, Archbishop of London, for advice.

After more talking, Vitalinus boarded a ship and sailed to Armorica (Brittany) to offer the position to Aldroen who was ruling Armorica at the time. But Aldroen did not want the job either. Instead he handed the job over to his brother, Constantine. This Constantine took 2,000 armed men with him and sailed with Vitalinus to Totnes, then marched to Silchester where a new council of the nobles was being held. The nobles hailed Constantine as king, and he promised to rule with their advice.

Now Geoffrey is always unreliable but there are some points of interest in his story. First, Vitalinus is thought to have been a real historical figure. According to later hagiographies, he was Archbishop of London at some unrecorded date before AD 450.

A man named Vitalinus is also listed in the genealogies of some Welsh nobles in a position that would fix his death somewhere between AD 380 and 430. These genealogies make him the grandfather of an important figure that we shall come to shortly, Vortigern.

Second, Vitalinus is said to have gone to Armorica and brought back a man to fill the position of Vicarius of Britain. It will be recalled that Armorica was the only other province to oust the officials of Constantine III. If the British wanted an outsider to become Vicarius, as was the custom, then Armorica was the only place to which they could turn. As for the name of the Armorican, Geoffrey may have got muddled with Constantine III. On the other hand, Constantine was a reasonably common name so it is not impossible that an Armorican official named Constantine was on hand to take up the invitation to become Vicarius of Britain.

Even if we ignore what Geoffrey writes, the overall impression from the written sources is that not much happened in Britain for some thirty or forty years after the diocese lost direct touch with the Emperors of Rome. So perhaps we should turn to archaeology.

The results of archaeological digs are unavoidably bereft of names and precise dates. They can, however, provide a reasonably accurate broad brush view of some of the changes that took place and approximately when they happened.

One significant trend found right across Roman Britain is that the construction of expensive private buildings declined sharply from around AD 390 and by around 430 had ceased completely. The work on large villas, houses with mosaic floors and private piped water supplies together with other high status buildings slowed, and then stopped. Of the large, luxurious rural villas that have been excavated, most continue to have been inhabited. However, there are signs that they were no longer being properly maintained, with some rooms apparently being converted to use for agricultural purposes and others left to collapse. One or two seem to have been abandoned altogether, perhaps being burned down.

At about the same time there was a disruption to the pottery industry. For most of the Roman period a relatively small number of large-scale potteries had supplied bowls, jugs and other domestic ware across Britain. Each seems to have supplied an area up to around fifty miles from its base, this presumably being how far it was economic to transport heavy pottery for sale. After about AD 400 this pattern of manufacturing starts to break down and by around 440 seems to have disappeared entirely. In its place was a large number of small, local potteries each of which supplied tableware to people living within only five or ten miles of the kilns.

Again at roughly this timeframe the number of buried hoards of coins increases. Before the age of banks, people often buried coins for safekeeping. The coins were, unlike modern coins, valuable in themselves since they were made of copper, bronze, silver or gold. They were not only money, but bullion. Even in the most peaceful of times some coin hoards were left in the ground and never recovered. In 1890 a elderly lady in Braishfield, Hampshire, suffered a stroke and died soon after. She had been quite unable to tell her son where she had hidden a large bag of gold sovereigns. So far as anyone knows they are still there. However, it is undeniable that people are more likely to be unable to retrieve buried wealth in times of war, revolution or social upheaval. A person killed in battle or forced to flee as a refugee cannot retrieve a pot of silver coins buried in his back garden.

Where coin hoards are more valuable to an archaeologist than abandoned rooms or new types of pottery is that the coins themselves can be dated quite precisely. It was Roman custom to stamp on to one side of a coin the portrait of the emperor who issued them. Knowing the dates when that man ruled gives a date for when the coins were minted. That does not, of course, mean that the coins were buried at that date but it does at least give us a date before which they could not have been buried.

The latest coins found in these British hoards are those of Constantine III. This is hardly surprising as he was the last emperor to hold sway over Britain, and so the date on which the hoards were hidden can be dated as after AD 410. It has been suggested that a more precise date can be gained by looking at how worn the coins are. The idea is that heavily-worn coins have been in circulation for much longer than less worn coins. This line of reasoning would seem to date the bulk of the hoards to around 420 or 430 since the coins show signs consistent with about ten to twenty years' wear.

The problem is that coins were not only used as money, they

were also used as a way to store wealth. Many silver or gold coins in particular could spend years just sitting in a pot. This tendency would have been even more marked in Britain in the fifth century as the functioning of a money economy is known to have gradually ceased. Bartering had always been used for low-value transactions in the Roman economy. With the supply of newly-minted coins cut off, bartering moved up the economic scale and soon was universal. Coins stopped being used as money and instead became used as a way to store wealth or for jewellery. Coins minted in AD 410 that show ten years' worth of wear might therefore not have been buried and lost until fifty or sixty years later.

Nevertheless, the archaeology does seem to show a marked and apparently quite sudden decline in prosperity. People had less money to spend on luxury items and trade patterns seem to have been at least partially disrupted. In many ways this is unsurprising. Much of the prosperity of Roman Britain had depended on exporting items to the rest of the Empire and on the spending power of the army stationed in Britain. With the export market effectively closed, there was bound to be a loss of prosperity.

But what of the army? Archeological finds show that the forts along Hadrian's Wall continued to be manned for some years, though it is unclear if they were occupied much beyond AD 430. Likewise the great fortresses of the Saxon Shore continued in use for some years, but not it would seem for all that many. The formal structures of the Imperial Roman Army were in a slow decline.

Very different were more local defences. Town walls were being repaired, enlarged or built anew. Not only that but earthen embankments and timber walls were being thrown up around villages and farmsteads. The old, pre-Roman hilltop forts were in several cases reoccupied and their defences repaired. Not every farm or village was fortified, but enough of them were for a general trend to be visible. Britain was becoming a more dangerous place in which to live.

Increasingly numerous were finds of military equipment in burials and in buildings that do not seem to have been specifically military. The belt buckles and other gear that has been found are of increasingly Germanic style as time passes. There are various ways this could be interpreted. We have already seen that the local armed police forces were becoming increasingly militaristic toward the end of the fourth century. It would not be unreasonable if by the early-fifth century they had become paramilitary in nature as each civitates sought to have its own defence force.

The Germanization of equipment might mean that these paramilitaries were copying the equipment, and maybe the tactics, of the German tribes that were proving themselves to be increasingly successful in wars on the continent. On the other hand it might mean that the men wearing and using the military equipment actually were Germanic. That raises the question of whether the foreign warriors were coming as invaders or as mercenaries. That conundrum takes us back to the written record.

Gildas, Nennius, Bede and the *Anglo-Saxon Chronicle* all pick up the story again with an incident that is usually dated to around AD 449. The key players in the drama are, on the British side, a Council and a leader named Vortigern, and, on the Saxons' side, a pair of mercenary brothers named Hengist and Horsa.

Before moving on to look at the events themselves, it is worth dealing with the main figures involved. According to Gildas, who was closest to the events, the trouble began with increased raids from the Irish and the Picts. He then says that

> A council was held, to deliberate what means ought to be determined upon, as the best and safest to repel such fatal and frequent irruptions and plunderings by the nations mentioned above. At that time all members of the assembly, along with the proud tyrant, were blinded.

In some copies of the book the 'proud tyrant' is named as 'Vortigern', in others he is not. However, all three later sources – Nennius, Bede and the *Anglo-Saxon Chronicle* – use this name so it is clear that the two are the same.

The picture painted by Gildas is very like that which we might expect if a Roman-style government bureaucracy was still functioning. Vortigern is taking the place of the Vicarius of Britain while the council seems to be a meeting of the assembled rectores. It has been suggested that this council and leader are not at diocesan level, but at provincial level and that Gildas is talking about events in the province where he lived, presumed to have been either Maxima Caesariensis or Britannia Prima. However, as events unfolded they had an impact across Britain as a whole, so it is more likely that we are dealing with a political body controlling the former Diocese of Britain. Moreover, while Gildas places great emphasis on the civil wars that would later rack Britain, he does not mention them as being a factor at this time. Again the implication is that Britain still had a unified political structure.

As for Vortigern himself, there has been much debate over both his name and the description of him by Gildas as a 'proud tyrant'. The word 'Vortigern' can be translated from the British language of the time as meaning 'Widespread Ruler', though its informal tone might be better captured by the tag 'Big Boss'. This has led to speculation that the name is really a title. However, no such title is known either in late-Roman government or in later early medieval Welsh. It is unique.

The vast majority of sources that use the name Vortigern come from Wales, or, like Bede, are clearly based on them. Throughout this time the inhabitants of Wales continued to speak British, even the richest and most noble persons failing to adopt Latin except as a second language with which to talk to Romans. It seems, therefore, that Vortigern was the name used for this man among the British-speaking population.

If Vortigern was occupying the position of Vicarius some forty years after the last letter from Honorius it is to be expected that, for formal business, he would have used the title of Vicarius. In much the same way, leaders of African countries still use the titles inherited from their former colonial masters such as President in former British colonies or *Presidente* in former Portuguese colonies. As I write none of them has started using titles drawn from their own culture or traditions. It seems likely that while Vortigern was known to the educated, Latin-speaking classes as Vicarius his British speaking followers would have called him Vortigern – the Wide Ruler.

We do not have to look far to see the importance of these informal titles. Throughout his years in power in Germany, Adolf Hitler occupied the formal constitutional post of *Reichskanzler*. This title is usually translated into English as Reich Chancellor, though it was more analogous to a British prime minister than to a British chancellor. But Hitler is not often linked to that title, he is far more often known by the informal title that he used as head of the Nazi Party: *Führer*. This translates as 'leader', but also has a secondary meaning as 'guide'. Perhaps Vortigern was also better known by his informal title than by the formal office of state that he held.

That leaves Gildas and his use of the term 'Proud Tyrant'. From elsewhere in his book we know that Gildas enjoyed wordplay and vicious insult on those he disliked or blamed for Britain's woes. Top of his list was this particular man, and his use of the phrase is most likely a calculated insult. In Latin the phrase 'Proud Tyrant' is *Superbus Tyrannus*. Now 'super' means wide or large, just as does the 'vor' element of the name Vortigern. But 'superbus' means proud or arrogant. Likewise 'tyrannus' is similar in sound to the 'tigern' part of Vortigern's name. The word tyrannus meant a ruler who had acquired his position of power illegally. Gildas is having another dig by punning the word with tigern. So Superbus Tyrannus is a pun aimed at men as educated and sophisticated as Gildas was himself.

A much later genealogy of Welsh noblemen states that Vortigern was the grandson of a man named Vitalinus, whose father was from Glevum (now Gloucester). There is no proof that this Vitalinus was the same Vitalinus who was Archbishop of London, though they would both have been alive at about the same time. Nor need we take too seriously Geoffrey of Monmouth's story that Vitalinus acted as powerbroker in choosing a new Vicarius. The links are suggestive, however, and may mean that Vortigern came from a faction favouring the agriculturally wealthy west, or one that favoured the Christian Church, or both, or neither if we choose to dismiss Geoffrey.

The position of Hengist and Horsa is rather more straightforward. They were mercenary leaders of a type well known elsewhere in the late-fourth and fifth centuries. Such men were tough warriors who recruited a band of young men and hired them out as mercenary fighters to whoever would pay them. Most sources agree that Hengist and Horsa were brothers and that they were Jutes, from what is now the southern end of the Denmark peninsula. Their men, however, may have been recruited more widely across northern Germany. Hengist and Horsa were mercenaries, not foederati, for they were paid in cash and in kind rather than being given land on which to settle.

All the sources agree that Hengist and Horsa came with three ships' full of men – perhaps 200 warriors. This may not sound much but they were all well-equipped and powerful fighters. According to Nennius they were based on the island of Thanet, while Gildas agrees they were stationed on the east coast. From Thanet, then truly an island off the east coast of Kent, the mercenaries would have been in a good position to stave off raids by Saxons or other Germans.

The ships and navigational techniques of the time were not well suited to long voyages out of sight of land, so most raiders would have come along the coast of Europe to what is now Cap Gris Nez, near Calais. From there they could either turn south for the coast of Gaul or turn north to attack Britain. From a base on Thanet, Hengist and his ships could have patrolled east to locate the raiders before they were a threat, then lain in wait to attack them.

Clearly the brothers did their job well. All the sources agree that before long Vortigern was hiring many more men through Hengist and Horsa. Nennius says that another sixteen shiploads, around a thousand men, came over. Another source says that some of these men were detached under the command of Hengist's son Oisc and stationed on the east coast near Hadrian's Wall to counter seaborne raids by the Picts.

So far, so good. The government of Britain was organized and behaving like any other late Roman diocesan government. They would soon learn what other dioceses had learnt. Gildas takes up the story:

> Thus the barbarians, admitted into the island, succeed in having provisions supplied them, as if they were soldiers and about to encounter, as they falsely averred, great hardships for their kind entertainers. These provisions, acquired for a length of time, closed, as the saying is, the dog's maw. They complain, again, that their monthly supplies were not copiously contributed to them, intentionally colouring their opportunities, and declare that, if larger munificence were not piled upon them, they would break the treaty and lay

waste the whole of the island. They made no delay to follow up their threats with deeds. For the fire of righteous vengeance, caused by former crimes, blazed from sea to sea, heaped up by the eastern band of impious men; and as it devastated all the neighbouring cities and lands, did not cease after it had been kindled, until it burnt nearly the whole surface of the island, and licked the western ocean with its red and savage tongue. In this assault, which might be compared to the Assyrian attack upon Iudaea of old. After a length of time the cruel robbers returned to their home.

Nennius has a less evocative, but more detailed account of events. According to this version, the second wave of mercenaries brought not only Hengist's son Oisc, but also his daughter – named by Geoffrey of Monmouth as Rowena. Vortigern then married Rowena and established very close links with the Germanic warriors. As part of the marriage contract, the civitas of Cantium (Kent) was handed over to Hengist. The leader of the civitas, Gwyrangon, was not consulted but merely told that in future he had to obey Hengist as overlord. The council does not seem to have been consulted, which would undoubtedly have caused ill will and disquiet.

This incident in which Hengist is given the civitas of Cantium is typical of what the barbarians were doing elsewhere across the Roman Empire. Isolated bands of warriors might be interested in loot and rape, but powerful men such as Hengist had much higher ambitions. They wanted to take over the role of the Roman civilian government, becoming masters of prosperous and efficiently run territories. Time and again barbarian invaders become kings of kingdoms the boundaries of which are those of a Roman province or civitas. It would seem that Hengist was after exactly the same thing.

In the account by Nennius, there then follows the uprising of the mercenaries after their payment was withheld, but Nennius does not mention the widespread destruction found in Gildas. Instead he writes:

Vortigern's son Vortimer fought vigorously against Hengist and Horsa and their people. Vortimer fought four keen

> battles against them. The first battle was on the River Darenth. The second battle was at the ford called Episford in their language and Rhydyr Afael in ours and there fell Horsa and also Vortigern's son Cateyrn. The third battle was fought in the open country by the Inscribed Stone on the shore of the Gallic Sea. The barbarians were beaten and he was victorious. They fled to their keels and were drowned as they clambered aboard them like women.

The *Anglo-Saxon Chronicle* records the same battles, though in a different order. The dates are not reliable and may be based on the date of AD 449 for Hengist's arrival, but the entries read as follows:

> 455: Hengist and Horsa fought Vortigern the king in the place called Agelesthrep. Horsa was killed and after that Hengist and his son Oisc ruled the kingdom.
>
> 456: Hengist and Oisc fought the Britons in the place called Crecganford. There they killed four companies. The Britons gave up Kent and fled to London in great fear.
>
> 465: Hengist and Oisc fought the Britons near Wippedesfleet and killed twelve ealdormen. One of their own thanes was killed, a man called Wipped.
>
> 473: Hengist and Oisc fought the Britons and seized countless booty. The Britons fled the English as one flees fire.

Hengist then vanishes from the *Anglo-Saxon Chronicle*.

These places can all be identified and they are all in Kent. Agelesthrep or Episford is Aylesford, and on the hill overlooking the ford across the River Medway is a large standing stone called the White Horse Stone. It is said to have got its name when Horsa was buried here by his grieving brother Hengist. The stone was painted blood red, then decorated with a white horse – the symbol of Kent to this day. Crecgnaford is Crayford, presumably the battle on the Darent in Nennius. Wippedesfleet or the Inscribed Stone is Richborough.

It seems certain that what these different accounts refer to is a rebellion of mercenaries in Kent led by Hengist. At first Hengist was successful, apparently wresting the civitas of Cantium from the control of the Diocese of Britain, but ultimately he was defeated and leaves the scene. The crisis seemed to have been averted.

In fact it was only just starting.

Chapter 3

The Power Shift

In case it should be thought that we can reconstruct an approximate chronological framework for British history during the fifth century, it is worth emphasizing the limits of our knowledge. Not only are there great gaps in what we know, but the dating of events of which we are aware is uncertain. As if to rub in how little we know for certain, there were events and people whose existence is definitely known, but quite how they fit in with each other or with the general flow of events is quite mysterious.

Take for instance the Strife of Guoloph, usually identified with Wallop in Hampshire. The only source for this event is Nennius who writes that 'From the start of the reign of Vortigern to the quarrel between Vitalinus and Ambrosius are twelve years, that is Wallop, the Strife of Wallop.'

The context in which the sentence comes means that whoever wrote the document that Nennius is copying clearly thought his audience would know of the event and would understand its background and importance, which was obviously great. We, however, are left guessing.

The first thing to notice is that once again the name of Vitalinus crops up. Given that this event occurred well into the rule of Vortigern, it is highly unlikely that this Vitalinus was the same Vitalinus who had been Archbishop of London around AD 410. Perhaps it is his son or grandson. It has been suggested that the Vitalinus referred to here is, in fact, Vortigern himself. The reasoning being that if Vortigern is a nickname given to the man by his followers then his actual name was something else, and since the genealogies make Vortigern the grandson of Vitalinus then maybe he was christened in honour of his grandfather the archbishop. So the Vitalinus who is recorded as quarrelling with Ambrosius at Wallop is, in fact, Vortigern.

The second thing to notice is that this is the first mention of the man Ambrosius Aurelianus who would feature prominently in Gildas and in Nennius. Ambrosius is portrayed as being hostile to Vortigern and taking over his position when Vortigern died. Perhaps the Strife at Wallop was an early flare up of whatever the disputes between the two men were.

Dating the Strife of Wallop is fraught with difficulties. Nennius tells us it took place twelve years into the reign of Vortigern. Elsewhere he says that that reign began in the year that Theodosius and Valentinian were Consuls in Rome, which we know to have been in AD 425. That would put the Strife of Wallop in 437. However, Nennius also tells us that Vortigern welcomed Hengist to Britain in the fourth year of his reign, which would be 429. But Bede, Gildas and the *Anglo-Saxon Chronicle* all put that event significantly later, in the 440s. As with so much about British history at this time we are uncertain about dates.

The third noticeable thing about the events at Wallop is where they took place. The Wallop stream is a tributary of the Test and it now runs through the three small villages of Over Wallop, Middle Wallop and Nether Wallop. None of these villages has ever been very important, and finds from late- or post-Roman times are negligible. The stream is, however, on the borders of two civitates, those of the southern Belgae and the Durotriges. Perhaps the argument was related to a dispute between the two civitates. One of the key roles of the Vicarius, it will be remembered, was to hear appeals on disputes between Roman citizens or organizations.

If there was a dispute of some kind between the civitates of the Durotriges and that of the southern Belgae then a natural place for the Vicarius to hear both sides and then give a judgement would be on the border between the two. In this scenario then Vitalinus may have been a rectore from one civitates and Ambrosius a rectore from the other. Alternatively, if Vitalinus and Vortigern were one and the same, then presumably he gave judgement against the civitas of which Ambrosius was rectore and this led to the Strife.

Either way, the location of the Strife of Wallop points to a disagreement between two civitates. It is not the only indication of such tensions. Archaeological finds seem to hint at something similar. One of the most impressive earthworks in Britain is the Wansdyke that runs from the coast of the Severn Estuary near Maes Knoll in Somerset east to end more than thirty miles away near Marlborough. It faces north and consists of a ditch that was originally eight feet deep backed by a bank that was thirteen feet tall and surmounted by a wooden wall or fence of some kind. In at least some places the ditch had sheer sides, held in place with timber revetments. This was clearly a formidable obstacle and had taken a good deal of effort to build.

The date of Wansdyke is uncertain. In one place it cuts through a Roman road, so it must be post-Roman. Its modern name is derived from the older form 'Woden's Dyke' and since the English habitually gave the names of their pagan gods to large structures that they found when they arrived it is thought that the dyke is pre-English. It must, therefore, have been built by during the years that we are studying. More precise dating is impossible, so it could date to anywhere between about AD 410 and 600.

Interestingly, the Wansdyke runs along the border between the civitates of the Durotriges and the northern Belgae. Again some form of tension between civitates is implied, and interestingly the Durotriges and the Belgae are involved in both.

Nor is that all. A string of small towns in the West Midlands gained some impressively strong fortifications. All of these lay close to the borders of the civitas of the Dobunni. A similar line of fortified towns lay around the borders of the Trinovantes civitas north of the Thames estuary. This may simply be an indication that the rectores of the various civitates were being selfish in their military expenditure and preferred to spend the money in their own territory rather than send it off to a vicarius to spend at the other end of Britain, but it might equally be indicative of growing tensions between the civitates.

Another indication of increasing fragmentation of military organization can be found in the distribution of military equipment. Under the Roman Empire, weapons and other military gear were mass produced in large workshops and distributed to army units. The result is that a Roman cavalry belt buckle found on Hadrian's Wall would be much the same as one found on the Rhine Frontier. But from about AD 420 onward there were increasingly clear local variations in military equipment. Not only was military gear being made locally, but it was not being exported to other civitates. Thus military gear in use within the Dobunni civitas was clearly different from that used in the Catuvellauni civitas next door. To call these pieces of equipment uniforms might be going a bit too far, but they may be indicative of other differences in terms of shield colouring, fabric patterns and so forth. At any rate, such visual differences would be noticeable to soldiers. A man from the Belgae military would be instantly recognizable as such. Again, a sign that the local civitates forces were becoming more military and increasingly separate from each other.

The finds of Germanic military gear dating to about AD 400 to 480 is also interesting. In the earlier period the finds crop up on Thanet, along the Thames estuary, in Norfolk, up the Lincolnshire coast and around the Humber. These are exactly where a centralized British government might be expected to put mercenaries in order to fight off seaborne raiders, whether they originated from Germany or north of Hadrian's Wall.

But there are concentrations of Germanic military gear in some unexpected places as well. There is a cluster of finds just south of London, another near Market Harborough and a smaller clump near Mansfield. But the largest of these inland sites is on the upper Thames between Wallingford and Abingdon. As with the fortified towns, these sites are all close to borders between civitates. Mansfield lies between the Brigantes and the Corieltauvi, Market Harborough between the Corieltauvi and the Catuvellauni, London between the Catuvellauni and the Regni and the upper Thames between the Catuvellauni and the Dobunni.

We have no way of knowing why these mercenaries were placed where they were. If they were hired by the central government of the Vicarius they might have been guarding administrative or financial bases. They might just as easily have been put in place to keep the peace between squabbling civitates. If they were hired by the civitates they might have a similar explanation to the fortified towns and local militias.

By the second half of the fifth century, the distribution has changed a bit, but not much. A new cluster of Germanic finds has sprung up on the south coast around Seaford and Littlehampton in the civitas of the Regni. Another new cluster can be seen around Ely and Cambridge and a few finds have been made near York. The already existing sites have all grown considerably, except for that south of London which seems to have shrunk.

Whatever the reasons for these assorted changes in military dispositions, there is a clear trend as the fifth century passes for the military to be moved from the exterior limits of Britain to inland sites.

Archaeology also tells us that during these years there was a continuing decline in overall prosperity. The industrial sectors of the economy were reduced to catering only for local needs. Agriculture and related activities continued, but again there seems to have been a reduction in scale. In particular some areas of less productive farmland were taken out of production and the sites where the workers lived were abandoned. This has been linked to the collapse of the grain export trade. Again, agriculture was moving more to cater for local needs as the economy of the Roman Empire fragmented and collapsed.

This in turn had a marked impact on the towns. The Roman lifestyle that had summoned the towns into existence was no longer so attractive, and prospects for lucrative careers in the imperial service had gone. Moreover the larger scale industries and export trades that had provided employment within towns had collapsed. The economic and political rationale for towns had gone and they went into a decline. There are signs that large areas within the town walls of many towns were abandoned, though the walls themselves seem to continue to have been maintained, repaired and, in a few cases, renovated.

One of the key archaeological features of Roman towns in Britain goes by the name of 'dark earth'. This is a layer, sometimes up to three feet thick, that lies immediately on top of the Roman remains and beneath later early medieval deposits. It is difficult to date as it usually contains little in the way of pottery, jewellery or coins. The few efforts that have been made to date the dark earth seem to place it somewhere between AD 500 and 700.

The cause of this dark earth has long been something of a mystery, but in recent years more detailed analyses have revealed high levels of ash, charcoal, animal dung, rotted wood and other vegetation. There have also been finds of high levels of pollen and seeds from plants that proliferated on empty bomb sites after the Second World War. The interpretation of what this dark earth means is controversial, but one particular picture is gaining ground.

This scenario envisages the majority of the residential and industrial buildings within Roman towns being abandoned as the urban, industrialized population left to find employment in the still functioning agricultural society outside the town walls. There are a few isolated examples of public buildings being apparently kept in use throughout much of the period of dark earth. Churches, temples and the more robust buildings seem to have escaped the general collapse. These buildings were usually made of stone or brick, while the less important buildings were of timber standing on stone or brick foundations. The rural population around the towns presumably had a use for these sturdier buildings – perhaps as meeting places, ritual centres or some such. The weeds growing on abandoned and collapsing buildings would have dated mostly from this period of general abandonment. How many years or decades this lasted is unclear, but it was clearly long enough to allow the stoutly built wooden houses, workshops and warehouses to fall down.

The fact that the rural population returned to the towns for some purposes and that the defensive walls were kept in good repair points to an origin of the dark earth. The dark earth may be the remains of flimsy, temporary structures made of wattle and daub, roofed over with thatch. These buildings would produce the organic-rich deposits, while cooking or heating fires used by the people living in them would give the ash and charcoal. The lack of pottery and jewellery is best explained by the buildings being only temporary. They might have been put up hurriedly, inhabited for a few weeks, then abandoned and allowed to collapse, only to be rebuilt the next time the rural population came to live in the town for a few weeks.

There is really only one likely scenario that would have produced this sort of large scale, but temporary occupation of the old towns: war. If the countryside were subjected to periodic bouts of raiding, warfare, chaos and violence then the farmers, herdsmen and their families would have flocked into the old towns to shelter behind the stout stone and brick defensive walls until the roving warriors had passed and it was safe to emerge once more. The lack of any secure dating for the dark earth means that archaeology cannot tell us when this extended period of occasional warfare engulfed Britain.

Turning to the written record for some clue, it may be best to start with three written references from the continent which, unlike the British accounts, can be dated securely.

The first of these is the *Chronica Gallica*, a chronicle which was kept in Gaul between the years AD 379 and 452. It was probably written in the Rhone Valley, or perhaps at Marseilles, and is concerned almost exclusively with what was going on in Gaul during those years. In 441 the chronicle records that

> The Britons even at this time have been handed over across a wide area through various catastrophes and events to the rule of the Saxons.

The disputes over what this entry means have been endless. The Gallic writer did not say that there had been an invasion, conquest or vast bloodshed. He said that parts of Britain had come to be ruled by the Saxons, and the Latin vocabulary used implies that this was done legally. The date might point us toward the career of Hengist. Certainly at one point Hengist came to rule all of Kent due to a perfectly legal agreement with Vortigern. Kent was that part of Britain most likely to be familiar to a man in Gaul, so what happened there may have loomed large in the mind of a man living down the Rhone valley somewhere. On the other hand, the phrase 'across a wide area' may seem a rather sweeping way to talk about Kent.

The second source is the book *Getica*, or *The Deeds of the Goths*, written in Constantinople by the historian Jordanes in about AD 551. The book is a shortened version of a much longer book about the Goths by Flavius Magnus Aurelius Cassiodorus, a high-ranking Eastern Roman senator and diplomat who had lived for some years among the Goths. The book by Cassiodorus has not survived, so we have only the abridged version produced by Jordanes to go on.

Jordanes included a lengthy section on King Euric of the Visigoths, who ruled what is now southern France from 466 to

484. Referring to about 470, Jordanes includes the following paragraph:

> Now Euric, king of the Visigoths, perceived the frequent change of Roman Emperors and strove to hold Gaul by his own right. The Emperor Anthemius heard of it and asked the Britons for aid. Their King Riotimus came with twelve thousand men into the state of the Bituriges by the way of Ocean, and was received as he disembarked from his ships. Euric, king of the Visigoths, came against them with an innumerable army, and after a long fight he routed Riotimus, King of the Britons, before the Romans could join him. So when he had lost a great part of his army, he fled with all the men he could gather together, and came to the Burgundians, a neighbouring tribe then allied to the Romans. But Euric, king of the Visigoths, seized the Gallic city of Arverna; for the Emperor Anthemius was now dead.

Most of the people and places mentioned here can be identified. Anthemius was the Western Roman Emperor from 467 to 472. Bituriges was the area around Bourges, south of the Loire. The Burgundians were a Germanic tribe that at this date occupied the area around Lyon in the Rhone Valley. Arverna was somewhere near what is now Vichy. It is only Riotimus who seems to be obscure.

In fact, he is not as unknown as some historians would have us believe. 'Riotimus' is a latinization of a title that means 'wide-reigning king'. This is very close to the 'wide ruler' that is the meaning of the title Vortigern. Of course, Riotimus lived about thirty years too late to be Vortigern but he would seem to have been using the same informal title as his predecessor. This would indicate that he was holding, or at least claiming to hold, the same official position – that of Vicarius of Britain.

Perhaps the most interesting thing about Riotimus is that he led an army from Britain to the continent to fight the Goths. No ruler willingly leaves his realm if there is not complete peace and stability, still less would he march off with what must have been a fairly sizeable proportion of his army. For whoever was holding this title to leave Britain, he must have been confident that all was well at home, that he faced no possible rebellion and that outside invaders would not take advantage of his absence.

This would indicate that in 470 the Diocese of Britain was coping reasonably well with the economic decline, worsening climate and declining population. The population may have left the towns largely abandoned during this time, but the chaos that led to the dark earth would not yet seem to have come. If Britain was poorer and less ordered than it had been, it was yet a functioning state living in comparative peace. It was not to last.

The paragraph in Jordanes leaves Riotimus having fled to the Rhone Valley for safety. We do not know what happened to him next. Maybe he stayed where he was, perhaps he died or he might have gone home. Whatever became of Riotimus his reputation for competence will have been severely damaged by the expedition and he would have lost a large number of men. If Britain had been stable before he left for Gaul, it does not seem have stayed that way for long.

We have three different versions of what happened next. Gildas, Nennius and the *Anglo-Saxon Chronicle* all describe an event. While there is no real proof that they are all talking about the same thing, it would seem likely that they are. As usual, Gildas is annoyingly vague talking about bloodshed, destruction and chaos. Nennius gives a much more detailed account, which runs as follows:

> After the death of Vortimer, Hengist being strengthened by new men, collected his ships, and calling his leaders together, consulted by what stratagem they might overcome Vortigern and his army; with insidious intention they sent messengers to the king, with offers of peace and perpetual friendship; unsuspicious of treachery, the monarch, after advising with his elders, accepted the proposals.
>
> Hengist, under pretence of ratifying the treaty, prepared an entertainment, to which he invited the king, the nobles, and military officers, in number about three hundred; speciously concealing his wicked intention, he ordered three hundred Saxons to conceal each a knife under his feet, and to mix with the Britons 'and when', said he, 'they are sufficiently inebriated, I will cry out, "Saxons, strike now", then let each

> draw his knife, and kill his man; but spare the king, on account of his marriage with my daughter, for it is better that he should be ransomed than killed.' The king with his company, appeared at the feast; and mixing with the Saxons, who, whilst they spoke peace with their tongues, cherished treachery in their hearts, each man was placed next his enemy. After they had eaten and drunk, and were much intoxicated, Hengist suddenly shouted as he had said and instantly his adherents drew their knives, and rushing upon the Britons, each slew him that sat next to him, and there was slain three hundred of the nobles of Vortigern. The king being a captive, purchased his redemption, by delivering up the three provinces of East, South, and Middle Sex, besides other districts at the option of his betrayers.

That is where Nennius leaves things before turning to give brief biographies of some saints. Clearly whatever source he had for this period of history stopped at this point. While it is a dramatic and exciting story, there is a problem with it. Both Gildas and the *Anglo-Saxon Chronicle* have Hengist leaving Kent after being defeated and not returning. However, Bede and the *Anglo-Saxon Chronicle* do mention a new Germanic mercenary leader whose deeds would seem to fit the events described so colourfully by Nennius. This is one of the more enigmatic figures in either source, and his name was Aelle. The *Chronicle* statements on Aelle are perfunctory, as are nearly all its entries for this early period. They read as follows.

> 477: Aelle and his 3 sons, Cymen and Wlencing and Cissa, came to the land of Britain with 3 ships at the place which is named Cymen's Shore, and there killed many Welsh and drove some to flight into the wood called Andredes Leag.
>
> 485: Here Aelle fought against the Welsh near the margin of Mearcred's Burn.
>
> 491: Here Aelle and Cissa besieged Andredes Chester, and killed all who lived in there; there was not even one Briton left there.

A later writer, Henry of Huntingdon, added on the basis of unknown authority that Cissa went on to live to the age of ninety and was granted the Roman city of Noviomagus Reginorum by his father. That city was then renamed 'Cissa's Chester', and is known now as Chichester. In early English the word '*chester*' was used to mean a Roman fortified place and probably derives from the Latin '*castrum*'.

As with all dates in the *Anglo-Saxon Chronicle* before 600 the dates given for Aelle should be considered to be only approximate, but, as they stand, they occur just after the expedition of Riotimus. We can, however, identify three of the places mentioned. Cymen's Shore was a patch of low-lying land south of Selsey Bill that now lies under the waters of the English Channel. Andredes Leag is the Weald forest and Andredes Chester is the great Roman fortress at Pevensey. Mearcred's Burn cannot be precisely identified, but the name means 'border stream', so it probably lay somewhere on the fringes of the civitas of the Regni. Together with Chichester all these places lie within the modern English county of Sussex, and within the old Roman civitas of the Regni.

The account as it stands in the *Chronicle* would seem to indicate that Aelle had a similar career path to Hengist, though he was more successful. It would seem that he came ashore as either an invader or as a mercenary hired by the Rectores of the Regni civitas. He then rebelled, fought a successful war against the British and grabbed power in Regni. He was then able to pass power on to his son Cissa and established the Kingdom of the South Saxons that in time developed into Sussex. As we have seen with Hengist, it was the aim of barbarians to take over a functioning Roman administrative region so that they could enjoy the tax revenues and other tributes. Raiding and pillaging was only a second best option.

However, Bede and the *Chronicle* state quite definitely that Aelle achieved far more than this, tying in with the account in Nennius of what Hengist did on his second incursion. Bede and the *Chronicle* both state that Aelle was the first of the English leaders to hold the title and authority of a position that would later be a constant ambition among English monarchs. In the *Chronicle* this title is given as '*Bretwalda*', an early English term that translates as 'wide ruler'. We have, of course, encountered this term before in the forms of Vortigern and Riotimus.

Bede renders the title as '*imperium*' over Britain. Bede was a careful scholar who knew his Latin, so his use of this word demands some attention. In later Roman constitutional usage, 'imperium' meant the legal right to exercise the power of the state. It was contrasted to '*potesta*', which meant the brute force to impose the power of the state. The emperors, of course, held the ultimate and unlimited imperium over the whole of the empire, but lesser government officials held imperium over their particular regions or duties. The Vicarius of the Diocese of Britain, for instance, would be said to have held imperium over Britain.

It would seem, therefore, that both the term Bretwalda and Bede's imperium are describing the same thing, which is the same thing indicated by the titles of Vortigern and Riotimus. They are talking about the office of Vicarius of Britain. We have seen that the Vortigern who dealt with Hengist over Kent ruled with the aid of a council over an apparently unified and generally peaceful state. Riotimus must also have had control over a similar situation in Britain or he would never have gone to Gaul. But now that position is taken by a Germanic mercenary named Aelle.

If we look again at the account in Nennius and substitute the name of Aelle for Hengist we might be getting close to what actually happened. The 'Vortigern' mentioned here might be a different man, but holding the same title, to the 'Vortigern' who invited in Hengist. After all, this event is said to happen after the death of Vortiper, son of Vortigern. Perhaps Nennius used the name of Hengist for a pagan Germanic mercenary who was nameless in his source. This is speculation, but it would explain why the English side of the story gave the credit of gaining control over Britain to Aelle, not to Hengist and would push the date more to the 480s when Aelle was active and after Riotimus had lost his army in Gaul.

However the sequence of events unfolded and at whatever date, all the sources are agreed that for a short period of time a Germanic mercenary held supreme power in Britain. It would seem that Aelle had hit the barbarian jackpot. He had got himself into a position of absolute power over a Roman diocese. If that diocese was not as rich as it had been, it was still comparatively prosperous and certainly made Aelle one of the most successful barbarian mercenaries in Europe.

But it was not to last. Gildas tells us what happened next.

> A remnant, to whom wretched citizens flock from different places on every side, as eagerly as a hive of bees when a storm is threatening, praying at the same time unto Him with their whole heart, and, as is said, 'Burdening the air with unnumbered prayers,' that they should not be utterly destroyed, take up arms and challenge their victors to battle under Ambrosius Aurelianus. He was a man of unassuming character, who, alone of the Roman race chanced to survive in the shock of such a storm (as his parents, people undoubtedly clad in the purple, had been killed in it), whose offspring in our days have greatly degenerated from their ancestral nobleness. To these men, by the Lord's favour, there came victory.
>
> From that time, the citizens were sometimes victorious, sometimes the enemy, in order that the Lord, according to His wont, might try in this nation the Israel of to-day, whether it loves Him or not. This continued up to the year of the siege of Badon Hill, and of almost the last great slaughter inflicted upon the rascally crew. And this commences, a fact I know, as the forty-fourth year, with one month now elapsed; it is also the year of my birth.

Nennius gives a similar picture of events, with a long protracted war in which the advantage swings from one side to the other before the British are eventually victorious. Nennius lists twelve battles fought during this war, with Badon Hill again being the last. He also gives credit for Badon to Arthur. Nennius says that 'Arthur fought against them (the Saxons) in those days along with the kings of the British, but he was their leader in battle.' Again we have the picture of an overall leader operating with a council of nobles. Arthur was, presumably, next in the line of Wide Leaders. The *Annales Cambriae* records Arthur's victory at Badon Hill under the year 516 and then under the year AD 537 records the Battle of Camlann in which Arthur and Medraut are both killed. It offers no explanations as to what was happening or why.

Geoffrey of Monmouth used this point in his story of the Kings of Britain to interpolate the long and complex cycle of stories about Arthur that formed so much of his book. Stripped of its romantic and clearly invented mass of details, Geoffrey's account is basically as follows. Vortigern is overthrown and replaced by Ambrosius Aurelianus who successfully fights against the Saxons, who are pushed back. Ambrosius is then poisoned by a Saxon spy and his throne is taken by his brother Uther. The Saxons return to rebellion and it is only after much effort that Uther defeats them. Uther is, however, already ill and dies after drinking from an infected spring of water. Uther's death sparks a fresh Saxon invasion, while the great council of Britain meets at Silchester and chooses Uther's fifteen-year-old son, Arthur, to be king. Arthur then fights a series of battles, similar in name and location to those given by Nennius, before defeating the Saxons. There then follows a long and glorious reign of peace before Arthur is killed during a civil war fought against his nephew Mordred – who is usually taken to be the Medraut of the *Annales Cambriae*. Mordred's sons are then killed and the title King of Britain passes to Malgo, who is clearly the Maglocunus or Maelgwn mentioned by Gildas as a ruler in northern Wales.

There have been many disputes about this most obscure of periods in British history. Understandably much of the interest and disputes have centred around the figure of Arthur. In later legend, Arthur grew in stature to be a mighty king of astonishing wisdom, power, chivalry and charm. Hundreds of stories were set in and around his court at Camelot and his kingdom. Figures such as Lancelot, Merlin, Guinevere, Gawain and Bedivere came to be associated with him. The vast majority of this is later legend totally unrelated to the historic character. The great fame and the romantic nature of the legends has had the unfortunate effect in recent years of causing many scholars to dismiss Arthur himself as being as much a fantasy as the bulk of the stories about him.

It is not the business of this book to argue for or against the reality of a historic Arthur. However, it is quite clear that somebody was leading the British during these years and that somebody commanded the British army at the Battle of Badon Hill. Some have suggested that this man was Ambrosius Aurelianus. Such an identification seems to be based on the fact that he is the only successful British commander mentioned by Gildas. But Gildas does not say that Ambrosius commanded at Badon. If he had done, then Gildas would surely have said so for Ambrosius is one of the few men that he is flattering about. There is only one person who is named as the commander at Badon, and that is Arthur. It would seem churlish to deny him the honour.

In any case, the overall picture that emerges from the various sources is consistent even if personalties and dates cannot be given with any real certainty or precision. The Diocese of Britain had been in decline for decades but in the early-sixth century it was still there. It was a few years after this that Gildas lived and worked. In his great book *On the Ruin and Conquest of Britain* he gives a very clear and concise picture of what Britain was like in his time. It was against this background that Ceawlin was to operate, so it is time to turn to what Gildas tells us about Britain in about 530. Gildas was clearly depressed by what he saw. And he had reason to be.

Chapter 4

The Arthurian Peace

Gildas makes it clear that after Badon Hill, there followed a lengthy period of peace between the British and the Saxons. 'Wars with foreigners have ceased', he writes. The *Annales Cambriae* record nothing except the deaths of various saints, bishops and rulers. Bede fills these years with an account of the theological dispute about the teachings of Pelagius on Original Sin. The *Anglo-Saxon Chronicle* mentions an eclipse of the sun and a couple of skirmishes in which 'a few men were killed'. Nennius records nothing other than a succession of births and deaths, though he does talk about a raid by the Irish on northern Wales.

The unmistakeable message from this lack of action in the various historic sources is that not much of any real importance was going on at this time. The years between the Battle of Badon Hill and the time that Gildas was writing have been termed the 'Arthurian Peace', after the name of the man who presumably commanded the British at Badon. But this overall impression of peace should not mask some disturbing events going on behind the scenes.

The *Anglo-Saxon Chronicle* as ever looks at things from the point of view of the Germanic incomers who would become the English. It records relatively little for the years after Aelle, but three incidents are perhaps of some importance. In AD 514 a group of Germanic mercenaries led by Stuff and Wihtgar take control of the Isle of Wight. In 519 Cerdic and his son Cynric take control of the civitas of the southern Belgae centred on Venta Belgarum (Winchester). Finally, in 547 Ida and a group of Angles seize the coastal fortress of Bamburgh and establish an independent kingdom.

None of these dates can be said to be at all accurate. However, they do show a general trend under which the centralized control exercised by the 'wide ruler' is starting to break down. Bamburgh and Wight are both peripheral and by themselves unimportant, though it is significant that the Germanic mercenaries are able to first establish and then maintain a grip on these isolated strongholds.

The role of Cerdic at Winchester is unclear. The *Anglo-Saxon Chronicle* says that he 'received the kingdom', and that he then fought a couple of battles against the British. It has been speculated that he was the Rectore of the civitas who grabbed dictatorial powers in a coup of some kind. If so, a similar feat may have been achieved at about the same time by Marcianus Gul (which means 'The Skinny') in the western part of the civitas of the Brigantes. This area covered the district north of the Dee, west of the Pennines and south of Hadrian's Wall. Marcianus Gul is known from Welsh genealogies as the ancestor of princes who ruled in the area.

If two rectores chose this time to stage coups that made them dictators within their own borders, though apparently not independent of the authority of the 'wide ruler', then others may have done so as well. It is worth asking why this change happened at this date. Whatever the chronology of late-fifth-century British history and in whichever order the historian cares to place the activities of Hengist, Aelle and Riotimus the general conclusion is that the central authority of the Vicarius or the Wide Ruler was slipping. In 410 he had been the undisputed head of the governmental system in Britain. By 500 he was not.

The local civitates were flexing their political muscles. It must be remembered that the civitates were based on what had been independent tribal kingdoms before the Romans came and it is likely that cultural differences remained between them. One needs only to look at the various states that in 1990 were part of the mighty USSR to see how the constituent parts of an apparently monolithic political state can preserve local cultures and rivalries. Georgia, Ukraine, Belarus and many others had been part of the Tsarist Russian state for generations before the formation of the USSR, but they all grabbed the chance of independence with alacrity as soon as they got the opportunity.

Moreover, in 476, Romulus Augustulus, the last Western

Roman Emperor abdicated under pressure from the Germanic kings who held real power across Italy. The regalia and other paraphernalia of imperial office were sent to Constantinople by the Senate of Rome along with a message that stated they no longer needed an emperor. The title and rights of Emperor of Rome were offered to the Eastern Emperor Zeno on condition that he did not interfere with affairs in Italy. Zeno accepted and so became the sole Emperor, although his power extended over only the Eastern Roman Empire. The incident is interesting as it shows that although the Senate, no doubt under pressure from the German hardmen, decided they no longer needed an emperor, they still felt that somebody needed to hold the imperial insignia. They could not yet free their minds of centuries of political habit.

News of this final collapse of the Western Empire will have filtered through to Britain eventually through merchants and travellers. It will have removed the final chance that the Roman Empire was ever coming back to Britain. Appoint your own officials until I can appoint some real ones, had been the final message from Honorius. Now it was clear that now real officials were never going to arrive. It also meant that no Roman armies were going to come to enforce the powers and authority of the Vicarius, the Wide Ruler. If he could not impose his rule for himself, nobody was going to do it for him. Local rectores and mercenary captains must have started to weigh up their chances. Cerdic, Marcianus and Stuff took their chance. Others remained loyal – for the time being.

Gildas himself was aware that things were not well. He covers these years in a single paragraph which makes for grim reading:

> But not even at the present day are the cities of our country inhabited as formerly; deserted and dismantled, they lie neglected until now, because, although wars with foreigners have ceased, domestic wars continue. The recollection of so hopeless a ruin of the island, and of the unlooked-for help, has been fixed in the memory of those who have survived as witnesses of both marvels. Owing to this kings, magistrates, private persons, priests, ecclesiastics, severally preserved their own rank. As they died away, when an age had succeeded ignorant of that storm, and having experience only

> of the present quiet, all the controlling influences of truth and justice were so shaken and overturned that, not to speak of traces, not even the remembrance of them is to be found among the ranks named above. I make exception of a few – a very few – who owing to the loss of the vast multitude that rushes daily to hell, are counted at so small a number that our revered mother, the church, in a manner does not observe them as they rest in her bosom. They are the only real children she has. Let no man think that I am slandering the noble life of these men, admired by all and beloved of God, by whom my weakness is supported so as not to fall into entire ruin, by holy prayers, as by columns and serviceable supports. Let no one think so, if in a somewhat excessively free-spoken, yea, doleful manner, driven by a crowd of evils, I shall not so much treat of, as weep concerning those who serve not only their belly, but the devil rather than Christ, who is God blessed for ever. For why will fellow-citizens hide what the nations around already not only know, but reproach us with?

As so often, Gildas is infuriatingly vague here. This is probably because he is talking about what was then recent history for his audience and so did not feel the need to go into too much detail. Everyone listening would know what he meant, but we do not. We have to pick at his words to find his meaning.

First, Gildas tells us that the cities and towns have been abandoned. He seems to be telling us that they have been utterly neglected, but that in his own time they are no longer neglected due to some fighting between the British themselves. This may be the start of the temporary reoccupations of the towns that shows up in the archaeological record as dark earth. We will look more closely at Britain in Gildas's own time later, but for now it is worth remarking that he says that towns lay abandoned for some years.

He goes on to say that this period of peace was so long that a new generation of men grew up to fill the assorted ranks of government – both secular and ecclesiastical – and that these men are not up to the job. This is, of course, only Gildas's view, but he does make clear that the old offices of state are continuing to be filled and occupied. The word translated here as 'magistrates' is, in Gildas, 'rectores', the highest office within the government of a civitas. In other words, the governmental bureaucracy of the late Roman state had survived, even if in the opinion of Gildas the men were not doing their jobs properly.

Other sources for these years are uncertain and often written down much later. Several of the hagiographies – biographies of saints that are generally thought to be unreliable – talk about Arthur in his role as great king or wide ruler. In the life of St Cadoc, who was Abbot of Llancarfan about AD 540, it is said that his father, Lord Gwynllyw of Gwynllwg (Glamorgan), abducted the beautiful daughter of Lord Brychan of Brycheiniog (Brecon). Arthur then stepped in to stop a war between the two lords and imposed a compensation payment on Gwynllwy, who then kept the girl to be his wife and, in time, mother to St Cadoc.

Another hagiography is that of St Paternus, Abbot of Llanpatenvaur in around 510. In this story, Arthur comes to the monastery demanding the payment of taxes. St Paternus refused on the grounds that the wealth of his monastery was for the glory of God and His priests, not for the use of secular authority. Arthur is furious and promises revenge, but St Paternus calls down divine intervention and sends Arthur away empty handed. All good hagiographic stuff that shows St Paternus defying secular authority for the benefit of the Church – an activity on which monks were very keen.

There are several other mentions of Arthur in these documents. Nobody is suggesting that the actual incidents related should be taken too seriously, but the attitudes underlying them are interesting. Arthur is shown acting as a good Vicarius should. He is raising taxes and mediating in disputes.

One final hagiography is worth a mention. It talks about a Pictish nobleman and warrior named Caw who lived around 490 or 520 and had his home near the River Clyde. Although Caw is not the subject of the work, he does rate a substantial mention. It is made clear that he has never submitted to any ruler, not even to Arthur. This may simply be a comment added generations later to emphasize how important Caw was, but it may also reflect the reality of the early sixth century. Roman control never reached beyond the Clyde, and Hadrian's Wall lay far to the south on the

Tyne. Assuming Arthur occupied the position of Wide Ruler, descended from that of Vicarius, his authority would not have extended north of Hadrian's Wall, which is the point made about Caw.

The authority of the Wide Ruler was also being tested in what is now southwestern Wales. Across an area from Aberystwyth in the north to Carmarthen in the south, and from Llandovery in the east to St David's in the west there is a dense scatter of place names of Irish origin, and archaeologists have turned up buildings and fortifications erected in Irish styles. These seem to date from about 430 to 510 and represent either hostile invaders or settlers coming peacefully.

An Irish history, written many decades after the events, records that King Illan mac Dúnlainge of Leinster fought nine campaigns in Britain. Illan ruled for twenty-two years and died in about 527, so presumably his wars took place around 510 or so. An independent, though equally late source from Wales records a war against the Irish led by a man with the very Roman name of Agricola taking place around 500 or so. Presumably these two accounts refer to the same war, seen from opposite sides. Perhaps Illan was trying to establish political control over the Irish settlers, or perhaps Agricola was seeking to conquer a mass of independent Irish settlers. Either way, both sides agree that the Irish lost.

Archaeology also shows us that there was an underlying and increasingly serious problem for the Wide Ruler. The climate was changing, and with it the prosperity of the people. For some 400 years Europe had basked in a climate generally warmer and drier than ours today. This had made large-scale grain farming a viable business, allowing farmers to grow much more food than they needed themselves. This surplus food had gone to feed the towns and cities, supporting the craftsmen, bureaucrats and soldiers who organized the empire.

Around AD 350 or so this began to change slowly as the climate became cooler and damper. At first it was not much noticed by farmers, but by 500 the process was well advanced and could not be ignored. Farmers in Britain gave up some crops completely, and yields of other crops declined. The productivity of British grainfields deteriorated, meaning that a farmer needed to keep a high proportion of his crop to feed himself and his family. There was, therefore, less surplus to feed craftsmen, bureaucrats or soldiers. Perhaps because of this, the population went into decline. Absolute numbers are difficult to judge, but it seems that the number of people living in Britain may have fallen by some fifteen per cent between 410 and 540.

Whatever challenges the Wide Ruler was facing in terms of foreign invasion, internal coups or discontent he was going to have increasingly slender resources on which to draw. Not only that, but as the years passed and agricultural output fell the civitates rectores were also going to find themselves short on wealth. They would become increasingly reluctant to share what they had with a Wide Ruler. The tension between the central government authority and local rulers was only going to get worse.

One of the thorniest problems about this period of peace regards the status of the Germanic settlers. It would seem most likely that the authority of Hengist over the civitas of Cantium was broken by Vortimer, son of Vortigern. However the later English kings of Kent traced their family back to Hengist and maintained that they had enjoyed a continual rule over Kent ever since his day. Archaeology shows Germanic peoples continuing to live in Kent through the years of peace, but only in certain areas. They are restricted to the offshore islands of Grain, Sheppey and Thanet, plus adjacent areas of the mainland. Most of Kent has few, if any, archaeological signs of the incomers.

The picture is repeated in Sussex, land of Aelle and his son Cissa. Again the written sources indicate that the invaders were driven out, but later English kings claimed descent from Aelle and that they had ruled the area since his day. And again, archaeology shows a definite, but limited settlement by the incomers. The Germanic finds are concentrated around the mouths of the Ouse and Arun rivers.

It is difficult to be certain about the status of these settlements. Perhaps they retained some form of independence from the Wide Ruler, as their dynastic leaders later claimed. Or perhaps they survived at all only by submitting to the political control of the newly triumphant Roman-style government.

Elsewhere in what had been Roman Britain, Germanic settlement seems to have been densest in what is now Norfolk, Suffolk, Lincolnshire and Nottinghamshire with smaller patches in

Yorkshire, Berkshire, Gloucestershire, Hampshire and elsewhere. There are no claims that any of these groups rebelled at any time, so it must be presumed that they had continued to be loyal foederati or mercenaries employed by the British. During the years of peace they presumably continued as such, or Gildas would surely have said so. The outlying fortress of Bamburgh, ruled over by Ida, lay north of Hadrian's Wall.

Those years of peace would become years of decline, a fact emphasized again and again by Gildas in his mournful work *On the Ruin and Conquest of Britain*. It is time to turn to that work and see what Gildas has to tell us about the state of Britain in the years when he wrote and when Ceawlin was born.

Chapter 5

The Britain of Gildas

In his great work *On the Ruin and Conquest of Britain*, Gildas gives his view of the political and ecclesiastical face of Britain at the time he was writing, probably around AD 530 or so. As ever with ancient authors, it is important to bear in mind the viewpoint of the author before taking his statements at face value. With Gildas this is more important than ever for he was writing a sermon with a clear message, not an impartial history.

Gildas himself is a rather shadowy figure, despite the fame of his book. There are two hagiographies of him, both written more than 300 years after his death. The two accounts of his life differ in some crucial respects, and at this distance in time it is impossible to know which (if either) is accurate. However there is some common ground between the accounts of his life and there are also clues in his various writings themselves that tell us much about him.

Everyone agrees that Gildas was a monk who came from a wealthy and noble family. He was well educated and well connected in both ecclesiastical and civic society. He was probably educated at the great Welsh monastery and school of Llan Illtud Fawr (now Llantwit Major) at the time when St Illtud was the leading teacher there. Gildas learned not only about Christianity and theology, but also about the wider learning of the ancient world. His later written works are filled with references and allusions to the writers and philosophers of Rome and Greece. He later went to Ireland, and perhaps Brittany, to continue his education. He may even have gone to Rome, but in any case was absent from Britain for some ten years. He came back an ordained priest and took up a preaching position in one or more unknown places. During these years Gildas wrote his famous book, but also got embroiled in a rather acrimonious dispute with St David (later to be patron saint of Wales). David taught that monks should cut themselves off from the world to lead a holy and austere life of prayer, while Gildas taught that monks should engage with the wider community in pastoral work. At some point he married and had three sons and a daughter. In his old age he retired to a small chapel on the remote island of Rhuys off the south coast of Brittany. There he died on 29 January. His burial place is claimed by both Rhuys and Glastonbury.

Other traditions about Gildas are more vague and colourful. He was said to come from a noble family from what is now North Wales and that his brother was executed by having his head hacked off on a stone in Ruthin – the alleged execution stone is still there. He is said to have been summoned by Ainmuire mac Setnai, High King of Ireland, to live in Ireland and undertake a thorough reform of the Christian church in his realm. He is credited with writing hymns, prayers, proverbs and several books, at least some of which were certainly written many decades after his death. His date of birth is generally thought to have been around 500 and his death to have taken place around 570, though these dates are not beyond dispute.

In writing his extended sermon, this well-educated and much-travelled man set out to get a simple message across to his audience. This was that Britain was in a state of terminal decline, that the reason for this was the sins of its social and government elite and that if those men returned to the righteous path of God they could overcome the decline and avert disaster. At the time such a message was not unusual; many churchmen blamed a person's ill fortune and failure on a lack of moral or religious probity. All Gildas was doing was extending the idea from an individual to a nation.

So far in this book we have referred to Gildas when he was writing about the years before his present day, probably about 530. But by far the longer part of his work is concerned with Britain as it was at the time he was writing his book, describing its problems and appealing for salvation. It was against this background that Ceawlin was to operate, so we shall now turn to this section.

Gildas divides Britain into three zones. The first is that part of

Britain that had not been part of Roman Britain in 410, the lands north of Hadrian's Wall and west of the Irish Sea. The second area of Britain covers those parts ruled over by men who have set themselves up as monarchs or dictators, apparently by illegal means. These lands are generally in the west and southwest. The third area of Britain is that part which still retains, at least in part, the later Roman governmental structures of rectores, bishops, councils and the like. Gildas has almost nothing to say about the first area, but moves on rapidly to the second.

According to Gildas there were five tyrants ruling in the west of Britain. Gildas uses the word tyrant to mean a ruler who has acquired power by illegal means. Each of them was a sinner doomed to Hell unless they repented. In each case, Gildas starts by making a series of allegations about the tyrant and his behaviour, then issues a call for him to return to the paths of righteousness. Of these tyrants only two can be located geographically with certainty. However, two others feature in the genealogical ancestor lists of later rulers and nobles so they can be placed reasonably well. It would appear from this that Gildas is following a route from north to south, which enables us to guess at a location for the fifth tyrant. It would appear that in four of the five cases the tyrant has control over what had formerly been a civitas.

First on his list is Constantine, Tyrant of Damnonia. This is one of the insulting puns that Gildas liked to deploy. He meant the civitas of Dumnonia, but by replacing the 'u' with an 'a' turns an area of southwestern Britain into the land of the damned. Gildas accused Constantine of a number of vaguely worded sins, such as adultery and bigamy, and of one very specific crime. Constantine had sworn a holy oath to protect two young boys from a noble family. The boys were placed into a monastery to be educated, with two bodyguards for protection. However, Constantine had then dressed himself up as an abbot to gain admittance to the monastery. While the community was at prayer in the monastic church, Constantine had drawn his sword and killed the two boys, one of whom reached the high altar before being cut down. Constantine had thus, said Gildas, broken his oath, murdered innocents and desecrated a church. He concludes:

> Return, I pray, though from the far-off secret haunts of sins, to the tender father who has been accustomed in gladness to kill the fatted calf and to bring forward the first garment and royal ring for the erring one, and with a foretaste of heavenly hope thou shalt feel how the Lord is kind.

Next to be mentioned is Aurelius Caninus, dismissed by Gildas as both a 'lion's whelp' and a dog. Again, Gildas is punning to good effect. Lions are golden in colour, and Latin for gold is 'aureus', while Latin for dog is 'canis'. Gildas does not say where Aurelius ruled, but he is mentioned in the ancestor lists of various families from southeast Wales. He probably ruled the civitas of the Silures, or perhaps that of the Dobunni. Gildas accuses him of assorted 'murders, fornications, adulteries . . . an iniquitous thirst for civil wars and repeated plunderings,' but mentions no specific incidents. Gildas goes on to call the wife of Aurelius a 'gallow's bird'. Again he concludes by calling on the tyrant to mend his ways

> Wherefore shake thyself from thy filthy dust, and turn unto Him with thy whole heart, unto Him who created thee, so that when His anger quickly kindles, thou mayest be blest, hoping in Him.

The third tyrant rules over the Demetae, the civitas of southwest Wales that had earlier seen intense Irish settlement. This was Vortipor, described as being as savage as a leopard, though he is growing old and has a head of grey hair. Vortipor is accused of generalized killings and sins, but then with one specific crime 'the violation of a shameless daughter'. The phrasing used by Gildas would imply that this was his step-daughter or a ward, but it is not certain. Certainly it is sexual sins that seem to be the key crime of Vortipor. The tyrant is compared unfavourably to his heroic father, who is not named by Gildas but is known from other sources to have been Agricola. Gildas concludes with the usual call to repent.

The fourth is named as Cuneglasus of Dinarth. Cuneglasus probably ruled the area between the River Dee and the River Conwy, that is the area that in pre-Roman times belonged to the Deceangli tribe, though he may have ruled all of north Wales. This area was never properly incorporated as a civitas by the Romans, being in that part of the western mountains that were left in the hands of the native dynasts. Gildas accuses him of 'crimes without number', but mentions only one in detail. Cuneglasus had driven his wife into exile and then married her sister, who had taken a vow of chastity after her own husband had died.

Gildas then turns to the most important of the five tyrants, the one about whom he writes the most. This is Maglocunus the Dragon of the Island. Gildas introduces him as 'first in wickedness, exceeding many in power and at the same time in malice, more liberal in giving, more excessive in sin, strong in arms, but stronger in what destroys thy soul – thou Maglocunus'. This Maglocunus is generally thought to be the same person as a ruler named Maelgwn who features in the genealogies of several families from north Wales.

Maglocunus is accused of murdering his uncle in order to seize power as well as assorted but unspecified sins. According to Gildas, Maglocunus then entered a monastery and turned away from sin. The wording here is obscure, so it is not clear if Maglocunus actually became a monk or merely took up a more morally admirable lifestyle. Whichever was the case, it turned out to be only temporary. He burst out of the monastery 'like a young colt, which, imagining every pleasant place as not traversed, rushes along, with unbridled fury, over wide fields of crimes, heaping new sins upon old'. Having got back power (if he had ever given it up), Maglocunus got married but then sent his wife away and instead married the widow of his nephew, and Gildas accuses him of murdering the young man to get hold of the wife. Alongside these sins and insults, Gildas manages to introduce some praise. He says that Maglocunus is well educated, wealthy, powerful and generous.

The location of the territory ruled by Maglocunus has been much disputed. When dealing with the rulers of southern Wales, Gildas had gone from east to west. If he did the same in north Wales, then Maglocunus would rule lands west of the Conwy. The description of Maglocunus as being 'Dragon of the Island' has been taken to mean he ruled Mona (Anglesey), which is west of the Conwy. On the other hand, Gildas may have been moving clockwise around Wales, in which case Maglocunus would rule lands east of the Dee, the civitas of the Cornovii. Just as noticeably Gildas does not mention the territory of the Ordovices, the most powerful tribe in western Britain before the Roman invasion. Perhaps Maglocunus ruled there.

Wherever his lands were, Maglocunus may have earned the title Dragon of the Island in an interesting way that has nothing to do with Anglesey. In the British language of the time a dragon was not only a mythical animal, it was also a type of military banner. This type of dragon took the form of a metal dragon's head with a wide open mouth, behind which trailed a dragon's body in the form of a hollow tube of fabric. The wind blew in through the metal mouth, then held the body up rather like a modern windsock. By extension a dragon was also the commander of an army unit. If Maglocunus was 'Dragon of the Island' in this context then he was the military commander of the island. This recalls the description applied by Nennius to Arthur, as the military commander of the forces of the petty states in Britain. The phrase also harks back to Vortigern who recruited and led armies to protect Britain.

Gildas goes further. He states that Maglocunus was responsible in some way for all the Christians of Britain. As Gildas used the term that meant the old Roman Diocese of Britain and its peoples, and specifically excluded pagan Germans such as Aelle and Hengist. He also states that Maglocunus was the greatest and most powerful warrior in Britain and that he had 'driven many tyrants from life as well as from power'.

The inescapable conclusion is that Gildas means that Maglocunus has some sort of authority over the other rulers of Britain. In other words, that Maglocunus is the Wide Ruler of his day. This identification is strengthened by the fact that our English sources do not specify who held the post in these years, implying that whoever did hold the rank of Wide Ruler, it was not a Germanic incomer. Gildas's subsequent condemnations of Maglocunus for failing to do his duty by his peoples and the Christians would imply that he had failed to protect Britain against the invading Saxons. Despite this failure, Maglocunus must have thought the title worth having, and his contemporaries clearly looked up to him as a result. He may have been an unworthy Wide Ruler, at least in Gildas's opinion, but he held the title and was the most powerful ruler in Britain.

There are scattered clues in later documents that Maelgwn held power outside his own civitas. Monasteries across Wales name him as having been a benefactor in the remote past. It may well have been that monasteries across Britain also were endowed by Maelgwn, but that the records were lost when the monasteries were destroyed in the wars that were to follow. Nennius states that he 'ruled over the Britons from Gwynedd'. Maelgwn also features in a wide variety of genealogies, indicating that his was a good family to marry into, or to take wives from, and hence that his power was widespread.

Gildas then turns to the rest of what had been Roman Britain. Here he does not describe any tyrants or monarchs, but instead refers to *rectores*, *publici*, *privati*, *sacerdotes* and *ecclesiastici.* None of these men is singled out by name, but are all discussed in general terms. Writers contemporary to Gildas use the word rectores to mean not only the holders of that specific office, but also heads of government areas in general. It is not entirely clear if Gildas uses the term to mean the head of a civitas, of a province or of any arbitrary area. What is clear, however, is that he considers the rectores to be legal holders of office – unlike the tyrants of the west.

The term publici means men holding public office and could refer to anyone in the government bureaucracy. Privati refers to private citizens, that is men who did not work for the government. It seems likely that the term privati excludes slaves, women and children and may also not refer to poor men. Perhaps Gildas is talking about men of substance when he uses this phrase.

Taken together the rectores, publici and privati are portrayed by Gildas as being far too busy to help save Britain. He castigates some for sins of greed, oppression and such like, but carefully makes the point that not all are to blame. Some of them are said to be enslaved by the Devil. This may simply mean that they are wicked men, but elsewhere in his sermon Gildas uses the term 'Devil' to refer to the Saxon warlords whom he blames for Britain's woes. This could be taken to mean that at least some of the rectores and the civitates they ran were subject to the overlordship of the Saxons. As yet, however, the basic administrative bureaucracy of the Romans had not fallen apart, it was just being run for the benefit of the barbarians.

How widespread barbarian rule was over crumbling civitates governments it is impossible to tell from Gildas, or from archaeology. The civitas of the Cantium (Kent) and Regni (Sussex) seem likely candidates. The dense settlements of Germanic families shown by archaeology to exist in Norfolk and Suffolk might indicate that the civitas of the Iceni had also gone under the barbarian yoke. However, there is no reason to assume that barbarian political control needed large numbers of barbarian families to be effective. A strong force of tough warriors could impose a barbarian ruler on a civitas that still had an overwhelmingly British population. Similarly a large number of Germanic settlers might be foederati or mercenaries still loyal to their local British paymaster. All that can be said with certainty is that Gildas is telling us that some, but not all, civitates in central and eastern Britain were under the domination of the Saxons.

Gildas is rather more forthcoming about the clergy of his time, the sacerdotes and ecclesiastici. The two terms may be interchangeable, but sacerdotes properly refers to clergy in general while ecclesiastici means the holders of specific offices. Gildas opens his attack on these people by declaring,

> Priests Britain has, but foolish ones; a great number of ministers, but shameless; clergy, but crafty plunderers; pastors, so to say, but wolves ready for the slaughter of souls, certainly not providing what is of benefit for the people, but seeking the filling of their own belly.

Gildas paints a picture of a church organization that is widespread, wealthy and corrupt. It is quite clear from his text that there are bishops resident in some of the Roman cities and that the wider Christian community is catered for by a large number of priests. There are many monasteries containing monks and led by abbots. He tells us that there are numerous churches and other Christian buildings, he tells us that there are extensive lands and much money at the command of church officials. The structure and organization appears to be healthy and large.

The problems come with the men who occupy Church offices. Again, Gildas makes it clear that he does not condemn all the churchmen of his time. Some do good work, others do their best under difficult conditions, but many are steeped in sin. Gildas tells us that some clergymen buy their way into office by paying money to more senior clergy, to the tyrants or to the Devil (again he may be talking about Germanic warlords here). Having bought their position, these men then use the wealth of the church for their own purposes and sins. They ignore their duties and allow the Church to suffer. Another sin ascribed to these unworthy clerics was that they had agreed to pay tribute to the secular authorities. In the later Roman world, the Christian church enjoyed many exemptions from taxation and other duties, such as providing men to repair roads and town walls. It would seem that the secular authorities in Britain had ended these privileges under the need to raise money for government. Gildas, as a good monk, condemned this, believing that Church wealth should be exempt from secular authority.

To what extent the sins that Gildas condemns were widespread in the British Church at this time it is impossible to say. Gildas himself makes the point that not all is lost. Having condemned the many sins of the clergy he writes

> Some may say: All bishops or presbyters are not so wicked as they have been described in the former part; because they are not defiled by the infamy of schism or of pride or of uncleanness. Neither do I deny this.

That there was a serious problem cannot be denied. Gildas was writing for a contemporary audience which would have seen the Church as it then was. If what Gildas claimed was totally untrue he would have undermined his whole purpose in writing. On the other hand, Gildas may well have been exaggerating for effect. He had a message to sell and condemning a large number of Church officials, but not the Christian Church itself, would have helped him.

Much of the rest of Gildas's famous book is taken up with scholarly and learned comparisons between the virtues of Biblical figures or men of ancient Rome on the one hand and the sins he has outlined as being common in his day. This long and highly rhetorical section would have impressed the educated listeners with how clever Gildas was and told them how seriously he took the matter in hand to have spent so long looking up obscure passages, but it does not get us any further in understanding Britain in about AD 530.

The overall image of Britain given by Gildas chimes remarkably well with what was going on in Gaul, Hispania, Italia, Africa and elsewhere. In those areas of the former Roman Empire the barbarians had taken over political control, and across some areas had moved in to occupy extensive areas of land. As in Britain the deteriorating climate led to a fall in population and drastically reduced prosperity. The collapse in civilization was as much due to the failing climate and economy as it was to the invasions of the barbarians.

But although they were politically dominant on the continent, the barbarians were very much in the minority in terms of numbers. The bureaucracy of most areas remained and continued to serve the new barbarian masters. Over time the Roman civil service changed dramatically, but there was no definitive break. The barbarians had taken over a declining province, but sought to keep it going for their own benefit and used the machinery of government that they had inherited to help them do this. Even some of the old Roman nobility continued into the new age; we know of at least two Roman families in Gaul that continued to hold extensive lands at least into the early 700s.

Gildas would have known all this, he was widely travelled. His purpose in writing was to stop the rot from spreading any further in Britain. The process of barbarization does not seem to have been so far advanced in Britain as it was in contemporary Gaul, Italy or Spain. Presumably this was because of the victories won when Gildas was a toddler, in particular the victory at Badon Hill. But now Gildas could see things slipping again. He was angry. He denounced the sinful, lazy and corrupt men that he saw around him.

But Gildas did something more. He offered hope and called out for help. He ends with the words 'the wrath of the Lord may be averted from you, inasmuch as He mercifully says: I wish not the death of the sinner, but that he may be converted and live.' What Gildas wants is for the peoples of Britain, and specifically their rulers, to abandon the sins that he has outlined and take up arms against the barbarians. Warriors and weapons alone will not defeat the Saxons, he says, only pure hearts and men free from sin can defeat the enemy that has been sent by God to punish the sins of the Britons.

The question was, who was going to achieve all this? Gildas had named and shamed the tyrants who were not stepping up to the challenge. First and foremost among these failures was Maglocunus, the Dragon of the Island. This was the man who had the legitimate authority to lead Britain out of danger, but he was not doing it.

It seems likely that Gildas was indirectly appealing to somebody not mentioned in his text. If all the people he mentions were not going to fit his role as divinely appointed saviour of the British race, then somebody else had to. Gildas must have thought that his audience would know who he was talking about. He must have thought that the person in question would know who he was talking about. But who was it? And was he listening?

Chapter 6

Britain in Decline

Gildas is our best, most contemporary and most detailed source for what Britain was like in around AD 530, but not our only one. Gildas portrays Britain as being in decline, rent by corruption, violence and sin. Perhaps our other sources will confirm that image, or contradict it.

These sources vary in quality, quantity and reliability. Archaeology can tell us a lot, but written sources fill in other sections. Much of this written evidence was written by and for churchmen, so it concentrates on the works of the Church and its employees, but it is nonetheless instructive for that and has much to tell us about social and economic conditions.

St Patrick died in 493 and is unique among early churchmen in having left us writings about himself that are undoubtedly from his own hand. There are many later legends and apocryphal stories about Patrick, but his own writings tell us much about him. He was born somewhere in western Britain, the son of a *decurio* – a man serving on the council of a civitas – and grandson of a Christian priest. At the age of sixteen he was captured by Irish raiders and taken to Ireland where he was sold into slavery. After six years as a shepherd, Patrick fled captivity, found a ship willing to carry him and managed to get home. He then embarked on a career in the Church, gaining a reputation for piety and learning but not achieving high office. At some point he had a vision of the recently deceased Bishop Victoricus urging him to return to Ireland. His appointed mission was to minister to the fledgling and growing Christian community in Ireland and to convert the pagan majority to the new faith. Patrick spent the rest of his life in Ireland converting pagans, ordaining priests and founding monasteries. Patrick's career has, over the years, become confused with that of other Christian missionaries to Ireland and there is some dispute as to just how important he really was. This does not affect the validity of what he has to say about the world around him, as he saw it.

Patrick's writings mention Britain only as background to his work in Ireland, but he does give some illuminating details. The Britain that he describes is a settled and generally peaceful place, despite occasional barbarian raids such as the one in which he was captured. He mentions in passing some officials with Roman-style titles who appear to be exercising the sorts of powers compatible with their positions.

Patrick also mentions a dispute with the bishops in Britain. This was certainly linked to allegations against Patrick of financial impropriety, but the real issue seems to have been who had authority over Patrick and the increasingly large and wealthy Christian community in Ireland. The British bishops clearly wanted to establish their authority over the Irish Church, while Patrick countered this by referring to the authorities in Gaul. This dispute could have importance only if the organization of the British Church was intact and functioning properly. If the Church authorities were in turmoil, riven by disputes or faced by collapsing authority they would hardly have expended so much effort and time trying to extend their reach. The problem is that we have no clue in Patrick's writings as to when this dispute occured. A later source says that it was referred to Rome for arbitration and that Pope Leo I decided to place Ireland under neither Britain nor Gaul, but to make it answerable directly to Rome. Leo died in the 460s, so if the later source is correct that puts the dispute in the mid-fifth century.

After Patrick, the conversion of the Irish was completed by other priests and bishops. The activities of these men are known mostly from later accounts and are concerned mostly with events and personalities within Ireland. There are, however, some facts relevant to Britain. Throughout the fifth century the leading lights of the Irish Church came from Britain or Gaul, indicating that a functioning Church still existed in Britain and had the energy to send men to Ireland. The first native Irish clergyman of any distinction was Ciaran of Saigir who was active in the 520s and 530s. There are also hints that between about 490 and 550 raids on Britain ceased to be made. No reasons are given for this, but the establishment of a strong and peaceful government in Britain would be a strong contender.

In Britain itself a key source is the *Life of St Samson*. Unlike most hagiographies, this book was written during the seventh century and was clearly based on an even earlier work. It is therefore considered to be much more accurate than most other hagiographies. We know from this book that Samson was ordained a priest in the year that the first day of Lent fell on the Feast of St Peter, which was 521. We know also that he attended a church council in Gaul in the 560s, when he was described by a Gallic writer as being elderly. Presumably he was born about 490 and died about 570, which makes him a contemporary of Gildas.

Like Gildas, Samson was unimpressed by the state of the Christian Church in Britain. While Gildas urged secular authorities to turn away from sin and take up arms, Samson set about reforming the Church from within. He travelled about preaching a message of redemption through personal austerity and devotion to duty. The reception he received seems to have been mixed. No doubt some Churchmen wanted to do right by their flock, but others preferred worldly luxury and viewed him as a troublemaker.

Samson's chance came in the ironic circumstances of a drunken dinner. Pyr, Abbot of the monastery on Caldey Island, held a celebratory meal one night and got heroically drunk. At the end of the meal he staggered out of the hall and headed toward his rooms. A few minutes later there came a loud shriek from the abbot as he fell headlong down the monastic well. He was pulled out by some of the more sober monks, but died a few minutes later. The monks elected Samson to take his place. As an abbot, Samson had a base from which to preach his message of reform. After some years of teaching eager young recruits to the reformist doctrine, Samson retired to live in an abandoned Roman fort somewhere in the Severn Valley. He was later hauled out unwillingly to become bishop of a town, probably in the civitas of the Cornovii. Samson later left this bishopric and moved to Brittany, where the clergy seemed to be more supportive of his message. After attending the Gallic conference he returned to Brittany and died sometime in the 560s.

In the ecclesiastical organization of the later Roman Empire, a bishop was appointed to head the Christian community found within a division of the secular government. This would mean that in AD 410 each civitates had had its own bishop. The bishop not only headed the community, but had important duties. He alone could consecrate new priests, or appoint existing ones to positions inside his civitas. Only a bishop could consecrate a bishop, with two bishops being needed to preside over the consecration for it to be valid. It was also the bishops who were in charge of the finances of an area, in theory using the wealth to support the needy or for other good works. It is this conventional structure that Gildas talks about and through which St Samson moved.

However, one of the problems mentioned by Gildas was that bishops were starting to be appointed by tyrants and rectores, not by their fellow bishops. Undoubtedly the formal ceremony was still presided over by two bishops, for if it had not been Gildas would have said so, but the real power to appoint had shifted to the secular rulers. From the point of view of Gildas and Samson, this was a dangerous move. It meant that the bishop was no longer answerable to either his Christian congregation or to his fellow bishops, but instead was dominated by the secular power. It would seem that bishops were increasingly being seen as the creatures of the secular ruler. The bishop was there to preside over religious ceremonies for the ruler, to ensure that the Christians behaved themselves and obeyed their ruler. It is in this context that Gildas complained of bishops paying taxes from which Church wealth should be exempt. A bishop appointed by a ruler was unlikely to resist a demand for tax payments. Perhaps this was why Samon was reluctant to become Bishop of the Cornovii.

The way forward for the Church in Britain was shown by a younger contemporary of Gildas and Samson named Paul Aurelian. Paul was born in the civitas of the Silures in about 510. Like Gildas and Samson he was the son of a rich nobleman and was sent to the school at Llan Illtud Fawr to be trained for a career in the Church. Unlike them, however, he soon despaired of the corruption and lax behaviour of his elders and turned his back on the formal Church. At the age of sixteen he left the school along with some like-minded youngsters and walked back home. He begged his father for a small farm where he and his friends could study the scriptures and lead a holy and austere life of virtue. Paul's father gave him a deserted farm and left the young men to get on with it.

Within a few years, the fame of the holy men had spread far and wide. Increasing numbers of men were attracted to come and join the small community, which grew rapidly. Paul was also consulted on theological matters by various churchmen and by local noblemen. Some time around 540 Paul received a messenger from a ruler named as Marcus Conomorus of Bannhedos. The name 'Conomorus' means 'Sea-hound' while Bannhedos was probably the hillfort near Fowey in Cornwall. This would indicate that Mark was the ruler of the civitas of Dumnonia. The messenger said that Mark needed Paul's advice on a matter of great importance. Paul travelled to Dumnonia only to find that Mark wanted Paul to be his bishop. Appalled, Paul fled. Realizing that his homeland would not be safe, he moved to Brittany to find solitude.

Where Paul had shown the way, others followed. His little community grew and soon gave rise to others. The cause of these small, ascetic monastic communities was to be taken up by St David, later to be the patron saint of Wales. David was born near Ceredigion (Cardigan) into a wealthy and noble family. Later tradition has it that he was a son of Prince Usai of Ceredigion, the area having emerged as a quasi-independent state carved out of what had been the tribal lands of the Ordovici. David began his schooling under St Paulinus at Whitland, near Carmarthen. Paulinus was a follower of Paul Aurelian and lived in a remote hut with just a few companions. David later moved to the larger and more famous school at Llan Illtud Fawr, but he does not seem to have got on well there. He left sometime around 540 or so to establish himself and some friends as an ascetic monastic settlement in the remote valley of Glyn Rhosyn, now St David's.

David proclaimed loudly a number of mottoes and watchwords, the most prominent of which were 'Comfortable ease is the mother of vice' and 'He that does not work, does not eat'. He drew up a set of rules for his community that was noticeably stricter and harsher than any other in Britain. The monks were expected to work from dawn to dusk at manual labour, be it in the fields or in workshops. The evenings were given over to reading, writing and prayer. Food was restricted to bread, water and vegetables, which earned David the nickname of 'Aquaticus', the 'water-drinker' from those churchmen who scorned his austerity. David allowed no personal possessions at all, everything belonged to the monastery and was owned communally by the monks. Anyone who so much as referred to 'my book' was punished.

David and his followers soon attracted another name. This was '*meliores*', which means 'the betters', and it seems to have been used as something of an insult with overtones of a holier-than-thou attitude. Gildas accused David of the sin of pride, saying that he was proud of his level of austerity and thus was more sinful than a bishop who travelled in a carriage. Gildas also accused David of putting his own pride and lifestyle above the duty of a Christian to minister to the community and of spurning those who did not match his own standards.

Despite such bickering, David was pointing the way forwards. The number of austere communities of monks or nuns increased dramatically. It was these monasteries that gained a reputation for learning and holiness, while bishops and priests were seen as poorly educated placemen obeying the orders of the local ruler. Indeed, the monasteries were ostentatiously outside the old, formal system of both Church and state. They refused to obey the instructions of bishops, decrying them as decadent hirelings, and refused to pay taxes arguing that the lands and wealth that they held were for the glory of God, not the squalid uses of secular rulers.

This attitude led to numerous disputes with rulers who wanted to impose taxation in kind or forced labour on to the monastic estates on a par with those extracted from secular estates. By and large the monasteries won the arguments because they had public support on their side. They were seen as beacons of learning and holiness in a world of declining harvests and falling prosperity.

We know that these new-style monasteries were widespread across what is now Wales, largely in areas outside the old civitates system. How widespread the movement became in the more settled and organized lands to the east is unclear. It would seem likely that they did not penetrate far over the Severn. The rulers in the wilder hills of the west might have been cowed by the formidable reputations of the holy monks, but the rulers of the established civitates had more efficient bureaucracies and larger armed forces. An appeal to God might not have got so far in such settled areas. There the rulers had a much stronger vested interest in maintaining the formal hierarchy of priests and bishops than did those in the west.

Corrupt, venal and lazy the clergy may have been, but they served the purposes of the secular rulers and so were kept in place. They did not, however, serve the needs of Christianity. The religion began to be seen as an arm of the state, and a not particularly nice one either. Paganism had never been eradicated in Britain and, although officially frowned upon, it remained. The Christian church and the Christian religion began to be seen as self-serving and decadent, although it remained a force in the land.

What little we know of what was going on outside the old borders of the Roman Diocese of Britain also comes from the writings of monks. They were spreading out to convert the northern pagans as well as those in Ireland. From these sources we know something of what was stirring. The tribe known as the Scots had been settling along the coasts of Kintyre, Arran, Islay and Jura around the mouth of the Clyde for some decades, but around the year 500 Fergus, chief of the tribe, moved his residence from Ireland to Kintyre. This was the start of Dal Riada, a state that would expand considerably in the generations that followed and eventually become Scotland. In 550, however, it was still relatively small, but determindly independent.

The Picts from the east coast north of the Clyde-Forth isthmus had long been formidable enemies of Roman Britain. Not much was heard of them between 450 and 500, perhaps because of internal civil wars or wrangles of some kind. These people are poorly known from the written sources, though much better understood from archaeology. They seem to have had a culture and a language that was broadly similar to that of the tribes living south of the Forth, though there were some important differences. The first Pictish king who is known by name was Drust, son of Erp, who died in about 458. He was celebrated in his own land as a mighty warrior, and was probably the ruler who led the raids into the northern parts of Roman Britain during the time of Vortigern.

When the Irish monk St Columb (often called St Columba)

came to Pictland in 563 the area was ruled by a man named Bridei. This Bridei was, if later traditions were to be believed, a younger son of Maelgwn, or Magolcunus, the Wide Ruler of what had been Roman Britain. It is known that the throne of the Picts passed from father to son-in-law, effectively allowing the reigning monarch to chose the next ruler by marrying him to his own eldest daughter. So far as is known, all earlier Pictish rulers had been Picts themselves so this seems to have been a break with tradition. On the other hand, Maelgwn is said to have had a Pictish grandmother so maybe Bridei had some royal Pictish ancestry.

Whatever his origins, Bridei proved to be a dynamic ruler. He tightened the grip of the central monarch on the various local lords, defeated the Dal Riada Scots in battle and captured the Orkneys. He was, of course, already a Christian and it may have been his accession that drew St Columb to try to convert the Picts. Columb was to make four missionary journeys to the Picts from his base on Iona. The work of conversion proved hard going and was far from complete when Columb died. The accounts of his travels, however, make it clear that Bridei was ruling a large but relatively united state.

Bridei was followed by Gartnait son of Domelch, who was in turn followed by a succession of solidly Pictish monarchs. These men seem content to have ruled over their own lands and, apart from squabbling with the Dal Riada Scots, did not fight many wars.

South of the Scots and the Picts was Ystrad Clud (Strathclyde), which covered the Clyde Valley and adjacent coasts. It was centred on a mighty fortress on the Dumbarton Rock. In the third century the northern border of Roman control had been moved north from Hadrian's Wall to the Antonine Wall which ran from the Clyde to the Forth. Even when the border moved back south, this area would have been in regular contact with the Roman authorities. If the Romans followed their usual practice they would have paid retainers to supportive rulers outside their borders in this area, and the monarchs of Ystrad Clud seem to have received Roman money. St Patrick wrote a letter to Coroticus of the Ystrad Clud in about 470. From the letter it is clear that Coroticus is a Christian and that there were at least some men at his court who could read Latin, or there would have been no point writing him a letter.

Coroticus was followed by his son Cinuit, of whom little is known, who was succeeded by his son Dumnagual. This Dumnagual ruled around the year 520 and seems to have expanded his lands east to Edinburgh and south into Galloway. The next ruler was Clinoch, followed by Tutagual, who was followed by Rhydderch Hael (the Generous) with whom the state really enters properly known history. Rhydderch died in 614 at which time he had firm control over the Clyde Valley and lands south to the Solway Firth.

East of Ystrad Clud was Goddodin, which stretched from Stirling along the southern coast of the Firth of Forth to the Lammermuir Hills. The royal fortress was probably on the steeply-sided hill of Traprain Law, in East Lothian, though at times the rock now crowned by Edinburgh Castle was used. Mynyddog Mwynfawr (the Wealthy) is the only known ruler of Goddodin, living about the year 600. Some think that Gwlyget was an earlier ruler of Goddodin, but this is unclear.

At various times there were smaller states in this area, though it is not certain whether they were truly independent states or were part of Ystrad Clud or Goddodin that achieved some form of self-rule for a while. These were Aeron around modern Ayrshire, Calchfynydd around Kelso and Novant around Carrick.

To the south of these states lay the militarized lands of the Roman frontier. Hadrian's Wall is the best known feature of this frontier, but there were large military forts and barracks south of the Wall and isolated forts and towers to the north. It has been presumed that the Wall itself formed a physical barrier, with movement through it possible only at a few guarded gates. The area to the north was regularly patrolled by detachments that stopped at the towers and forts to the north. The main army strength of the area was based in the large fortresses to the south, with the major supply base being located farther south still at Eboracum (now York).

Much of the Roman army in the north was stationed in the lands of the Brigantes, a tribe that put up a fierce resistance to Roman occupation. In Roman times it is unclear if the Brigantes formed a single civitas, or two with one lying east of the Pennines and one west of the mountains. It is equally unclear if the Dux Britanniarum commanded only the soldiers in this area or if he had any sort of control over the civilians and towns in the area as well. During the fourth century there is evidence that the Wall itself was less used than it had been and some of the milecastles were dismantled. It would seem as if the Roman army was relying more on a mobile force based behind the wall to defend the frontier than on the Wall itself.

The history of this militarized zone is even more poorly known than that of the rest of Britain. All of our written sources come from the south or west. The only written sources for this area are much later in date and say very little about what went on here before about 590. When this area does emerge into written history it is broken up into a number of small states, each ruled by a royal family that claims to share an ancestry with the others. The common ancestor of all these royal families is given as Coel Hen (the Old). Counting back the generations in the ancestor lists gives a date of about 420 for when Coel Hen was alive.

There has been a lot of dispute over who Coel Hen might have been. Some scholars view him as a mythical ancestor figure invented by court poets to give a spurious respectability to the claims to power of a man who grabbed power by force. Others think that he may have been a real person and have set about looking for a likely historic character to match him. The lack of written sources for the years around 420 have made this a fruitless effort, but the area where his descendants ruled covers what in 410 would have been the civitas of the Brigantes and the militarized zone around Hadrian's Wall.

It is possible that Coel Hen may have been a man in a position of authority in one of those units of Roman administration who siezed power for himself in the years after 410. Some have suggested that he was the Dux Britanniarum, the military commander of the Wall area, who used his soldiers to make himself independent of the civilian authority of Vortigern. Others had suggested that he may have been a descendent of the old Brigantian royal family who had enough popular appeal to get himself elected to be rectore of the Brigantes, and then to use this as the basis for a power grab.

Whoever Coel Hen was, we do not need to accept that it was he who staged a coup to make himself independent. It is a well-known feature of this period in Europe that rulers will claim as an ancestor the person who established the legitimate authority of a dynasty whether or not that person was actually an ancestor. Several Welsh families claimed descent from the Emperor Magnus Maximus who in 383 formalized a new structure of devolved government in the Welsh mountains outside the civitates system. So far as is known Magnus sired no children in Britain, but he did appoint a cluster of local dignitaries whose descendents remembered him as the originator of their family's power and hence thought of him as an ancestor. Perhaps Coel Hen was the Dux Britanniarum back in 410 and it was from the legitimate power of his office that the later dynasties traced their right to rule.

In any case, it is worth considering what happened to the large, well-trained and well-equipped Roman army that manned the Wall and adjacent forts in 410. It does not seem to have followed Constantine III to Gaul for there was no immediate invasion from the north. We know that in about 405 this northern command consisted of a legion based at York, plus a large number of auxiliary units stationed at forts south of the Wall and a few on the Wall. The size and composition of the various units is unclear, but there were at least some cavalry and light infantry units as well as heavy infantry. These men were fulltime soldiers, paid wages in coin and supplied with food and equipment by the Imperial government. As elsewhere in Britain there would have been part-time militia equipped and paid from local resources.

When contact with the Emperor Honorius was cut off in 410, the professional soldiers would have been left without a source of pay and supply. The first thing to have happened was that a new Dux Britanniarum would have been appointed by the council of representatives of the civitates at the same time as they were appointing other temporary officials to tide Britain over until Honorius could send proper officials. That temporary commander would have looked to the temporary Vicarius of Britain for pay and supplies for his men. At first this was presumably supplied readily enough from taxation raised in Britain that was no longer being sent across the Channel to the Imperial treasury. As time passed, however, the declining economy will have reduced the amount of taxation that could be raised and the civitates seem to have become increasingly reluctant to hand it over to the Vicarius or Wide Ruler.

In better documented areas of the Empire we know what happened to the army units similarly cut off from imperial pay and supplies. In 460 Aegidius, commander of Roman forces in northern Gaul, used his men to set himself up as a tyrant over the civitates of the area where his men were stationed. The state, known today as the Domain of Soissons, stretched from the Atlantic coast at the mouth of the Loire to the Rhine at Cologne The civil bureaucracy continued to function, raising taxes to pay the army. Aegidius died in 464 and was succeeded by his son Syagrius who ruled until he was killed in battle against the Germanic Franks in 486. Throughout this time Aegidius and Syagrius claimed to be Governors of a Roman province, though they ignored any instructions sent to them and kept all taxes for themselves.

Elsewhere the army men continued to live in or near their forts, but turned to farming to feed themselves. At Passau in what is now Austria one community of such men was still calling themselves a Roman army unit, using ranks to distinguish themselves, as late as 477, some thirty years after their last pay packets had arrived. In Egypt several army units survived as part-time militia until 640. They had long since given up any pretence at being full-time professionals and were instead a civilian militia, but they retained their Roman unit name and titles.

It seems likely that as tax revenues paid to the Vicarius declined over the decades, so the money available to pay the northern army also declined. Perhaps the Dux Britanniarum set himself up as a tyrant to ensure the flow of tax revenues from the civitas of the Brigantes. Or perhaps the proud army units gradually dispersed to become farmer-militias before vanishing entirely. We simply do not know.

But of one thing we can be absolutely certain. In 547 Britain suffered a catastrophe compared to which the problems complained of by Gildas were minor indeed. It was an event that was to leave its mark across the whole of Britain and Europe, a mark that was never to be erased. It began in Egypt. In 541 some men from the east arrived in the port of Pelusium, near modern Suez. A few days after arriving they fell sick and died. Within days locals were falling ill and dying in large numbers. The mysterious, but deadly, disease spread quickly across Egypt. Within a few weeks of the outbreak in Pelusium a sailor from a grain ship died in Constantinople. Before he died he has spread the contagion to the capital city of the Eastern Roman Empire. Disaster followed.

The disease spread rapidly through the packed tenements of the crowded city. People began to fall sick and writhe in agony as the infection took hold. The horrified onlookers noted two key symptoms; the first was a hideously painful and deforming malformation of the hands and feet, that spread up the arms and legs. Known today as necrosis, this is formed by the rapid death of individual cells of the body, resulting in the loss of limbs. If the limb is not rapidly amputated the infection spreads to the body and death results. For the terrified citizens of Constantinople things did not get that far. Before the spreading necrosis could kill, the victims developed hideously painful puss-filled boils and growths formed around the neck, armpits and groin. Within a couple of days these turned black, then ruptured causing agony and death.

The spread of the disease and the death rate was simply astonishing. About sixty per cent of the population of the city went down with the disease, and of them over eighty per cent died within a week of thier first symptoms. At one point 10,000 people died in a single day. The city simply could not cope with the vast number of corpses being created. The bodies were simply dumped outside the western gates of the city and left to rot. The Emperor Justinian himself contracted the disease, but after two weeks of agonized prostration he threw off the infection, though it was weeks before he was up and about again. For this reason the event became known as the Plague of Justinian.

As the sheer scale of the horror in Constantinople began to be clear, anyone who could leave did so. Merchants, sailors, rich families and the desperate fled on ships, horses and carts. But they could not outrun the infection that they carried with them. All the exodus achieved was to spread the disease far and wide. By the spring of 542 there was not a port in the Mediterranean that was not suffering massive loss of life from the disease. The infection spread more slowly inland, but its advance was inexorable. It reached Britain in 547 and Ireland in 548. The death toll was again horrific, with Maelgwn or Maglocunus being only the most famous victim.

It is thought that between fifty and sixty per cent of the population of Europe and North Africa was wiped out in the ten years or so that the plague raged. The disease would return several times in the generations that followed, though these secondary attacks were never as devastating as the first occurrence. Modern scholars generally believe that this terrible disease was a particularly virulent form of the bubonic plague. The Justinian Plague probably began in central Asia, spreading west along trade routes, but this is not known for certain.

The effect of the plague was dramatic. Populations slumped and with them tax revenues paid to governments. A writer in Constantinople recorded the aftermath for Justinian.

> When pestilence swept through the whole known world, wiping out most of the farming community and of necessity leaving a trail of desolation in its wake, Justinian showed no mercy towards the ruined freeholders. Even then, he did not refrain from demanding the annual tax, not only the amount at which he assessed each individual, but also the amount for which his deceased neighbors were liable.

Despite such drastic measures, the imperial government almost imploded. Military plans to invade Italy and North Africa and to build a new church in Constantinople were first shelved, then abandoned.

In Britain the tyrants, rectores and others lacked the resources of Justinian. They could not hope to forcibly raise the taxes to which they were due. Everywhere governments would have been in crisis, societies in turmoil and populations reeling from the shock and the horror of the massed deaths.

And into this world of decline, chaos and death strode Ceawlin.

PART II

Cometh the Man

Chapter 1

The Lands of Ceawlin

Ceawlin came from the House of Cerdic, the dynasty that was to provide the Kings of Wessex and would later provide the Kings of England and so is ancestral to our current monarch. If we are to understand Ceawlin, his motives and his actions we must first understand where he came from.

Our prime source of information about the yearly generations of the House of Cerdic is the *Anglo-Saxon Chronicle*. This account of the dynastic origins of the Kings of Wessex can be supplemented by comments found elsewhere, but primarily we must rely on the *Chronicle*. Unfortunately the writers of the *Chronicle* were not content merely to collect together the information they found in their sources. Like Gildas before them they were writing with a purpose.

The *Chronicle* was produced by order of King Alfred the Great in AD 891. The aim of the *Chronicle* was to bring together all the known historical facts about the English peoples in order to celebrate Alfred's defeat of the Viking invaders. A team of scholars worked for months, perhaps years, to bring together chronicles, biographies and histories from monastic houses all over England. They also gathered heroic poems and genealogical lists celebrating kings and warriors of the past. For the more recent years they seem to have interviewed men who had been present at the battles, treaties and other events that they described. All this information was brought together into a single volume that ascribed each event to a year and then placed the years in order. Once the task was finished, a small army of scribes produced dozens of copies of this monumental work. Each cathedral and all the larger monasteries were sent a copy of the *Chronicle* for their libraries. Clearly the intention was that each copy would continue to be updated year by year by its new owners. The nine copies that have survived are more or less identical up to 891, then vary widely as the new owners put in whatever information they thought was of interest. One version continued to be kept up to 1154.

Historians are generally agreed that Alfred's team of scholars did a reasonably good job of compiling the material that they had to hand. However, there were some inevitable problems, especially in the earlier sections before about 650, by which date the skills of reading and writing had spread widely across England. Before that date, the scholars depended on heroic verse, genealogies preserved in the memories of successive royal historians and on what monks writing in the late seventh century had recorded about the earlier centuries. This material was unavoidably of mixed quality in terms of historical accuracy.

The histories of royal dynasties was preserved by men whose main tasks were to praise the current monarch and to entertain the ruler and his court of an evening. The historian had a motive for being selective as to the material he preserved. Battles made for good evening entertainment for warriors, marriage alliances less so and records of harvests even less. Each dynasty was interested in the battles it had won, denigrating or ignoring those that it lost.

A key problem faced by the scholars was ascribing dates to events. Many oral historical accounts of battles and campaigns simply did not mention the date when they took place. At best they might record the age of the king who led the campaign, or state that it took place when he had been on the throne for a set number of years. Most royal genealogies not only listed the previous kings, but also stated how long they had reigned for and how they were related to the previous king. The scholars therefore had to act as detectives to ascribe dates to events, working back from a known date through the years different kings had ruled and in which of those years the event had taken place. The further back in time they went the harder this task was.

With the royal house of Wessex, Alfred's scholars had a particular problem. Their employer was from that royal dynasty and wanted a suitably heroic past for his family. In the context of the ninth century a family was ranked as much by the length of its ancestry as by the exploits of its members. For this information they were dependent on the royal historians of the court, and they were under some pressure to produce a coherent and orderly ancestry. For other royal families they could, and did, leave gaps where they knew nothing or recorded conflicting information when their sources were inconsistent, but for Wessex they succeeded in documenting an unbroken line of kings from earliest times to their present day. They went further, ascribing a series of legendary and mythical ancestor figures to the royal pedigree that went back to the pagan god Woden, and beyond him to Biblical figures and so to Adam and Eve. It was an impressive feat. Unfortunately for our purposes we do not know to what extent their records of the early years of the dynasty are accurate and to what extent they glossed over inconsistencies. There are clues, of course, and we will come to those.

Another point about the *Chronicle* is that it was written by and for men living in the 890s. To make their work easy to understand, they used contemporary titles for positions held by people and institutions and, whenever they could, modern place name spellings. This has served to obscure the true picture of relationships in the earlier centuries, though at places it is possible to see what the ninth-century scholars did and pick away their changes.

It would be tedious and unproductive to go into huge detail on these linguistic gymnastics, but it is worth looking at one key word in some detail to show what was done across the board. The word 'king' is one that we are all familiar with and one that has a meaning that in the twenty-first century is widely and clearly understood. The writers of the *Chronicle* use the word fairly widely to describe the ruler of any of the English states, called kingdoms, that they write about. In origin, however, the king was the leader of a people in war, a meaning that might be better conveyed to modern people by our term 'commander in chief'. It was in this sense that the word was used of Germanic leaders on the continent by Roman writers in the second and third centuries. The Germanic peoples, from whom the English came used *wealden* (powerful one) or *rica* (strong one) to refer to the man who held supreme political power over a people.

It seems that the early Germanic arrivals to Britain termed their leaders kings because they were war leaders heading a group composed mostly of warriors and their families. At first, up to about 750 or so, the word king did not necessarily mean the supreme head of an independent state. It could also mean the head of an area or a tribe that was part of a larger political state. Long after some of the smaller kingdoms were conquered by a large one they continued to have 'kings' who headed up the local tax collecting systems, led the local men to war and so forth. Modern historians refer to these men as 'sub-kings' to make their inferior status clear, but in their own day they would all have been 'kings'. The *Chronicle* refers to all such men as kings, so it is not always easy to work out who was an independent ruler and who was not.

Not only that, but the *Chronicle* used the word 'king' to describe a person in the past who had the powers or status of a king as it was understood in the 890s. Those men would never have used the word king to describe themselves and would have been puzzled to be called such a thing.

Perhaps the most important and confusing thing that the team of scholars which drew up the *Chronicle* did was to give an entirely spurious origin to the ruling dynasty of Wessex. In the 890s Wessex was a thoroughly English state, populated by people who spoke only English and ruled by kings who acted, behaved and thought as Englishmen. The dynasty therefore needed an English origin. The scholars knew full well that the English had come to Britain from Germany after the fall of Rome. By studying the royal background of other English dynasties, they would have known that all these men arrived as the leaders of groups of warriors who came either to raid and plunder, to settle and farm or as mercenaries to work for the British. But the Wessex dynasty did not have this sort of an origin. Either Alfred's scholars or the source they relied on had therefore invented such an origin by inserting into the historical record one single entry:

> 495: There came to Britain to the place called Cerdicesora two ealdormen, Cerdic and Cynric his son, with five ships and on the same day they fought the Welsh.

Cerdicesora was probably Calshot on the Solent, though this is not certain.

With this entry, the Wessex royal family was made to be English from the very start. The picture is of Cerdic and Cynric arriving with a band of warriors on the south coast of Hampshire, then fighting their way inland to establish a small independent state. This gave Alfred a solidly respectable ancestry of impeccably English origins, but it does not make sense when set against the other records of the early generations of the dynasty. Nor does it square with the archaeology of the area. It has caused endless confusion among historians. But if it is discarded, the history of the House of Cerdic makes a lot more sense, becoming consistent not only with its own records but also with what other people wrote about it.

What seems likely is that the scholars found a genuine reference to Cerdic being at Cerdicesora in command of some ships, and twisted it to suit their purposes by making the entry read as if he had arrived by sea. In fact, as we shall see, it is much more likely that he was in command of a post-Roman flotilla of warships based at Cerdicesora.

The key figure is clearly that of Cerdic. It was to Cerdic that later generations of the dynasty looked back, and for a man to rule in Wessex it was necessary for him to be able to prove that he was descended from Cerdic. The first thing to state about Cerdic is that he was not a Germanic incomer, he was a Briton. 'Cerdic' is simply an anglicized version of the name 'Caradog', which is a name that crops up several times in early British history. The is a male form of an early British word that means 'caring' or 'protecting' and is similar to the Latin '*caritas*' from which we derive the word 'charity'. In some sources he is given the nickname of Vreichvras, which means 'Strong Arm'. So the name Caradog Vreichvas could be loosely translated as 'He who protects with a strong arm'. Once it is realized that Cerdic was a native Briton, his story and that of his dynasty starts to make more sense.

The *Chronicle* gives Cerdic's ancestry as follows:

> Cerdic, son of Elesa, son of Elsa, son of Gewis, son of Wig, son of Freawine, son of Freothogar, son of Brand, son of Balda, son of Woden, son of Frithuwulf, son of Finn, son of Godwulf, son of Geat, son of Tetuua, son of Beo, son of Scyld, son of Scef, son of Noah.

The line then follows the ancestry of the Biblical Noah who built an ark and so survived the great flood reported in Genesis.

Some of these ancestors can be identified, some cannot. Wig and Freawine are known to have been semi-legendary German heroes of the fourth century, who were said to have ruled what is now Schleswig and to have fought a war against the equally legendary Athisi of Sweden. Freothogar is otherwise unknown. Brand is not known from other documents, but it is a fairly common element in northern Germanic names such as Wedgrand, Ingibrand or Gechbrand. Balda, Woden and Geat were all pagan Germanic gods, while the earlier part of the pedigree was simply copied from the genealogies of other royal families that claimed descent from Woden. Quite clearly the names from Wig back were entirely false, being added simply to give the dynasty a longer history than it otherwise had. Our interest should therefore focus on Elesa, Elsa and Gewis.

Gewis is probably derived from the Gewisse, a shadowy people mentioned in various early sources. They were a group of Germanic warriors and settlers based around Dorchester on Thames that were active by AD 550 and possibly much earlier. The name is of Germanic origin and means 'reliable'. We have already seen that archaeology has placed one of the anomalous inland groups of Germanic military settlers on the upper Thames between Wallingford and Abingdon. These finds of Germanic military gear date back to perhaps as early as 410. It must be presumed that the Germanic warriors located by archaeology and the Germanic warriors mentioned by written sources were one and the same. This would mean that the Gewisse were in place very soon after imperial control was lifted from Britain, and that they remained permanently.

As we have seen, the reasons for these inland groupings of Germanic warriors at such an early date is open to different interpretations. The mercenaries may have been hired by one of the civitates to guard its frontiers, perhaps from aggression from another civitates. On the other hand they may have been recruited by the central power of the Vicarius to forestall trouble between rival civitates. A third probability sees them as being placed by the central authority for some reason that we do not know – perhaps to guard a taxation gathering headquarters, the site of an important office of government bureaucracy or some such.

For the Gewisse of the upper Thames we do know who

employed them, though not exactly why. Bede and other later sources state that by around 710 the Gewisse and the West Saxons were almost identical and could be treated interchangeably. Quite clearly the Gewisse had been employed for a great many years by the dynasty of Cerdic. It is very likely that they had been brought to Britain in the first place by that dynasty. The very name Gewisse – the Reliable Ones – hints at some long-term relationship.

All the early information puts Cerdic and his immediate successors in what had been the civitas of the Belgae, so the Gewisse must have been hired by the Belgae. The position of the Gewisse is indicative of the reasons that they were there. The Thames around Dorchester on Thames marked the boundary between the civitas of the Belgae and that of the Atrebates. The Gewisse must surely have been employed by the Belgae to guard the border crossings, either to prevent incursions from their northern neighbours, or to launch raids. Dorchester on Thames had been a small Roman town and could be easily defended for it had the river on three sides. The combination of easy defence and pre-existing buildings would have made it an ideal base for a group of mercenaries hurriedly moved into position around 410 or so.

The use of the name Gewis in the official ancestor list of the Cerdic dynasty was probably derived from the knowledge that in its early years the state the family rule had depended on support from this group of warriors.

The next two names in the list are Elsa and his son Elesa. The names are clearly very similar and some have suggested that they represent a confusion over a single man whose name cropped up in different contexts, leading later generations to think he was two people. On the other hand it would not be the first time that a father had chosen a similar or identical name for his son. In the absence of other evidence we should accept that Elsa and Elesa were father and son.

One brief glimpse we have of Britain in about the year 445 comes from an account of a visit to Britain by St Germanus of Auxerre, a Gallic bishop charged by the Pope with stamping out the heresy of Pelagianism. This heresy had arisen from the teachings of a British monk named Pelagius who had been working in Rome around 400. The heresy was the belief that original sin did not taint human nature and that mortal will is capable of choosing good or evil without special Divine aid, and it seems to have been popular in the monk's native Britain. The heresy had been thought in Rome to be in decline by 440, but fresh reports of heretical teachings in Britain brought Germanus over the Channel.

The accounts of Germanus's journey do not say exactly where he landed in Britain, but we can guess. In the mid-fifth century most of Gaul was still under a Roman government of a sort, albeit with frequent raids by barbarians and some local control falling into the hands of barbarians. However the lands north of the Marne and Somme were falling into the rule of the pagan Franks, who would eventually take over all Gaul and rename it France after themselves. Germanus would most likely have avoided the Frankish lands, travelling down either the Seine or the Loire to reach the sea and then sailing thence to Britain.

If he used the route of the Seine, Germanus would probably have landed at Portus Adurni (now Portchester) or Clausentum (Southampton). The route down the Loire may have led him to land at Isca (Exeter) or Glevum (Gloucester). Wherever St Germanus landed he was met on the dockside by a nobleman named Elapheus, described as being '*regionis illius primus*' or 'leader of that region'. From what we know of Britain at about this date – when Vortigern was in power – such a phrase would most likely mean that Elapheus was rectores, or head of the council, of the civitas in which he lived. At Portus Adurni or Clausentum, that civitas would have been that of the Belgae.

Elapheus brought with him his son who was suffering from a crippled leg. The priests following the Pelagian heresy had been unable to cure the young man, but Germanus 'passed his healing hand over the afflicted leg and at his touch health was swiftly returned'. In gratitude, Elapheus had the heretical priests arrested and bundled on to a ship so that Germanus could take them to Gaul so that 'they could be brought to recognize their errors'. Now free of heresy, the British cheered Germanus and promised 'to live better and shun all error'.

It has been pointed out that the name of Elapheus is not too dissimilar to that of Elesa. In fact, it is likely that both derive from the Celtic name Eliavres, with Elapheus being the latinized version and Elesa the anglicized version. If this is the case, it would indicate that perhaps Germanus did land in the civitas of the Belgae. If so, this would emphasize the British ancestry of Cerdic and establish that his family had possessed political influence among the Belgae for at least two generations.

Until recently this was about all that could be said about Cerdic and his ancestors. However, close study of genealogies recorded in Wales has turned up new evidence that seems to confirm that Cerdic was a local nobleman from a rich and influential family based in what is now Hampshire. The Welsh stories mention a man named Caradoc Veichvras, son of Eliavres (sometimes given in its diminutive form of Ellyr or Llyr) Merini, son of Einion Yrth. This Caradoc ruled a territory somewhere in southern Britain in an area of the country that had been lost to the English by the tenth century when our version of these tales was written down.

This Caradoc has two stories told about him. The first is that his father, Eliavres Merini, was a powerful wizard who lusted after Ysaive, wife of the ruler of Portus Namnetum (now Nantes), a great port at the mouth of the Loire in Gaul. Eliavres used his magical powers to smuggle Ysaive out of Nantes and away from her husband so that he could bring her to Britain and marry her. This marriage was improper since Ysaive's husband was still alive, but nobody in Britain knew of this. Caradoc was born of this illegal marriage, and grew up unaware of his illegitimate birth. As a young man he married a woman named Tegau Eurfon, which means 'she of the beautiful golden hair'. In time Caradoc heard rumours that his mother was properly married to a ruler in Gaul and confronted his parents on the subject. Eliavres then magicked up a serpent that wrapped itself so tightly around Caradoc that he could not move. It took the combined efforts of his wife Tegau Eurfon and his brother Cador to pull the snake off him.

The second story is much shorter. It states that Caradoc was sent a magical drinking horn by Mangoun of Moraine that had the power to show whether or not a wife was faithful to her husband. Only a husband whose wife was faithful could drain the horn of wine in one go without spilling a drop. Caradoc managed this feat and so proved that his wife was entirely faithful.

In fact this lady, Tegau Eurfon, is relatively well known in early Welsh legends. She appears several times in the triads, which are preserved in a number of documents dating to the eleventh to thirteenth centuries. The triads take the form of three people or places that have something in common. They are thought to have originally been used by bards who worked entirely from memory to remember links and connections between different stories. Although in their final form the triads are quite late, they are referred to in much earlier documents and poems. A typical example would be 'Three Men Who Received the Wisdom of Adam: Cato the Old, and Bede, and Siblo the Wise. They were, all three, as wise as Adam himself'.

Tegau is mentioned in two triads. The first is when she is named as one of 'Three Faithful Wives of the Island of Britain'. The second mention is when the marriage between herself and Caradoc is named as one of the 'Three Bonds of Enduring Love of the Island of Britain'. Her final appearance comes when her dress is named as one of the 'Thirteen Treasures of Britain'. The dress would remain floor-length when worn by a faithful wife, but would magically shrink to the knee if worn by an unfaithful wife. When coupled with the tale of Caradoc's drinking horn it is clear that Tegau was a famously loyal wife.

The ancestry of Tegau is given as Tegau Eurfron daughter of Nud Hael, son of Senyllt, son of Kedic, son of Dyuyniwal Hen, son of Edneuet, son of Maxen Wledic. This lineage is from central or northwestern Wales somewhere, though it cannot be placed precisely. The Maxen Wledic named here is the usual Old Welsh name given to the Roman Emperor Magnus Maximus, who ruled in the 380s. Magnus Maximus reorganized the organization and defences of western Britain to counter raids from Ireland. In what is now Wales he placed power and defence in the hands of a number of local noblemen, who thereafter tended to remember him as an ancestor since he had given their family the basis of their power and prestige.

The family link to Wales is continued in other tales where the children of Caradoc and Tegau are named. The first of these was Kowrda, or Cawrdaf, who inherited his father's lands. The next three sons were St Gadfarch of Llyn, St Dangwn of Llangwm and St Amaethlu of Carneddawr. These saints are very poorly known, but the places with which they are associated are all in northern Wales. Presumably they settled on lands belonging to their mother's family.

Caradoc also features in a triad by himself when he is mentioned as being one of the 'Three Battle-horsemen of the Island of Britain'. He is also mentioned fleetingly in several old Welsh stories. In each of these he appears as a great warrior, usually mounted on a particularly fine horse or fighting from horseback.

The second name of Merini given to Eliavres in the Welsh version of the ancestry of Caradoc/Cerdic means 'of the sea'. In the story of Caradoc's birth, Eliavres is said to have kidnapped his wife from Nantes, so presumably he spirited her away by sea. We know that the two ports of the Belgae, Portchester and Southampton, traded extensively with Gaul in later Roman times and that Nantes traded with Britain. It must be presumed that ships sailed between these ports frequently and profitably. It might be that Eliavres/Elesa/Elapheus was a rich and powerful merchant whose ships traded with Gaul in the years around AD 450. We need not believe that he kidnapped his wife to accept that she came from Nantes. Perhaps he met her there on a trading voyage, or perhaps the marriage was arranged as part of a trading agreement.

The father of Eliavres is named in the Welsh genealogy as being Einion Yrth. Einion was a not uncommon British name of the time, while Yrth means 'rash' or 'impetuous'. Interestingly another Einion Yrth is named in Welsh sources as being the grandfather of Maelgwn, the Maglocunus of Gildas. Whether this was the same Einion Yrth is open to question as the two sources are separate and do not refer to each other at all. It remains, however, an interesting link.

Before leaving the Welsh sources, at least for the time being, mention should be made of Caradoc's eldest son Kowrda. This is very similar to the name of the man named in the *Anglo-Saxon Chronicle* as being one of the sons of Cerdic, Creoda. We thus have two distinct sources that give a grandfather-father-son trio with what are effectively identical names. In Welsh these are given as Eliavres-Caradoc-Kowdra, and in English as Elesa-Cerdic-Creoda. Moreover, the English *Chronicle* makes Cerdic the ruler of the lands around Winchester, the old civitas of the Belgae, while the Welsh sources describe Caradoc as ruler of lands somewhere in southern Britain. And both Caradoc and Cerdic are dated to around the years 400 to 420.

The chances are that what we have here are the same three men, but remembered through very different routes. The *Anglo-Saxon Chronicle* remembers Cerdic as the founder of the West Saxon royal dynasty and so dresses him in English clothes, while the Welsh documents recall him as the ruler of a land later lost to the English and so depict him in British form.

Before following the subsequent careers of Cerdic and his offspring we must look at the lands that he is said to have ruled, the civitas of the Belgae. This was undoubtedly one of the oddest civitates in Britain, perhaps in the Roman Empire as a whole.

The Romans never drew any accurate maps of their Empire, but they did leave extensive written records. From these we know in most cases which towns and cities in Britain lay in which civitas. The vast majority of the civitates were based on the territories of the pre-Roman tribes, and most of these had borders that could be easily defended such as rivers or ranges of hills. The civitas of the Belgae, however, was different.

This civitas appears to have been formed artificially by carving sections out of the territories of two distinct tribes. The southern part of the civitas was based on the fertile valleys of what are now the Test and Itchen, reaching inland from the Solent to the high chalk hills now called the Marlborough Downs. It then stretched in an oddly shaped dog-leg to the northwest over the barren heights of Salisbury Plain to include the valley of the Somerset Avon that extended on to the coast on the southern edge of the Severn Estuary. It is an odd shape, and odder still when considered in the light of archaeology.

Before the Roman invasion the southern part of the Belgae civitas would seem from archaeological finds to have shared a strong cultural affinity with the upper Thames Valley where lived the Atrebates. This tribal state had been minting coins in the Roman fashion since about 30 BC and seems to have had numerous cultural exchanges with the continent, perhaps by way of ports on the Solent. In about AD 40 the Atrebates were conquered by their long-term enemies the Catuvelauni to their east. Verica, ruler of the Atrebates, fled to Gaul and appealed to the Roman Emperor Claudius for help in recovering his power. Claudius gleefully took up the cause and launched the Roman invasion of Britain using Verica as a pretext. Verica was given

an.
an. cccxl. Vastatio brittonum cum offa in estate.
an.
an.
an.
an.
an.
an.
an.
an.
an.
an.
an. ccc.l.
an. Primus aduentus gentilium apud dexterales ad hibernia.
an. Offa rex merciorum et morgetiud rex demetorum morte moriuntur et bellum rudglann.
an.
an. Caratauc rex guenedote apud saxones iugulatur.
an.
an.
an.
an.
an.
an. ccc.lx.
an.
an.
an. Argen rex cereticiaun

moritur.
an. regin rex demetorum et cadell powis moriuntur.
an. Elbodg archiepiscopus guenedote regione migrauit ad dominum.
an. Combustio miniu.
an. Eugein filius margetiud moritur.
an. De cantoriu ictu fulminis comburitur.
an. Bellum inter higuel ... uictor fuit.
an.
an. ccc.lxx.
Tonitruum magnum fuit et incendia multa fecit.
Trifun filius regin moritur.
Fe griphiud filius cincen dolosa dispensatione a fratre suo eli sed post interuallum duorum mensium interficitur. higuel de mona insola triumphauit et cinan de ea expulit cum contritione magna exercitus sui.
an.
an. higuel iterum

demonia expulsus est.
Cinan rex moritur.
an. Gueith lanmaes.
an.
an.
an.
an.
an. Arce decantoru a saxonibus destruitur et regionem poyuis in sua potestate traxerunt.
an.
an. ccclxxx.
an. higuel moritur.
an.
an.
an.
an.
an.
an. Laudent moritur et satubin hail minui moritur.
an.
an.
an. ccc.xc.
an.
an.
an.
an.
an.
an. Nobis episcopus in minui regnauit. an. an. ludguoll moritur.
an.
an. cccc. mermin moritur. gueith cetill.

A page from the *Annales Cambriae*. This early medieval document is a key source for events in Britain during the fifth and sixth centuries. Unfortunately controversy surrounds the earlier entries.

A statue of Gildas, author of the only surviving contemporary description of Britain in the sixth century. Gildas later moved to Brittany where he died in about AD 570. This statue stands outside a church that he founded in Brittany.

The ruined gateway to the Roman fort at Birdoswald on Hadrian's Wall. These forts continued to be manned for some decades after the end of Roman rule in AD 410, suggesting that the military continued to exist long after our written records of them cease.

A stretch of Hadrian's Wall. This stone fortification was erected to keep the northern tribes out of the Roman diocese of Britain. It marked the northern limit of the authority of the Vicarius appointed by the Emperor, and of the Wide Rulers who were elected by the British after the end of direct rule from Rome.

A Roman road cuts straight across the hills in Yorkshire. Roman roads remained the best marching routes for armies for centuries after they were first built.

The city walls of Canterbury, capital of the civitas of the Cantii. Most of the stonework visible is medieval in date, but they are built on the original Roman foundations with their distinctive semi-circular bastions.

The city walls of Colchester, capital of the civitas of the Trinovantes. This stretch of the original Roman defences stands to a height of about ten feet and continued to protect the city right up to the eighteenth century.

The Roman Emperor Honorius as shown on a contemporary ivory plaque. It was Honorius who lost direct rule over Britain and advised the British civitates to elect their own officials until he could appoint somebody. In the event Roman rule never returned, so the British continued to appoint their own officials.

The Hugin Ship that stands on the shore near Ramsgate in Kent. The ship is a modern replica of the type of ship that brought the Saxons to Britain in the fifth century. It was sailed from Denmark to England in 1949 to commemorate the 1500th anniversary of the voyage made by Hengist and Horsa.

The bridge at Aylesford in Kent. Before the present bridge was constructed there was a ford here over the Medway. It was here that Horsa was killed fighting the British in about 455.

The White Horse Stone near Aylesford in Kent. The early Germanic mercenary leader Horsa is said to be buried near this great boulder. As part of the funeral rites, Horsa's brother Hengist painted the stone red and decorated it with a white horse – the symbol of Kent to this day.

The Roman Bath at Bath, Somerset. This ritual complex fell into ruins in the fifth century as it was fought over by the Belgae and the Dobunni. The war ended with the annexation of the city and surrounding lands by the Dobunni.

The massive Roman walls around the naval fortress of Pevensey. This fort was captured by Aelle of the South Saxons amid great slaughter. Aelle went on to become perhaps the most successful of the early Germanic leaders.

A romantic Victorian illustration of King Arthur and Merlin the wizard. Both men were real enough figures in the fifth or sixth centuries, though it remains controversial precisely what their roles were in the turbulent decades as Roman Britain gradually disintegrated.

A Victorian stained glass image of St Patrick. The patron saint of Ireland was born and brought up in Britain. His career helps to illuminate the state of Christianity in Britain during the fifth century.

(Below) The cathedral of St David in Wales. The beautiful medieval cathedral was built over the site of the small monastic centre founded by St David where he sought to live a holy and ascetic life away from the temptations of the world.

A head of the Romano-British goddess Sulis-Minerva. This goddess was revered in Bath where the hot waters were sacred to her. The worship of pagan gods survived into the fifth century, but Christianity was a rising force and would come to be a key ethnic feature of the British.

The Tor at Glastonbury. As a young man Ceawlin came to Glastonbury to be educated. Later legend asserted that he had a weird encounter with the otherworld on the top of the Tor. (Photo: Adrian Pingstone)

The great gate at Portchester. The central square tower is medieval, but most of the walls and round towers here are Roman. The fortress guarded a naval harbour and was the site of one of the great victories won by the Belgae.

The interior of the Roman fortress of Portchester. The church and buildings in the foreground are medieval, but the curtain walls and towers are Roman. The fleet stationed here sallied out from the Solent to patrol the Channel and seek Germanic raiders. After Roman rule ceased, the Belgae garrisoned the fort and probably operated warships from here. (Photo: Charles Miller)

The earthwork defences at Old Sarum, Salisbury. The Belgae ruler Cynric won a great victory here that crushed the neighbouring Civitas of the Durotriges. It is likely that Cynric annexed the lands of the Durotriges in the wake of this victory.

Ceawlin fought his first battle alongside Cynric at Barbury Castle high on the chalk downs south of the Thames valley. It would appear that Ceawlin lost this battle, though it would not be long before he got his revenge.

King Ethelbert of Kent was later commemorated by the Christian church for being the first English king to become a Christian. But when he was defeated in Surrey by Ceawlin he was a young and inexperienced ruler.

The defensive ditch at Dyrham. It was here that Ceawlin won a spectacular victory that allowed him to sweep over the lands of the Dobunni and install his own garrisons and governors on the rich lands of the lower Severn. (Photo: James Frankcom)

The tower of the medieval church of St Collen at Llangollen. Ceawlin's grave lies beside the church.

Bamburgh Castle. The present building is medieval, but the coastal rock on which it is perched was the stronghold of the mercenary Ida in 547. Ida's successors would establish English control over northern England.

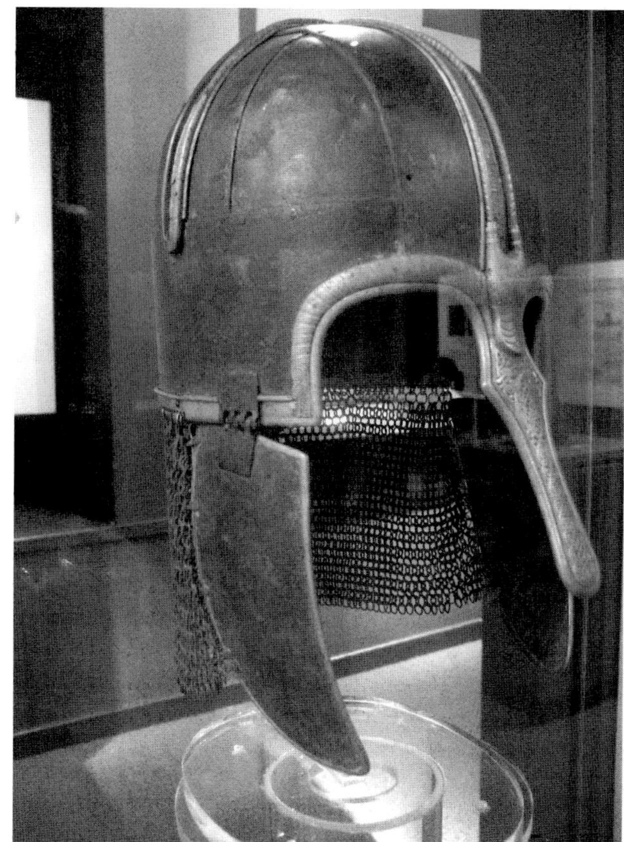

A helmet found in northern England. It is thought to date from the eighth century and is typical of the sort of high status armour used by nobles. (Photo: Christian Bickel)

A Saxon king and a supporter go into battle. The shields, mail shirt and helmets shown here were typical of the seventh and eighth centuries.

back his lands, and his son Cogidubnus succeeded him, but after that the division of the Atrebatic lands took place. The lands in the Thames Valley became the civitas of the Atrebates, centred around the town of Calleva Atrebatum (now Silchester in northern Hampshire).

The Avon Valley area, by contrast, shows up in archaeological digs as having the culture shared with the Dobunni. This tribal state was centred around the lower Severn Valley, though it extended over various adjacent areas. The Dobunni were famously prosperous farmers who preferred to defend their lands, rather than to invade those of others. When Claudius invaded Britain, the Dobunni sent messengers to the invaders offering to surrender in return for lenient terms. We do not know what terms were granted, but the Dobunni did not fight so presumably they were reasonably content with whatever deal they were offered in AD 43.

In about AD 96, however, the Dobunni and their territory were reorganized by orders from Rome. The bulk of the tribal lands were formed into a civitas based on the new city of Corinium Dobunnorum (now Cirencester). Corinium was to become the second largest city in Britain by 300 and was the centre of a prosperous and sophisticated society. In 96 one part of the lands of the Dobunni was taken by Rome to be given as land to retiring soldiers, a type of settlement called a colony. The official name of this tract of land was Colonia Nervia Glevensium, but it is more usually called Glevum (now Gloucester). The section of Dobunni land on the southern shore of the Severn Estuary south of Glevum were then taken and lumped together with the southern Atrebatic lands to form the civitas of the Belgae.

Why Rome should have created this apparently artificial political entity is unknown. It may be that they thought the Dobunni to be too large and powerful to be left as one civitas, but the smaller Atrebates do not seem to have been in a position to pose a threat of any kind. Whatever the reason for the move, the Belgae civitas was established by about AD 100 and thereafter became a highly prosperous area.

The largest city in the civitas was Venta Belgarum (now Winchester), the name of which means 'Market Place of the Belgae'. Before the Roman invasion there had been a fortified settlement here on a hill overlooking a ford across the River Itchen, probably the first non-tidal ford over the river. The Romans laid out an extensive grid street pattern on the west bank of the Itchen and surrounded it with earthern and timber defences that were later to be replaced in stone. Inside the city were built a forum, a basilica and at least two large temples – one dedicated to Jupiter and the other to the local horse goddess Epona. Archaeological digs have uncovered a number of luxurious town houses in Venta Belgarum, indicating that it was a prosperous town at least as late the 380s. Venta Belgarum covered 144 acres, making this the fifth largest city in Roman Britain.

The second largest town in the civitas was Aquae Sulis (now Bath). Unlike Venta, Aquae Sulis seems to have been more religious in character than commercial. The hot springs that still bubble to the surface here were no doubt the reason. These were dedicated to the local goddess Sulis, whom the Roman identified with their goddess Minerva. The extensive temple complex at Aquae Sulis was based around the baths where supplicants could bathe in the healing waters.

A third city in the civitas of the Belgae was Iscalis and has never been firmly identified, but may have been the smaller town based around extensive lead and silver mines on the Mendip Hills south-west of Bath. The site is now known as Charterhouse-on-Mendip and lies on top of a steep slope looking south over the Somerset Levels. The site was clearly important as there was a small fort, apparently garrisoned by the II Legion, in the early days of Roman control. There was also an amphitheatre a hundred feet across and extensive housing. The site has never been properly excavated so we do not know much about it. An inscription on a large stone block mentions that the building it was part of was opened during the time of the emperor Caracalla. That would date this impressive structure to about AD 217.

The two identified cities were linked by a road that ran north-west from Venta Belgarum to the small fortified town of Cunetio (now Mildenhall, Wiltshire). From there the road ran west to another small fortified site called Verlucio (now the hamlet of Sandy Lane, Wiltshire). There were longer road connections, but that via Calleva Atrebatum (Silchester) ran through the civitas of the Atrebates, and that via Sorviodunum (Salisbury) went through the civitas of the Durotriges.

The road links between Roman sites dominated maps and discussions of the Empire. This is largely due to the fact that roads are solid great things that are easily found by archaeologists, are often still in use today and were used by the government machine that left written records of the roads' conditions. This does not mean that they were especially important to the people who lived in Roman Britain.

The roads built by the Roman state, and maintained by the local civitates, had to be kept clear for the use of the army and of government officials. The roads went where the army needed to send its men on duty or along routes frequented by tax collectors, imperial messengers and other workers of the state. They did not go where private individuals wanted to travel, still less along prosperous trade routes. In any case, road transport was expensive and slow at this date. Anyone wanting to send grain, pottery or wine could send their goods five times as far by water as by road for the same cost and (if the wind was favourable) quicker as well.

It was for this reason that trade routes tended to go along rivers or along the coast. Nearly every sheltered bay on the coast held a small harbour to service the needs of the farms and villages in the locality. Many rivers were improved in Roman times by the insertion of locks to hold back water and keep the river navigable by barges in dry weather or by being straightened out to cut off lengthy loops and bends. The Trent, Nene, Ouse and Cam are all known to have been improved in this way, and undoubtedly other rivers were likewise adapted for barge traffic. The civitas of the Belgae was divided by the high hills of the Marlborough Downs and Salisbury Plain. This may not have been an issue for the army and government that used the roads, but for merchants, farmers and other civilians it was an awkward division.

Archaeology can tell us something of what was happening about the time that Cerdic lived. For the two great cities of Venta Belgarum and Aquae Sulis we have only a partial view of events since both are still inhabited and archaeologists can get at sites only when they are redeveloped. Inevitably only a few areas in both cities have been excavated by archaeologists. These do however, seem to fit a general pattern.

In Venta Belgarum the great prosperity of earlier years seems to have declined after about 370. No new buildings of any size seem to have been erected after that date, though the existing ones remained in use. The stone walls around the city were kept in good repair and sometime around 420 were strengthened. At some point in the mid-fifth century the complex drainage systems that the Romans had dug to channel and control the Itchen at this point collapsed. This would have led to periodic flooding of the lower sections of the city so the buildings closest to the river were abandoned and the remaining population moved to live further up the hill. Along with all Roman cities, Venta Belgarum saw a general fall in population over the fifth century and by 520 at the latest seems to have been almost totally abandoned. The defences were, however, kept in good repair.

Aquae Sulis saw a faster and apparently more complete decline. The great bath seems to have gone out of use around 390, but the thermal springs continued to be used and most of the buildings within the city walls were inhabited. By about 420 several buildings were abandoned. Then, in the mid-fifth century something dramatic and violent must have happened here. Many of the buildings went out of use in apparently violent circumstances. The unburied body of a teenage girl was found by archaeologists beside what seems to have been a baker's oven. The baker's shop collapsed on the oven and body soon afterwards, showing it was abandoned when the girl was killed and never reoccupied.

What this violence may have been is open to conjecture, but it is probably relevant that the great earthwork defence of the Wansdyke was built on the hills only a mile from Bath, facing north. We know that by around 560 this area was no longer ruled from Venta Belgarum but was instead part of the Dobunni territory. Given that in pre-Roman times this area was part of the Dobunni territory it may be that the Dobunni at some point moved to regain their lost lands.

We know that Glevum, the great port town separated from the Dobunni, was taken over by the civitas of the Dobunni sometime in the fifth century. Moreover archaeology reveals that Glevum suffered none of the damage found at Aquae Sulis. The city remained inhabited, albeit with fewer people, certainly as late as the 530s and perhaps much longer. The city walls were extensively renovated in the 400s, with stone towers being added to the four gateways. Since there are no signs of violent damage to the city in the early-fifth century it must be assumed that this strongly fortified city rejoined the Dobunni peacefully.

Aquae Sulis was violently retaken, and it must be assumed that the rest of the Avon Valley fell at the same time. It would seem that the Wansdyke may have been a defensive work put up by the authorities of the Belgae in a vain effort to hang on to their prosperous western areas. There is some evidence, though it is controversial, that the Durtoriges extended their power north into the lands south of Bath at about this time. Perhaps the Durotriges and Dobunni had ganged up on the Belgae. Thereafter the civitas of the Belgae included only its southern sections.

It is worth pausing there to recall that Gildas, writing about 530 or so, condemned what he said were civil wars between the Britons. Given that he was probably writing in southern Britain in either the territories of the Belgae or Durotriges at the time he may well have had this sort of conflict in mind. He condemns Aurelius Conanus, perhaps of the Dobunni, for 'an iniquitous thirst for civil wars and repeated plunderings'. If Gildas was in the territory of the remaining Belgae as he wrote, his audience would have relished the accusation.

Chronology is difficult to fix for certain in these vague years, and while it would be tempting to suggest the end of Belgae rule in Aquae Sulis led to the end of democracy (such as it was) in Belgae lands the dates do not seem to fit. Archaeology would suggest that Aquae Sulis and the Avon Valley was lost to the Dobunni around the middle of the fifth century. The *Anglo-Saxon Chronicle* places the coup of Cerdic to the very early sixth century. Depending on how one reads the evidence there might have been as much as sixty years or as little as thirty between the two events.

That does not mean that it was not a crisis that prompted the change of government in the Belgae. We know that the last Western Roman Emperor had abdicated in the 476, we know that the Belgae lost their western lands somewhere between 440 and 460 and we know that Riotimus lost his battle and much of his army in the 470s. Finally, Aelle had grabbed the title of Wide Ruler, or Bretwalda, for the English in about the 480s. Although it had subsequently been taken back by a Briton (be it Aurelianus or Arthur), the status of the once mighty office of Vicarius had been badly damaged. In the circumstances it was perhaps surprising that something had not happened earlier. It was certainly happening now.

Chapter 2

The Wars of Ceawlin's Family

The *Anglo-Saxon Chronicle* introduces Cerdic and his son Cynric in AD 495. The date need not be taken too seriously and may be up to thirty years too early, at least for Cynric whose death is recorded in the year 560. The *Anglo-Saxon Chronicle* regularly links father and son, or uncle and nephew, in this way. There are three ways to interpret this feature. It may be that the younger man could indeed have been present with his father, or uncle, at the event being recorded. It was not unusual for boys to enter the public arena in a junior capacity as young as eight or nine years old both to gain experience and so that other men could get to know them. Alternatively it may be that the career of the younger man has been deliberately falsified in later years to try to accrue extra glory to his name. By including his name alongside that of his father at some event that took place when he was a toddler, the younger man can associate his name more closely to the achievements of his dynasty than if he merely claimed the event as a triumph for his father. Finally, it was not unusual for rulers to seek to secure the succession to their son by including the son in events, giving him positions and even having him crowned while he was still too young to be an effective politician, administrator or soldier. We are ignorant of which was the case in the early years of the Cerdic dynasty, but something of this kind must have been going on to account for the otherwise unfeasibly long careers of some of its members.

The other interesting thing about Cerdic and Cynric when they first appear is that they are described as being '*ealdormen*'. The *Anglo-Saxon Chronicle* was, of course, written in the ninth century for a ninth-century audience. The title would not have existed in 495, so authors were probably using a then modern word to explain an archaic title that they had found applied to the two men. We need to look to the 890s for a meaning.

In the later-ninth century the word ealdorman could have two meanings. It might be used as a loose term for a nobleman, but its more specific meaning was quite precise. When used in governmental documents it signified a nobleman who was the king's representative in a specific area, usually a county. As the king's representative, the ealdorman could carry out most of the duties and powers of a king within his designated area. He could command the local militia, he could raise and inspect taxes, he could charge customs on imports and exports and he could sit in judgement in legal cases. Often the only appeal against a decision of an ealdorman was to ask the king to remove him from office.

Peering back to the late-fifth century the closest equivalent to an ealdorman of a shire would be a rectore of a civitas. While an ealdorman was appointed by the king, a rectore was elected by the curia of the civitas. Their duties, however, were not dissimilar. It may be that the scholars compiling the *Chronicle* came across the word rectore and substituted that of ealdorman to make the obsolete title meaningful for their audience.

In the notice for 495 Cerdic and Cynric are said to have 'come to Britain with five ships to a place called Cerdicesora and on the same day they fought the Welsh'. As we have seen it is likely that the arrival in Britain with ships full of warriors was a later fabrication to claim a fictitious English ancestry for Cerdic, but Cerdicesora is a real place. It is generally identified with Calshot, which stands on a low-lying headland on the western shore of the mouth of Southampton Water where it enters the Solent. There is a sheltered lagoon here with shores of sloping sand and mud.

The position would have been ideal as a base for the type of shallow-draft warships that were common at the time. We know that Cerdic's father later had a reputation for having been a sea-wizard so it is likely that the family was a seafaring one. If Cerdic was not a German invader, but a local civic leader then he may have had command of a small flotilla of warships based at Calshot. From this base he could easily command both Southampton Water and the Solent. Together these waters controlled the ports of Portus Adurni (Portchester) and Clausentum (Bitterne in Southampton). The port of Noviomagus

Reginorum (Chichester) of the neighbouring Regni civitas was not far to the east and might have been blockaded by ships from Calshot. The Regni might at this date have been subject to Cissa, son of Aelle, making the area an early English state.

Perhaps the entry in the *Chronicle* records a genuine battle fought here by Cerdic as commander of a flotilla of Belgae warships. The battle may have been on shore at Calshot, or may have been a naval battle out at sea somewhere.

Whatever Cerdic's exact links to Calshot may have been, the next entry in the *Chronicle* to the lands of the southern Belgae ignore him completely. That entry reads:

> 501: Port came to Britain with his two sons Bieda and Maegla and two ships to the place called Portchester and they killed a young British man, a very noble man.

It is likely that the name of the man Port was invented to explain the name of Portchester. We know that the name came from the Roman name for the place, but this type of invented correlation between a place name and personal name is not unusual at this date. Bieda and Maegla are more interesting. Maegla is an anglicized version of the British name Maglos, but Bieda is a Germanic name. It may be that what we have here is a band of Germanic mercenaries led by Bieda operating as part of a Belgic army under the overall leadership of Maglos.

Rather unusually we can almost certainly see this same battle recorded from the other side in a very early Welsh poem called 'Geraint son of Erbin'. The poem as it was written down in the 1250s seems to have been produced in the ninth or tenth centuries. However, the Gereint who is the hero of the poem lived much earlier, probably sometime between 450 and 550, and hailed from either Dumnonia or southern Wales.

The section about this battle places it as having taken place at Llongborth. This is a Welsh term that translates as 'ship-harbour'. The element *Llong* comes from the Latin *longis navis*, a type of shallow-draft oared galley used in the third and fourth centuries in coastal waters and on larger rivers. Llongborth would therefore translate as 'port for coastal warships', which is a fairly accurate description of Portchester's role in the late Roman defensive system for Britain. Gereint was certainly 'a young British man, a very noble man', so the battles of Portchester and Llongborth would seem to be the same event.

Quite what a warrior band led by a nobleman from Dumnonia or southern Wales was doing fighting at Portchester is a bit of a puzzle. One clue comes from the Welsh triads where Gereint is said to have been one of the 'Great Seafarers of Britain'. If he were from Dumnonia and he was a great seafarer then he may have been trading with the continent, in which case the Belgae would have been serious commercial rivals. An attempt to wreck the fleet of the Belgae would have made sense, so perhaps he came to Llongborth/Portchester by sea only to be faced by a Belgic army invigorated by Germanic mercenaries under Bieda (possibly the Gewisse), and harried by a flotilla of oared galleys under Cerdic operating out of Calshot. The ships could have cut off Gereint's retreat, leaving him to be killed.

On the other hand the battle may have been an attempt by the Wide Ruler of the day to curb growing Belgic independence. Perhaps the Belgae were already getting restive under the rule of a distant Wide Ruler and needed bringing to heel. This is all conjecture, but something was happening.

So far as the *Chronicle* is concerned, Portchester/Llongborth was not the only battle fought between the Belgae and other Britons at this time:

> 508: Cerdic and Cynric killed a British king named Natanlaod and five thousand men with him. After that the land was known as Natanleag up to Cerdicesford.

The place names here can be identified. Natanleag is now known as Netley. It stands on the east shore of Southampton Water, about halfway between the Solent and the port of Southampton, near the mouth of the River Hamble. Cerdicesford has been identified as Chandler's Ford, a spot where a Roman road crosses the Monks Brook just north of Southampton. The rather more distant Charford on the Avon near Salisbury has also been suggested as the location of Cerdicesford.

Other than this brief mention in the *Chronicle* there is no talk of Natanlaod, or any similar name, in any other document of any kind. For this reason many historians have come to the conclusion that both he and the battle in which he died were invented by the scholars who were trying to invent an English ancestry for Cerdic. However, the entry makes no mention of Cerdic and Cynric arriving by ship nor of their leading Germanic warriors. It is possible that the battle really did take place at Netley, though perhaps the name of the enemy leader was invented.

If this were the case it must surely have been part of the same war that saw Gereint killed at Portchester. Again, the Belgae were victorious. The fact that the *Chronicle* records that 'After that the land was known as Natanleag up to Cerdicesford' would imply that the pursuit of the defeated invaders was continued to Cerdicesford, wherever that was. If Chandler's Ford is meant then the chase went on for eight miles in a northwesterly direction. The retreat northwest would indicate that the enemy here were men of the civitas of the Durotriges, or at least had advanced from that territory. A distance of eight miles is quite in order for a pursuit by men on foot chasing a defeated enemy up to dusk on the day of battle.

A pursuit to Charford is again in a northwesterly direction, implying an enemy from the Durotriges. The distance is, however, a more impressive eighteen miles. For an infantry army to chase a defeated enemy for such a distance without either losing cohesion, stopping to plunder or being evaded is a much more impressive feat. It would imply strong discipline, inspired leadership or both. Alternatively, the pursuit may have been carried out by mounted warriors who would have been able to cover the distance much more quickly. By implication those on the run would also have been mounted. We will look at the conduct of warfare at this period in our next chapter, but for now it is enough to note that whether this battle really did take place or not, an organized pursuit over some miles was considered perfectly feasible for an army of this date.

The next *Chronicle* entry about the southern Belgae comes in AD 514 when it is recorded that 'Stuf and Wihtgar fought with the Britons and put them to flight'. This is another annoyingly vague entry. It comes just after a reference to Cerdicesora (Calshot) and so may mean that the battle took place there. This would make it just one more battle in the war that had already seen conflicts at Portchester and Netley. It seems the Belgae were hard pressed, fighting a succession of battles around Southampton Water at the very heart of their lands. Both Stuf and Wihtgar are Germanic names, so they must be presumed to have been leading a mercenary force.

Then in 519 comes the really key entry. It is rather longer than the usually terse entries typical of the *Chronicle* at this early date and reads as follows:

> Cerdic and Cynric undertook the rule of the West Saxon Kingdom, and the same year they fought the Britons in the place now called Cerdicesford. The royal line of Wessex ruled from that day.

Again we are reading a late ninth-century version of an early fifth-century reality and need to read carefully to understand what is meant. By the ninth century Cerdic's dynasty ruled over the English kingdom known as the West Saxons. The last sentence can be understood as being an addition from the scholars creating the *Chronicle*. They are emphasizing that their patron, King Alfred, is a direct descendent of Cerdic and that his ancestors have been royal rulers ever since 519. A battle at Cerdicesford – be that at Charford or Chandler's Ford – would probably mean another battle against the Durotriges. The phrase 'West Saxon Kingdom' is another explanatory gloss put on by the ninth-century scribes to explain which kingdom it was that Cerdic and Cynric undertook to rule.

It is the phrase 'undertook to rule' that is most interesting and contentious. The precise wording in the Old English version is '*rice onfengun*', a phrase that is used nowhere else in the *Chronicle*. The usual phrase when a ruler inherits a kingdom is '*feng to rice*', which is usually translated as 'received the kingdom'. Clearly the ninth-century scribes meant something different from the usual run of the mill inheritance of power when it came to Cerdic in 519. They were not referring to the establishment of a new state, for when Ida founded Bernicia in 547 the phrase '*feng to rice*' was used. The meaning is obscure, but it clearly indicates that something different happened with Cerdic.

We have seen that in the years running up to this key event the

Belgae were under serious military pressure, mostly from the civitas of the Durotriges, but also from an army led by a noble from Dumnonia or southern Wales. The Belgae had already lost the western half of their state and now seem to have been threatened with extinction. In the circumstances it would have been natural for them to turn to a military leader of proven ability to lead them out of trouble.

At this distance in time it is impossible to know quite what happened. It is unlikely that the curia of the Belgae would have granted to Cerdic absolute power in perpetuity, still less that they would have made the office hereditary – though that is how things turned out. It is more likely that they would have followed Roman precedents in some way. They may have made Cerdic a *Dictator*, that is a person who could rule by dictat (speaking) rather than having to bother with getting motions passed by the curia and other democratic but time consuming processes. On the other hand he may have been given a title akin to *Magister Militiae*, or supreme military commander, a rank that brought with it power to recruit men, enforce the provision of supplies and other powers necessary to keep an effective army in the field.

Whatever the formal constitutional title and powers granted to Cerdic it would seem that he quickly converted it into one of near absolute rule in the Belgae territory and one that was hereditary within his family. It would have been for this reason that later rulers of the state placed such emphasis on their descent from this man.

Meanwhile, Cerdic would soon have nothing to rule if he did not secure the borders of the southern Belgae. As pointed out he fought a battle in 519 at Cerdicesford, then in 527 we read 'Cerdic and Cynric fought the Britons at the place called Cerdiceslea'. The location of this battle is uncertain. There is nowhere today in the then lands of Belgae called anything like this, but over the years the name may have been forgotten and replaced. The only place in England that is similar is Chearsley, Buckinghamshire, which appears in the Domesday Book of 1086 as 'Cerdeslai'.

The location of Chearsley is interesting as it stands close to the River Thame, a tributary of the River Thames, on what was in 527 the far northern edge of the civitas of the Atrebates. The relationship between the Atrebates and the Belgae had always been close. In pre-Roman times they had shared a culture, and perhaps a ruler, while in the fifth century the border between the two was settled by the Gewisse. Perhaps Cerdic led a contingent of Belgae men to fight alongside the Atrebates against the Catuvellauni. Or it may be that Chearsley is a mistaken identification and the battle took place closer to home for Cerdic.

In 530 Cerdic and Cynric are recorded as invading and capturing the Isle of Wight. As ever the exact year should not be taken as certain here, though it is likely that the order of these events is correct. In Roman times the island had been called Vectis, but there is no indication of to which civitas it belonged. The island lay off the coast of the Belgae, but the Regni might have conceivably had a claim to it. The fact that Cerdic had to capture it in around 530 would indicate that at that point it was not part of the Belgic state.

Four years later it is recorded that Cerdic died and that power passed to Cynric, though the recently conquered island of Wight was given to Stuf and Wihtgar. This move has caused most to conclude that Wihtgar never existed. He is only ever mentioned alongside and second to Stuf, while his name is used to explain the name 'Wight', which we know is in fact descended from the much older 'Vectis'. Stuf, however, seems to have been real enough. He is identified in the *Chronicle* as being a nephew of Cerdic. Given his Germanic name this is at first sight unlikely, although he may well have been the son of a sister of Cerdic who was married to a German war leader for political purposes. Whatever the case, Stuf and his descendants ruled Wight until 661. Throughout this time they seem to have had some sort of loosely defined status inferior to that of the main Cerdic dynasty.

Cynric, meanwhile, had succeeded to power in the lands of the Belgae. His early years in power were quiet. The *Chronicle* mentions only events in other parts of Britain and, for 540, a solar eclipse. We know from Gildas and elsewhere that this was the time of the five tyrants, of the decline of the British church and of the Plague of Justinian, in which Maelgwn the Dragon of the Island died. All these events passed the *Chronicle* by, for in these years it seems to have been concerned only with Kent to the east, Bernicia to the north and the Belgae to the west. Presumably Alfred's scholars had access only to documents from these areas for these years.

The *Chronicle* is clearly a bit confused about the precise relationships within the family of Cerdic at this early date. In most entries Cynric is said to have been son of Cerdic, but one entry states that he was the son of Creoda, who was the son of Cerdic. At first sight this would mean that Cynric was both the son and grandson of Cerdic, which does not make sense. However, the year by year accounts of the *Chronicle* make it clear the Cynric succeeded Cerdic in power. This might mean that Creoda did not for some reason take power – perhaps he died before his father or was judged unfit to rule for some reason. It would therefore be easy for later generations to assume that Cerdic was succeeded by his son, thus mistaking a list of kings for a list of fathers and sons.

The Welsh genealogies can help out here. They record that the son of the Caradog identified as Cerdic was 'Kowrda' and that his son was 'Kydeboc'. Given the differences in pronunciation and spelling conventions, Kowrda and Creoda are identical while Kydeboc and Cynric and very similar. This would indicate that Cynric was Cerdic's grandson. In turn this would make more sense of the long timescale accorded by the *Chronicle* to the careers of these two men. Cynric is said to have died sixty-five years after Cerdic is first mentioned as an ealdorman. This is possible for a father-son relationship, though somewhat unlikely given the low average ages of men in this period, but it is much more likely if the pair were grandfather and grandson.

The Welsh genealogies also record another branch of the same family. In this version, Caradog had a son named Meuric, who had a son named Erbic who had a son named Erb who became the ruler of Gwent, and from whom were descended the later rulers of Gwent until 1091. Erb is generally thought to have died around 560 or thereabouts. Gwent covered the lands, now in southern Wales, that lay between the Usk, Wye and Severn rivers. It therefore stood on the opposite side of the Dobunni from the Belgae. Given the apparent battles and bloodshed between the Belgae and the Dobunni over Aquae Sulis, a dynastic marriage between the house of Cerdic and a powerful family in southern Wales might make sense. The precise date when the civitas of the Silures in this area broke up into the states of Gwent to the east and Morganwg to the west is unknown. If the split was the work of Erb in the 540s he may have been emulating the success in establishing a dynastic rule of his great grandfather Cerdic and cousin Cynric.

The early years of Cynric's rule may have been quiet, but the peace was not to last. In 552 the *Chronicle* records that 'Cynric fought the Britons at a place called Salisbury. And he won.'

By Salisbury the *Chronicle* means the massive hilltop earthworks known today as Old Sarum, not the more modern city in the valley below that dates back only to 1220. These earthworks were an important pre-Roman fortified settlement that seems to have been largely abandoned during the Roman years. There was a military posting station called Sorviodunum on the site, but the local farming population was shifted out of the fortifications. The site seems to have been partially reoccupied sometime after 450, though the date is uncertain. This may represent a move by the civitas of the Durotriges in their long-running conflict with the Belgae. The site is in the far northeastern corner of Durotriges territory, right on the border with the Belgae. If they had begun to refortify and garrison the old ramparts, Cynric would have seen it as a provocative move. This may be what prompted the campaign, or maybe if the refortification had taken place earlier it may simply have been a pre-emptive strike by the Belgae.

Whatever the motives, the battle was a clear victory for Cynric. The emphasis on his winning might indicate that it was a particularly impressive victory, but might just as easily indicate that it was the first real success for the Belgae against the Durotriges. Given that all the earlier battles had been fought deep inside Belgic territory, this latter interpretation may be the more accurate. The change of ownership of Sorviodunum does not seem to have affected the place much. The refortification continued apace and there was a growing, though still small, population. This might represent a garrison installed by Cynric, though at least some of the settlement seems to have been agricultural in character.

The gaining of Sorviodunum was an important strategic gain for Cynric. The fortress commands the junction of five river valleys – those of the Nadder from the west, the Wylye from the northwest, the Till again from the northwest, the Dorset Avon (not to be confused with the Somerset Avon that flows through Bath) from the north and the Bourne from the northeast.

Sorviodunum also marked an important meeting point for Roman roads, at this date still by far the best way to march armies around Britain. The first road began at Venta Belgarum (Winchester) then ran west through Sorviodunum to reach the coast near what is now Weston-super-Mare. The other main road started at Durnovaria (now Dorchester) the capital of the civitas of the Durotriges, ran northeast to Vindocladia (now Badbury) then on through Sorviodunum to Calleva Atrebatum (Silchester), the capital of the Atrebates, then pushed on to Londinium (London).

The capture of Salisbury was the first aggressive move made by the Belgae. It was not to be the last, for Ceawlin was about to enter the scene and tear Britain apart.

Chapter 3

The Face of War

Ceawlin was a great warrior and it was with warfare that he destroyed post-Roman Britain and created England. To understand why his wars had the impact they did, it is necessary to appreciate how wars were fought in his time and why they could have the devastating impact that they did.

As we have already seen, the fifth century was a time of decreasing population and of a drift from towns to countryside. Both trends were to be hastened in the mid-sixth century. The Plague of Justinian that hit in the 540s was devastating enough, but in 535 and 536 there was a severe winter and a cold summer that were probably caused by a gigantic volcanic eruption sending up enough dust into the upper atmosphere to block a high proportion of the sunlight. Crops failed across the world and famine stalked the land. It is thought that between 400 and 550 the population of Britain fell from around six million to around three million.

This disastrous fall in population was mirrored by a general collapse in trade. The quantity of goods being moved both within Britain and from Britain to the continent decreased spectacularly. As much as ninety per cent of the value of trade may have vanished. Increasingly the economy was based on subsistence agriculture producing a small surplus of food and wealth to be used for other purposes.

In this sort of situation, governments and rulers were faced with collapsing revenues in terms of cash, produce and manpower. A prime motive for warfare at this time was, therefore, to gain control of economically productive areas of land. This could be done either by conquering an area and annexing it to the dominant power, or by enforcing the payment of tribute on to a defeated ruler or government. Slaves captured in warfare were also a valuable commodity, not only because they could be sold but also as they could be put to work on the lands of the conquerors to increase the area under cultivation and so boost productive output.

Wealth could also be gained by the more basic method of looting and stealing anything that could be captured as an army moved through an area. On the whole, however, looting and raiding was an admission of weakness as it implied that the aggressor would not be able to hold on to the lands being attacked. Capturing an area with its infrastructure and population intact was much preferred.

Archaeology can tell us rather a lot about the weaponry and other military gear in use at this time. The military equipment in use in Ceawlin's time seems to have been an odd mixture of Germanic and Roman styles. While the overall pattern of weapons and equipment was becoming increasingly Germanic, the styles and designs were very often derived from those of the later Imperial age. It is almost as if men still hankered after the look of a Roman soldier for prestige and glamour but, when it came to the serious business of killing, they preferred the brutally effective functionality of the Germanic weapons.

A large number of male burials from about this time contain weapons, indicating that fighting was something expected of a man. These weapons tend to include a long spear, a shield and a hand weapon of some kind. So ubiquitous is this trio that it seems to have been standard, and may have been laid down by the state as the equipment necessary for a man to join the army.

The spear was clearly the primary weapon in combat. It was usually about nine feet long and used for thrusting. The shaft was thick and often made of ash, which is strong under compression. The iron blade was broad, flat and shaped rather like a leaf. The socket was comparatively short, not extending far down the shaft. There was only rarely a metal butt spike.

The shield was usually round, though occasionally oval, and was up to forty inches in diameter. It was flat, being made of several planks of lime wood glued together with some variety of tongue and groove or pegged joints. Lime wood was preferred as it had a sticky characteristic that caused it to grip on to any object, such as an arrow, pushing through it. The rim of the shield was bound with iron or boiled leather to keep the wooden sections together and to protect the vulnerable rim from wear and tear. There was a large central boss of iron, which contained the hand grip. Opinion is divided as to whether the face of the shield was covered with boiled leather or not. If it were the shield would have been greatly strengthened for only a minimal increase in weight. However, evidence for this is lacking.

We know that in later Roman times each unit had its own shield design. This served both to identify the men from a distance, but also put on a more visually intimidating display facing the enemy. By the eighth century at least, this practice had ended but it may have still been in use during the sixth century.

The hand weaponry found in graves is very mixed. Hand axes have been found, as have long bladed hunting knives and daggers. It seems that these secondary weapons were very much a matter of choice. Some of them are indistinguishable from the sorts of knives or axes that might be used on a farm, and probably were household tools.

Armour and helmets are found only very rarely, but there are indications that they were not unusual. Many graves contain buckles, studs and other metal fittings that seem to indicate that the man originally wore boiled-leather armour that has rotted in the ground. Comparisons with examples known from continental carvings and written accounts would indicate that this leather armour took the form of a solid breastplate and back plate linked over the shoulders by metal or leather clasps and at the sides by smaller buckles. Straps of leather hung down over the upper arms from the shoulders and over the groin and upper thighs from the bottom of the breast and backplates.

This boiled leather is also known by its medieval name of *cuir bouilli*. It was frequently backed by quilted layers of cloth and was more effective than it might sound. The process starts with leather tanned using natural vegetable tanning chemicals. The sheet of leather is then plunged into a large pot of boiling water and cows' urine. After about thirty seconds the leather darkens in colour and shrinks, becoming thicker. The longer the leather is left in the water/urine mix the more it shrinks, the thicker it becomes and the harder, but also the more brittle the final result will be. Once it has been boiled for the appropriate time, the leather needs to be pulled out and then the hard work begins.

The treated leather is supple and flexible, but remains so for only about twenty minutes or so. In that time the sheet of leather needs to be stretched over a form for the desired shape, trimmed to size and then held in place with clips. The leather is then left to dry and cool, hardening over the form as it does so. A skilled worker can thus produce pieces of boiled leather of any three-dimensional shape and size required. Top quality breastplates were even produced with imitation muscles, belly buttons and nipples. Larger pieces of armour tended to be boiled for less time to result in a hard, but non-brittle sheet of leather. Smaller pieces were boiled for longer as they could be more easily replaced if they broke in action.

The quilted padding that so often lined the leather armour was crucial to its success. The leather would stop most blows from edged weapons, but did nothing to stop the brute force of the blow. The quilting served to spread the force of the blow over a larger area of body, reducing bruising. It also helped to stop arrows from penetrating through to the flesh.

Helmets seem to have often been made of boiled leather with padded linings. They had a rounded crown, often with cheek pieces and a flap down over the back of the neck. Fixings for a crest of coloured horsehair are not unusual.

We know from written sources that mail shirts were usual for richer men, but they are very rarely found in graves. Presumably they were so astonishingly expensive that they were passed on from one generation to the next rather than wasted on the dead. Mail was composed of a huge number of small interlocking rings of iron or steel, often sewn on to a supple leather lining which may have been quilted like the leather outfits. Mail was much more effective at stopping edged weapons than was leather, but not noticeably better at deflecting arrows. It was, however, hugely impressive to look at. The iron was usually kept brilliantly clean by being rolled in barrels of sand and vinegar so that it gleamed and sparkled in the sunlight. A man in mail was an impressive sight indeed.

Richer men not only wore mail, but were equipped with swords in place of daggers or hand axes. These swords were generally based on the Roman *spatha* style that entered service around 300, at first with the cavalry but later with other troop types. It was a straight-bladed weapon with a sharp point and finely honed edges that could be used to thrust as well as to slash. The blade was about thirty-two inches long and three inches wide where it joined the hilt. The hilt tended to be simple, with a heavy pommel to help balance the weight of the blade in the hand. The hilts and scabbards were often highly decorated with ivory, silver or even gold ornamentations.

The helmets worn by wealthy men were of iron, often decorated with gilding or with silver ornaments. Again, the helmet would have been kept brightly polished to be as impressive and intimidating as possible. A very few prestige helmets had face guards, some decorated with embossed moustaches, beards, eyebrows and noses. Most helmets made do with a simple bar projecting down over the nose, if that.

We know that infantry also threw light javelins, but it is unclear if every man had a few javelins to throw or whether some men were equipped as outlined above, while others went to war as specialist javelin throwers. If such men did exist, as we know they did in the later Roman army, they would have lacked the large spear and shield, and probably the armour as well.

From archaeological sources it is difficult to distinguish between a wealthy man richly equipped as an infantryman and one who fought on horseback. A war horse was a very expensive object to purchase, but even more costly to train properly and to maintain in top condition for campaigning. Training a horse to remain calm and obedient when surrounded by the noises of battle, the flashes of weapons and the smell of blood takes many months of dedicated work. Just getting on a normal riding horse and going into battle is a certain way to get thrown and so be a helpless victim of the enemy. Consequently men who rode to war were invariably rich, and this severely limited the numbers of men who could fight as cavalry. This was always the case, but increasingly so in the resource-poor post-Roman world.

Cavalrymen from this date on the continent wore metal helmets and mail shirts. They carried an oval shield that was about half the size of an infantry shield, but of similar construction. Each man had three or four light javelins to be thrown at the enemy and a *spatha* for close-quarter fighting. War horses at this date seem to have been quite small compared to later breeds, perhaps only slightly larger than a modern Exmoor pony.

Much cheaper than a war horse was a riding horse. It seems likely that many men could afford a nag on which to ride off on campaign. No doubt such mounted men were used to scout ahead of the main army, or to launch small-scale raids. It may also be that men in the main army rode horses on the march, but dismounted to fight. Certainly food, sleeping blankets and other gear would have been carried on packhorses, mules or small carts whenever possible.

Such was the equipment of the men raised by a post-Roman British state like the Belgae or the Durotriges. The Germanic mercenaries used equipment that was broadly similar, but there were some differences. The thrusting spear tended to be a bit shorter, at about seven feet in length, and armour of any kind was significantly rarer among the rank and file. The shields were also smaller being about thirty inches or so in diameter. There is some dispute about the grip on the Germanic shield, but it seems to have been a single-handed grip behind the boss. This allowed the shield to be used offensively by punching it forward at the enemy, not just as a passive defence. While helmets were rare, the men seem to have often worn a padded cap which may have been able to cushion a blow to the top of the head.

One distinctive weapon of the Saxons, though other Germanic tribes used it, was the *scramaseax*, a word that means 'wounding-knife'. This was a large, single-edged knife with a broad blade. The blade was up to fourteen inches long and although only one side was sharpened it was often symmetrical in shape. The edges were straight for most of its length, then suddenly curved in to form a point. A few examples had a notched or bent back. These blades often had a design scratched into them, frequently a serpent or a boar. The tang, that part of the blade that fixed it to the handle, was invariably on the centreline of the blade and was enclosed in wood or horn.

One thing that all these weapons have in common is that they demand a fair amount of physical strength to use. Having handled modern replicas, I can assure you that they are heavy and often cumbersome objects. Balancing a nine-foot-long spear in one hand (the other being used for the shield) is not easy, and that is without trying to thrust it at somebody. Campaigning must have been a tiring business with hours each day being spent tramping along roads carrying all this gear. And battles must have been simply exhausting. No doubt a sixth-century warrior was more accustomed to these weights than I am, but even so going to war was not an easy option for anyone.

Archaeology can tell us much less about the military organization of states at this time, and still less about the size of armies. We know that in later Roman times fighting wars was not considered to be the role of the mass of the population. Peasants, craftsmen and landlords paid taxes in money or in produce to the government, which then recruited soldiers or hired mercenaries to do the fighting. This was certainly the case in Britain in AD 410 for we have the army lists to prove it.

It is clear that at least in the early years of its existence the office of Wide Ruler had as a key duty the security of Britain. The Wide Ruler hired mercenaries, paid soldiers and presumably organized their training and dispositions. He must, therefore, have had a stream of incoming revenue to pay his men. Quite how effective this role remained by the mid-sixth century is uncertain. The individual civitates had always had their local militias to man town defences, enforce law and order and to patrol boundaries. It is likely that as the central authority of the Wide Ruler diminished the strength of local armed forces increased. As we have seen wars, or at least armed struggles, between the civitates had begun to break out fairly early and, if Gildas is to be believed, became widespread by the 510s. These wars can have been fought only by the local armies and by mercenaries hired by the civitates governments.

It is possible that by the 550s most of the hard work of fighting was still being done by units of fulltime soldiers, or by fulltime mercenaries. However, given the falling supplies of money it is unlikely that any government could afford to keep a large standing army in existence. It is much more likely that the professionals formed an armed core, while farmers were called up to serve in the army as and when needed. In an agricultural society, such as Britain had become, men cannot afford to be away from home for very long or they risk the essential farmwork going undone. Many years later a period of thirty days absence a year was fixed upon, but it is unlikely to have been formalized as early as the 550s. However long they served, these part-time warriors had to bring not only themselves and their weapons, but also enough food to keep them going while they were away.

It is likely, but unprovable, that long-range campaigns into enemy territory were the business of the professionals while guarding bridges, patrolling borders and guarding the Roman walls around towns was left to the part-time amateurs. Perhaps there was some form of rota system so that different villages had their men called out at different times, ensuring that guards and patrols were active throughout the summer campaigning season without anyone needing to be away from home for very long.

The size of armies at this date is a matter of great dispute. The *Anglo-Saxon Chronicle* often gives figures of between 4,000 and 8,000 for the numbers of men involved. Other written sources seem to agree that the small states could field armies of about this size. It is likely that these figures refer to the full armed might of a state such as the Belgae. Equipping a man for war was expensive and beyond the reach of most peasant families. Most likely four or five families would club together to buy the gear needed to equip one man, who would then march off to campaign. The full-time professional core of an army of this date would have been much smaller.

The hints and clues in later heroic poems are scanty, but it does indicate that at this date the professional bodyguard of a ruler was organized in units of 100 men. Mention of these units are always in multiples of 100, and very often in multiples of 300. We know of one ruler who had 900 men in his bodyguard and another who had 600 men. A large and prosperous civitas such as the Dobunni might have been able to afford as many 1,500 fulltime professionals, an apparently smaller and weaker state such as Cerdic's Belgae maybe 900.

We have even less idea of the organization of a Germanic mercenary group at this date. The little evidence that we have implies that the smallest unit was a group of ten men, five of whom went to make up a 'keel', or ship's company.

When it comes to tactics we are dependent on written sources, most of which were recopied much later. There is no way of knowing how much of this detail has been updated by the later copyists to refer to their own times and how much goes back to the original sources. With that caveat in mind, the sources do seem to present a generally consistent picture of how battles were fought.

It would seem that battle tactics could be a good deal more flexible and sophisticated than is often thought. The three basic troop types available to a commander such as Cerdic, Cynric or Ceawlin would appear to have been: heavily-armed infantry with shield, spear and some armour; lightly-armed infantry with javelins and no armour; and cavalry with javelins and swords. The mix seems to have been broadly the same in other former Roman provinces of the western empire. We know rather more about tactics used there, and there seems no obvious reason why British armies would have been any different.

The basic blocking force of an army was the heavy infantry that formed up in the centre. The men would have stood shoulder to shoulder and been arrayed as much as fifteen or as few as six deep depending on the circumstances. Those in the front rank presented their shields to the enemy, overlapping them as much as possible to form a solid wall of wood and leather. They would have used their spears to jab over the top of this shield wall at the enemy, with the second and third rank joining in when they could. The rear ranks provided muscle power in the shoving match to come, and replacements to step forward to replace the dead and wounded.

The lighter javelin men would have formed up either on the flanks of the heavy infantry or in front of them. The formation of these men would have been much looser, with each man choosing his own spot and being some distance from his fellow. The cavalry were positioned in loose clusters on the flanks or rear. They do not seem to have formed up stirrup to stirrup, but to have preferred a more open formation. The commander usually placed himself behind the central mass of infantry, usually to one side. He kept back from the front line a number of heavy infantry and horsemen who were under his personal command.

An idealized battle plan would seem to have gone something like this. Having formed his army up, the commander would push forward his main block of heavy infantry at a walk toward the enemy army. The javelin men would have scampered ahead of the shield wall, raining their weapons on to the enemy formation in the hope of causing casualties and disrupting its tight formation. The cavalry would meanwhile be cantering about at high speed, dashing forward to throw their javelins at the enemy and then wheeling away to get out of range before retaliation came. As the main shield walls came into contact with each other a slow grinding contest would begin. The men in the front ranks would attempt to kill each other, while those behind pushed and shoved as if engaged in some deadly rugby scrum. The idea was to get some forward momentum going at some point that would push the enemy shield wall back, breaking it open and allowing the front ranks to get into it and start killing. All this time the javelin infantry and cavalry would have been skirmishing around the flanks.

The commander would, meanwhile, have been watching events. The key decision for him was to decide when he needed to push forward his reserves, and in what numbers. He may have needed to send forward infantry to push back a dangerous bulge in his own lines, or to enlarge and extend one forming in the enemy forces. The cavalry reserve seems to have been kept for the final stages of the battle. If the enemy broke and fled, the cavalry would be unleashed to pursue, harry and destroy. In defeat, the cavalry would move up to try to hold back the enemy cavalry long enough to allow the infantry to get away. It would appear that pursuing cavalry were in two groups. One force moved forward fairly slowly and in good order to attack enemy cavalry, break up groups of infantry and do most of the killing. The other group was sent galloping ahead at high speed, bypassing any enemy troops and getting as far ahead as possible. They were seeking either to block the enemy retreat at a ford, bridge or defile or to capture the enemy baggage and supplies.

Of course, such an idealized battle rarely took place. More often the battle would happen on broken country, at a ford or where at least one flank was unsuitable for cavalry. Moreover, not all armies had a balanced mix of troop types so the commander might not have had enough cavalry for an organized pursuit, or not enough infantry to have formed a proper shield wall.

The Germanic mercenaries employed by the British states, or

fighting on their own account, seem to have been composed overwhelmingly of heavy infantry. There were some light infantry armed with javelins or light bows, but they were very much in a minority. When serving the British as mercenaries, the Germans seem to have been used in the shield wall. The skirmishing and pursuit would have been left to the British.

The mercenaries may also have been used for second order duties, such as patrolling borders or guarding bridges, thus freeing up the depleted manpower resources of a British state to serve in the field army. Mercenaries are notoriously unreliable when in a bad position. If they could be kept away from any major battle they were unlikely to be put into a position where deserting to the other side was too tempting to resist. One key feature of employing mercenaries is that they should, whenever possible, be under the command of an utterly reliable officer. If that is not possible then a pretext for having a liaison officer with them at all times should be found.

The Belgae seem to have understood this for at the Battle of Portchester/Llongborth the mercenary Bieda had the Briton Maegla alongside him. Once Cerdic became supreme ruler we do not hear of any mercenaries operating alone, so presumably they were always closely under the eye of the ruler. In any case, Cerdic's dynasty seem to have been employing the Gewisse – the reliable ones.

But whatever tactics were employed, one thing is clear: the vast majority of fighting was done hand to hand, at very close quarters. This sort of fighting is uncompromisingly brutal. Men are not killed by a bullet half a mile away, but two feet in front of you. Their blood splatters over you, as does that of your comrades dying beside you. The emotional strain of close combat is terrifyingly intense. Adrenalin pumps through the body, driving men on to take risks in order to get at the enemy, to hack and slash, to kill and maim without a thought. Combined with the physical exertion of handling the weaponry of the time, this combines to make pitched battles utterly exhausting experiences. While the action is going on, the excitement keeps a man fired up, but once the battle is over the reaction can be intense, leading to a stupor that can last hours.

If the general tactics of the time can be drawn from continental sources, the strategies can be deduced from British records. The majority of battles were fought either at fortifications on the boundaries between states or at river fords. In both cases it seems that the aggressor was seeking to enter enemy territory, presumably with the intention of either looting it or of annexing it. The defender sought to block the advance at the first opportunity, choosing an easily defended position at which to do so. There do not seem to have been many attempts to strike fast and deep into an enemy territory either to capture his royal base or to kill the enemy ruler. If wars were generally about controlling areas of land, then so too was war strategy.

Warfare was not only about pitched battles, though understandably the surviving accounts are dominated by these events. Wars have always involved a large amount of scouting, raiding and patrolling. Anyone who has served in the armed forces will know that the military life is composed of long periods of intense boredom broken by short periods of intense danger. There is no reason to suspect that warfare at the date we are looking at would have been any different.

Winter campaigning was generally considered impossible, except for a few small-scale raids. The problem was generally the weather. Men cannot sleep outside in snow and driving rain for very long before falling sick and being unfit for military duty. Moreover the short days mean that there is only a limited amount of time during which it is safe to march over unfamiliar territory before night draws in. And since most winter nights are overcast, there is no moon or starlight to enable men to see where they are going. Before the days of modern tents, modern night vision and modern clothing fabrics, a winter campaign would have been suicidal.

Spring, summer and autumn would therefore have been the war seasons, but even then things were not that simple. In a basically agricultural society men were needed to work on the farms during the times when grain crops were sown and harvested. Moreover the summer was often a time of hunger when last year's crop was running out and this year's crop was not yet in. Wise commanders would be wary of setting off on campaign with empty supply bags. It would be all too easy to advance into enemy territory only to run out of food and starve. The best campaigning season of all was late summer and early autumn. At such times men were well fed and fit after gathering in the harvest, supplies could be guaranteed and, in enemy lands, food could be easily pillaged or extorted under threats of violence. For this reason August and September have always been the most dangerous months in Europe.

Warfare was not only fought on land. A much ignored aspect of war at this period is the role of marine combat. We have already seen that Cerdic's first military appointment may well have been the command of a small war flotilla on the Solent, and that Gereint may have travelled to the Battle of Portchester/Llongborth by sea. We also know that although cross-Channel trade was much reduced from Roman times, it was still economically important to the rulers of the time as a source of taxation and wealth. Controlling the sea lanes would have brought wealth and income to a ruler.

If Gereint was from Dumnonia, as seems likely, his reputation as one of the three great sea travellers of Britain means that Dumnonia was probably a major player in the international trade of the time. Cornish tin was no doubt the main export, but the Dumnonian merchants may also have acted as carriers for wool or grain from Dobunnic lands. The rulers of Kent would later establish very close links with the Frankish rulers of what is now northwestern France. Given the short distance over the Channel from Dover to Calais it is inevitable that they would have sought to control the seaborne trade out of the Thames estuary and from southeastern Britain. The Belgae had two major Roman ports in their territory, and Cerdic's father had a reputation as a sea wizard so it is likely that they too had a role in the import-export trade.

The great Roman galleys were by this date a thing of the past, so the various states would have relied on a very different sort of ship for sea fighting. The basic pattern would seem to have been what is today termed a Nydam ship, named for the site where a well-preserved example was found by archaeologists. These ships were about ninety feet long, had a maximum beam of some fifteen feet and a draft of only two feet. In shape, they are identical at both ends, with stem and stern forming a gentle upsweeping curve. The rear was distinguished by a steering oar on the right, or starboard, side. In form the ships were effectively very large, open rowing boats.

Propulsion seems to have been mainly by oars. Along each side were positions for as many as twenty oars, each one being hauled by a man sitting on a bench just inboard of the bulwark. The keel was formed of a large, broad plank laid flat side down, which made it easy to haul such a ship up on to a beach. The planks were tied to the ribs with leather thongs and laid in an overlapping pattern known as clinker-build. At least some ships had a single mast erected amidships from which was hung a single, square sail. The combination of square sail and flat keel meant that such ships could take advantage of the wind only if it was blowing from more or less the stern.

When used to transport warriors, a ship like this could carry fifty men along with their weapons and enough food to keep them going until they could capture some more. For trading voyages, the crew would have been reduced to perhaps a dozen men. This would have greatly reduced rowing speed and made the ship more dependent on a favourable wind.

Although surviving records contain many references to warriors travelling by sea and arriving in ships, there are no accounts from this time of naval battles. It is likely, therefore, that such naval fights as did take place were small in scale, though not necessarily in importance. If trade was a valuable source of income to a government, then it could decide the ability of that state to pay for an army. It is at least possible that the success of Cerdic and Cynric in fighting off invasions from other civitates was based on their ability to pay their Gewisse allies and to afford a standing army of their own. Given the apparently small size of the rump Belgic state after the loss of Aquae Sulis, the most likely source of that wealth would be trade. And successful trade at this date meant a force of military ships to protect it.

It is worth remembering at this point that the Welsh genealogies give Cerdic a mother from Nantes. In one story, which admittedly dates from much later than this time, Cerdic owned lands at Vannes, near the mouth of the Loire. Whether these links to western France survived Cerdic's death to serve his descendents is unclear. We do know, however, that Christian priests and scholars from Britain were travelling routinely to Brittany and other parts of what had been Gaul, so it seems unlikely that the Belgae would have willingly relinquished contacts that brought them both wealth through trade and useful contacts abroad.

It is time to look at who Ceawlin was and how he was able to make best use of his lands, wealth and family contacts.

Chapter 4

Ceawlin the Man

Ceawlin was a man of his time. Although we know very little about his younger years, it is unlikely that he would have had an upbringing very different from that of any other young man from his class, area and background.

For such an important man, a key fact would have been his ancestry. We have this in two versions, that given in the *Anglo-Saxon Chronicle* and that given in the *Welsh Genealogies*. We have already looked at the correlations between these two sources, but in regard to Ceawlin there is a difference.

In the *Welsh Genealogies*, Ceawlin is recorded as Collen or Kollen, son of Gwynoc, son of Kydeboc. We have already seen that Kydeboc is identical to the same man as the Cynric recorded in the Chronicle, so the Welsh make Collen (Ceawlin) a grandson of Cynric. It is usually said that the *Chronicle* declared Ceawlin to be the son of Cynric, which would contradict the Welsh accounts, but this is not quite the case. The earlier *Chronicle* entries do not mention the relationship between Ceawlin and Cynric, saying only that the two men led joint military expeditions and that when Cynric died Ceawlin inherited power. It is not until AD 685 (more than a century later) that Ceawlin is claimed to be the son of Cynric. It is possible that by 685 the exact relationship between Cynric and Ceawlin had been forgotten. If that were the case then the fact that Ceawlin succeeded Cynric in power might be enough to lead to the assumption that he had been Cynric's son. On balance, therefore, it seems likely that Ceawlin was grandson of Cynric and son of Gwynoc.

Again according to the Welsh sources, Ceawlin's mother was Ethinen, daughter of Matholwch Lord of Ireland. The identity of Matholwch is uncertain. His name is given in some manuscripts as being Mallolwch, which translates as meaning something like 'Still Waters' or 'Placid River' but his Irish Gaelic name is not known. As Ceawlin's grandfather he should have been ruling in Ireland sometime around the 500s, but no ruler of this name is known. It must be admitted, however, that our records for Ireland at this time are scanty to say the least. Very likely Matholwch was a ruler of a smaller state the records of which have not survived. An alternative suggestion has it that the name is not that of the man, but of the state he ruled over. If this were the case than 'Placid River' would suit any of several lowland areas of what is now the southern half of Ireland. 'Still Waters' may suggest a harbour, and so a link to the maritime trade routes that we know the Belgae used. Perhaps Gwynoc was married to an Irish heiress to secure some sort of trade alliance or to gain the aid of Irish warships to protect Belgic merchant shipping.

Be that as it may, Ceawlin was born somewhere in the Belgic lands in about 530 or 540. He was thus born into a Britain that was in serious decline as regards both population and economic prosperity. The bulk of the old Roman lands were still under the authority of Christian British rulers, whether they were tyrants, rectores or civitates councils. The Belgae Civitas in which Ceawlin was born would seem to have been under the personal rule of a dynasty of men whose power was based on their military prowess and ability to hold the enemies of the Belgae at bay.

Undoubtedly the young Ceawlin would have been taught all there was to know about fighting and warfare. This training would have begun when the boy was only a toddler as he was told tales of battles, campaigns and heroic actions. Later he would have been given child-sized blunted weapons with which to play and a pony on which to ride. Being fit and strong was essential to warfare at this date since battles were physically exhausting events and campaigns involved sleeping out in all weathers. A young nobleman would therefore be expected to spend hours every day engaged in outdoor exercise of various sorts to prepare his body and mind for the long and arduous exploits to come. Hunting was a favourite way to pass the time.

A more formal military training would have begun when Ceawlin was about nine years of age. We do not know quite how this was structured, but it may have followed a similar pattern to that in use a few generations later. Ceawlin would have been put under the charge of a distinguished older warrior. There he would have learned to care for the armour, arms and campaign equipment of his teacher. By the age of twelve he would have progressed to being a shield bearer, that is an assistant to his master on campaign. He would have ridden a horse and been responsible for ensuring that his master was fed, watered and provided with any equipment he needed as and when it was required. Training in the use of weapons would have been carried on throughout, with Ceawlin being given his first set of adult weapons by the age of about fourteen.

Given his parentage, Ceawlin would have been trained for command in the field. This involved his learning about battle tactics, war songs and banners. He would also have needed to understand those often neglected arts of early medieval warfare supply and morale. These features do not often make it into the written record, but no war leader could hope to succeed without them.

Supply at this date is poorly understood in Britain, but analogies from elsewhere give us a clue as to how an army was fed and maintained in the field. Assuming that most fighting – other than local defence – at this date was done by mercenaries or a professional militia, it was up to the commander of a force to provide food and drink for his men. When operating in enemy country it was often possible to steal food or to cajole locals into revealing where their supplies were hidden. This was not always feasible, and in any case could not be relied upon in friendly territory.

On campaign supplies were probably carried on pack horses or light, two-wheeled carts. Roman roads were necessary for the latter, though the former could follow anywhere that men could march. Such supplies would have needed to be securely packed into leather bags or wooden barrels to protect them against rain and sun. Working out how much food to take and how to transport it was a key command skill that Ceawlin would have learned at an early age.

Ceawlin would also have needed to know how to get the supplies in the first place. Given that the cash economy had vanished by this date, Ceawlin would probably have fallen back on what was known as the *annona*. This system of raising military supplies was named after the pagan goddess Annona. Usually shown holding a cornucopia and a grain measure, Annona was the personification of the government's ability to care for the people and, particularly, to feed them. By extension she came to symbolize the emperor's care for his servants, and so the name was adopted for the system by which a ruler fed his army.

The system relied upon an administrator, named a *Cais*, operating in each district and knowing intimately the lands in his area. Each year at harvest time the Cais would tour the district to assess how good the local crop was and how productive the livestock had been. He then assessed each landowner for the annona. Usually this took the form of a list of agricultural produce to be handed over, but sometimes a landowner would be assessed in terms of having troops billetted on his lands for a set number of nights. The annona was not always taken up by the ruler, at least not fully, but represented the maximum that a landowner would be expected to hand over if required to do so.

The annona was massively unpopular with landowners. This was not only because it could represent a great drain on their wealth, but also because of its erratic nature. The annona was assessed each year, but only imposed when needed. Inevitably some lands found themselves handing over the annona more often than others – perhaps those close to a civitas capital or a garrisoned border fortress had to pay up more frequently. It gave landowners a real interest in trying to keep the army as small and as inactive as was possible, at least in peaceful times. When war came, of course, they clamoured for the army to protect their lands.

Ceawlin would have learned early on the skills needed to balance the demands of a hungry army with the need to placate resentful landlords. Those landowners were rich and influential men, many of whom would have been relatives or friends of Ceawlin, and yet the army was necessary both to defend Belgic lands and, perhaps, to keep Ceawlin in power. It was a delicate balancing act that any ruler at this time had to manage carefully.

Among the landowners who resented the annona most openly and vociferously was the Church. The Christian Church as it existed in Britain in the mid-fifth century is well described by Gildas, and can be tracked in other sources. Gildas describes a late-Roman hierarchy that was clearly still in place and was effectively organizing both the spiritual and worldly aspect of the Church. Gildas, of course, denounced those who use religious office to benefit themselves or who fail to carry out the duties of their office, but there was no doubt in his mind that such positions existed and had duties. We have seen that in the less organized areas of what later became Wales many saints successfully opposed exaction of taxes, including annona, on Church lands. This does not seem to have been the case in more settled area such as the Civitas of the Belgae. There the Church paid its annona and taxes, but under protest.

There is a possible link between Ceawlin and Gildas. It is impossible to be accurate with dates for this period, but it is generally thought that Gildas was writing some time in the 530s or 540s. Ceawlin emerges as an adult man in 556 when he fights his first battle. Now by the conventions of the day Ceawlin may have been as young as fifteen when he first went to war, which would put his date of birth around 540. Of course, he may have been older when he first fought a battle, making his date of birth earlier. It is possible that he was a child of up to ten when Gildas wrote his history of the decline of Britain. We know that Gildas was living somewhere in southern Britain when he wrote his book, and it is certainly possible that he was working in the lands of the Belgae. Is it too fanciful to imagine a ten-year-old Ceawlin sitting at the feet of the aged scholar Gildas, listening to his words of anguish? Well, perhaps, but it is not impossible.

Ceawlin was undoubtedly a Christian, though as a ruler he would have had no scruples about taxing the Church as he would any other landowner. The *Chronicle*, seeking to portray Ceawlin as an English king, is silent on his religion, but the Welsh sources are more revealing about Ceawlin (or Collen).

The purported biography of Collen, the *Buchedd Collen*, is contained in a manuscript dating from about 1350. The biography as we have it is short and is clearly based on an earlier work which was updated by the fourteenth-century copyist, but it is impossible to tell how faithfully the newer work followed the older version. Nor is it clear how old the original version was. The text as we have it may be entirely unreliable, and as we shall see it contains some sections that are clearly fantastical embellishments drawing on Welsh folktales. That said, it does have a few facts that may date back to Collen's own time.

The first of these states that Collen was sent to live in Orleans, France, for six months to learn about Christianity. At this date Orleans was the centre of a Frankish kingdom ruled by Childebert I, a son of the great Clovis I. This claim of a visit to Orleans is interesting. The Welsh sources claim that Cerdic's mother had come from Vannes, near the mouth of the Loire, and Orleans stands on the middle reaches of that same river. It may be that the family still had links to the area, family at this date being considered to be enormously important. It is not inconceivable that Ceawlin went to visit relatives. As the grandson of a ruler in Britain he would have been more than welcome.

Religiously the visit was also important. At this date the Franks had recently converted from the Arian form of Christianity (traditionally treated as a heretical doctrine) to the more mainstream Catholicism. It was this form of Christianity to which the British adhered. The British had, however, been as cut off from the Pope in Rome as they had been from the Emperor. As we have seen those British clergy who travelled far did so to Ireland, Scotland and Brittany where they were assured of finding other priests who shared their brand of Christianity. The Arian nature of those Germans who had converted to Christianity made them unwelcome to the British.

Ceawlin's alleged stay in Orleans may have coincided with the period of time when the great teacher Mesme was active in the city. Mesme was the sister of Bishop Maxim, who died around AD 525, and is known to have outlived him for some time. She worked tirelessly to boost Catholicism among the newly-converted Franks and was a famous teacher. It would have made sense for Ceawlin to come to Orleans to be taught by her, or perhaps by one of the pupils who kept her school going after her death.

At any rate, a stay in Orleans would have put Ceawlin in more direct touch with Rome. At this date the papacy was nowhere near as important as it would later become. The Bishop of Rome was acknowledged to be the successor to St Peter, but at most this made him a first among equals with other bishops. Like many other bishops, a new Bishop of Rome was elected to office by the clergy in his diocese and like most others in the Mediterranean that new bishop had to be confirmed in office by the Emperor in Constantinople before he could be consecrated. However, Rome was a great centre for theological learning and debate. A sojourn in Orleans would have enabled Ceawlin to meet men who had been to Rome and learn the latest trends in Christian thinking.

The visit to Orleans could have been important for another reason that would only become apparent many years later. Childebert I had grabbed Orleans in 524 as part of a murderous feud within his own Merovingian royal dynasty. The Merovingians were a famously fractious and violent family, and the events of 524 were brutally typical. In 511 Clovis I had died and divided up his kingdom among his four sons. In 523 the second son Chlodomer died and left his lands (including Orleans) to be divided among his three sons, who were placed in the care of his mother along with a daughter. But in 524 Chlodomer's three brothers hatched a plot to murder the children and divide up their lands.

The youngest son, two-year-old Clodoald, escaped the massacre by pure luck and was spirited away by his nurse to be raised by relatives in Provence. As a teenager young Clodoald became a priest, renounced all claims to lands or position and symbolically shaved off his beard – the Merovingian Franks viewing beards as being synonymous with masculinity. He moved to Paris and by the time Ceawlin came to Orleans was running a small monastic house at what is now Nogent-sur-Seine. He subsequently lived a long and uneventful life as a monk and priest famed for his learning and piety. He is today better known by the shortened version of his name and has been canonized as St Cloud. Ceawlin may well have met St Cloud, the king who was ousted from his kingdom, but saved his life by entering a monastery. Perhaps the meeting made an impression on him.

Welsh sources also maintain that Ceawlin lived for a time at Glastonbury Abbey. Glastonbury was one of the most important religious houses in Britain, having a reputation for learning and for sanctity. It was certainly the burial place of some very important people, and possibly of Arthur – the Wide Ruler who died about twenty years before Ceawlin was born. It would have made sense for a young nobleman to be sent to stay at Glastonbury for a while to further his religious education. But there may have been more to the visit than that.

Glastonbury stands on what was then an island among the vast marshes of the Somerset Levels. That position put it almost precisely on the boundary between the civitas of the Durotriges and what had been the western lands of the Belgae. We do not know on which side of the border the island lay. Nor do we know what happened to this area of Somerset in the internecine wars between the civitates that saw Bath apparently fall to the Dobunni in the mid-fifth century.

Whatever the political status of the surrounding lands, however, Glastonbury was a holy island in the hands of the Church. Since the abbey there had been founded in late Roman times when it certainly fell under the Belgae, it would have been endowed by the wealthy Christians of that civitate. Ceawlin's family was rich and prestigious at least as early as the 440s and probably much earlier. They may well have given lands or money to the abbey at Glastonbury, which would have made Ceawlin a welcome visitor.

Whether the rulers of the surrounding lands would have been quite so keen to see him there is another question. Perhaps the visit was an attempt to remind people of the links between the Belgae and the western lands that they had lost.

There are two interesting stories told about Ceawlin's time at Glastonbury. The first relates that he had been studying there for only three months when the monks decided to elect him as their abbot. Ceawlin accepted, but then received 'a letter from his home parish' instructing him 'to pursue a harder path than being an abbot'. Ceawlin then stood down as Abbot of Glastonbury and left the precincts of the monastery. He did not go far, building himself a small stone hut on the slopes of the Tor where he could study and contemplate God.

The story of his sudden election to be abbot might, of course, be a later invention to portray Ceawlin as a popular and well educated young man. The sudden renunciation of the title in the story would be necessary since Ceawlin did not feature on the lists of Abbots of Glastonbury that might have been current when the *Buchedd Collen* was written.

On the other hand the event may have had some basis in fact.

Assuming Ceawlin did visit Glastonbury as a young man he would have come as the wealthy and well connected heir to a ruler, albeit a not terribly powerful one. The monks may have calculated that by electing him to be their abbot they might persuade Ceawlin's family to lavish gifts and lands on the abbey. So long as young Ceawlin was a reasonably competent scholar and was no more sinful than most other young men, the move would not have been out of place in sixth-century Britain. Young Ceawlin would not be the first young man from an influential family to have his head turned by flattery and to believe that such flattery was due to his own talents, not to who his father was. Perhaps he believed the monks when they told him that they wanted him for abbot because they had been so impressed by his learning, his intelligence and his piety.

But the elevation of a leading member of the Belgae to be Abbot of Glastonbury would have been fraught with political difficulties. Neither the Durotriges nor the Dobunni would have welcomed the move, perhaps seeing it as part of some plot to expand Belgae influence back into the area. We know that both these civitates had fought the Belgae in recent decades, so they would have been touchy about the actions of young Ceawlin. In any event, grandfather Cynric may have had plans for Ceawlin, and they would not have involved the young man being an abbot on an island in a marsh. Hence the swift letter from home telling Ceawlin not to be so foolish and to get back to his studies.

The second event recorded about Ceawlin's time at Glastonbury is altogether more mysterious. It concerns an encounter with a man named Gwyn ap Nudd. In Welsh folklore, Gwyn ap Nudd is usually described as being the chief of the fairies, but he is in origin a pagan deity of the Celts. As a pagan god, Gwyn ap Nudd was ruler of *Annwn*, the Otherworld. This Annwn was generally described as being a wonderful place of perpetual summer, plentiful food and eternal youth. Its inhabitants are all beautiful and young, clever and wise, healthy and joyful. It was probably originally the place to which people went after death. Opinion differed as to whether it lay underground or was an island far out in the western ocean.

Gwyn ap Nudd was son of Lludd Llaw Eraint (Llud of the Silver Hand), a Celtic god linked to hunting, healing and the sea.

There are various legends linked to this shadowy god, but one of the few facts known about him is that a temple to him once stood on top of the hill in the centre of the city of London. When the Roman Empire turned Christian this temple was rededicated to St Paul, and its site still contains St Paul's Cathedral. The nearby Ludgate was named after the god. Gwyn married his own sister, Creiddylad, having abducted her on her wedding day.

In Welsh mythology, Gwyn ap Nudd has some interesting relatives. His father's sister, Penarddun married Llyr, God of the Sea, who thus became Gwyn's uncle by marriage. That Llyr has a name almost identical to that of Llyr Merini (or Elesa) the father of Cerdic. Penarddun and Llyr had twin, a boy named Bran and a daughter Branwen. Bran will re-enter our story near its end. Branwen, meanwhile, married Matholwch, a poorly-known Celtic god who seems to have been linked to quarrels between members of a family. Matholwch, of course, shares the name of the father of Ceawlin's mother Ethinen. None of these names were especially uncommon at the time, so there is no need to read too much into them. It may simply be that whichever monk inserted the tale of Ceawlin's encounter with Gwyn ap Nudd into the *Buchedd Collen* was aware of the coincidence of names and thought it an amusing addition to slip in.

In the story of his encounter with Ceawlin, Gwyn ap Nudd behaves very much like a ruler of the fairies, but the encounter seems to be an allegory for the triumph of Christianity over paganism. Perhaps whoever developed this tale was aware of Gwyn's pagan origins. The story begins after Ceawlin (Collen) has stood down as Abbot of Glastonbury and retreated to his stone hut.

> As Collen was within his secluded cell, one day he heard the sound of voices approaching. As they came nearer he heard that they were discussing Gwyn ap Nudd, his talents and his wealth. Unable to bear any more Collen stuck his head out of his cell and reproached the men saying 'Hold your tongues, quickly, for they are no more than devils'. The strangers turned to face him and one of them looked at him sternly, saying: 'Hold your tongue, foolish man, or you will receive your reproof from him in person'.

At this Collen merely huffed before retreating into his cell and shutting the door as before.

Not long after Collen heard a knocking on the door of his cell and a voice enquired if he was within. 'I am', responded Collen. 'Who is it that asks?'

'I am the messenger of Gwyn ap Nudd', responded the voice, 'and I have come on the behest of my Lord to command you to come forth and meet him at the summit of this hill at noon.'

But Collen ignored the summons, returning to his devotions instead, and the next day, at the same time, the messenger returned – once more ordering Collen to attend his master at the top of the hill. This time the messenger added 'Who are you to be so rude about our Lord, after all are you not a guest in this land? Maybe this time you will not be so rude in your response to this request.'

But once more Collen had no intention of answering the summons and he returned to his devotions. But the next day he was disturbed once more by loud knocking on his cell's door. This time the messenger began with: 'Little man, our Lord will not wait forever. But he kindly requests that you put away any hostilities that you have against him and that you but attend his court and his table. He is eager to make the acquaintance of such a wise man as you and merely desires to talk of your God. He gives his promise that no harm will come to you. Again he asks for your audience at noon on the summit of this hill.'

This time Collen decided to go and visit Gwyn ap Nudd so he responded: 'It seems that I will gain no peace until I go. Tell your master that I will come at noon. Now, begone!'

A little before noon, Collen prepared himself by donning his robe though as a precaution he filled a bottle with holy water which he secreted in the folds of his robe. Then taking his staff he made his way towards the summit of the hill. When he reached the hilltop he was disappointed to see that nothing and no one was there, despite the sun being at its zenith. But almost at the instant he had this thought a castle appeared before him and the air was filled with the sound of joyous celebration and the rich scents of roasting meats.

Before the castle stood an honour guard of troops arrayed in ranks, their armour shining in the sun. Before them danced musicians playing flutes, drums, lyres and all manner of instruments that he had never seen nor heard before. It was almost as if he were being serenaded as the music danced upon the breeze.

As Collen walked towards the castle gaily-dressed people danced about him and young men rode across the hilltop, each colourfully arrayed in clothes of red, green and blue. These were the most graceful and beautiful people that Collen had ever seen. Even within the court there was such merriment and happiness that Collen believed they must be celebrating some special event or occasion. He was greeted by a courtier arrayed in blue shot through with gold and he was ushered into the great hall.

Gwyn ap Nudd was there to greet him, seated as he was on golden throne covered with snakes and the arms of his chair were fashioned into the forms of two great ram-horned serpents. Gwyn's golden hair glittered and his green eyes sparkled as they turned to look upon his guest. Then he spoke, his deep voice booming against the rafters of the hall. 'Welcome, wise man,' he said, 'I am pleased that one so honourable and knowledgeable as you would agree to accept my invitation.'

'I agreed only to rid myself of your troublesome minions and to regain my peace and solitude,' Collen replied.

'Were they wearisome, did they annoy you?' Gwyn asked. 'No matter, for that is past. Come, join me, and all you see before you is yours dear saint. Come, partake of my food and of my drinks and I am sure that you will agree that this repast is the finest that you will ever have tasted.'

'I am neither hungry nor thirsty', Collen responded, his visage showing no delight at the delicacies he saw before him.

'It matters not,' replied Gwyn, 'for I can regale you with the finest poets, the most diverting conversation, the best dancers and musicians – all to entertain you.'

'I do not wish to talk,' responded Collen, 'nor do I wish to hear music and singing nor to listen to music. Neither do I wish to see any more of your kingdom!'

> 'You refuse everything I offer?' Gwyn asked in wonderment. 'Is this land not a pleasant one, does not the singing and music delight you. Do not my young men amaze you in their splendour!'
>
> 'Your land is pleasant enough,' replied Collen, 'but the raiment of those youths you speak of reveal the truth of your realm. For the red of their garb is nought but the flames of hell and the blue of their cloaks reveals the true coldness of this place.'
>
> This said the saint leapt to his feet and taking the bottle of holy water from his garments he unstoppered it and cast drops of the water in a circle about him. Instantly Gwyn vanished along with his courtiers the table the knights the musicians, minstrels and dancers. Finally the court itself faded away into nothing leaving Collen alone upon the hill.
>
> The saint made his way back to his cell, resumed his meditations and was not troubled by the fairy folk any more.

The story is clearly more related to folklore than to history, but it is interesting that Collen (Ceawlin) was considered to be a worthy opponent of Gwyn ap Nudd and a representative champion of Christianity.

As a young man who had spent more than a year being educated in monastic houses, Ceawlin would almost certainly have been able to read and write. By this date the skills of literacy were much less widely spread than they had been in Roman times. The purposes for which reading and writing had been used in Britain were, by and large, no longer relevant. Reports from government departments were no longer sent to Rome, tax returns were no longer compiled to be checked against central accounts in Rome and the complex bureaucracy of the Roman army was no more. The much more limited demands of the local civitates governments could have easily been met by non-written methods such as tally sticks, public declarations and sworn oaths. However, it remains likely that literacy continued among the better educated classes since it remained a useful skill, if no longer a necessary one.

It was among the churchmen that literacy remained widespread, but that was for basically religious reasons. Christianity is a book-based religion so its priests need to be able to read the Holy Book in order to interpret its teachings to their congregations. The vast majority of books in monastic libraries were Bibles or theological works.

It has been suggested that the only reasons young men, such as Ceawlin, spent time in monastic houses was in order to learn to read and write and to become familiar with Roman tracts on good government, battle tactics and other practical matters. This is not necessarily the case. People took religion seriously, and nobles were expected to play a role in religious as well as in secular society. There are indications that Christianity was being used as something of a cultural marker to distinguish between civilized, Roman-style people and pagan barbarians. In a Britain with a growing population of restive Germanic pagan incomers, at least the outward signs of Christian faith would have been essential to Ceawlin.

As grandson of Cynric, ruler of the Belgae, Ceawlin would have been a man of prospects. However, it was by no means certain that he would inherit either his grandfather's wealth or his power. At this date, and for many generations to come, it was not usual for a British man to leave his entire wealth to his oldest son as it was among the English. Instead he was most likely to divide up the inheritance among his children, giving to each whatever he felt was most appropriate. This worked best in terms of money and objects. A helmet and mail armour could be left to the son who showed military promise, a Bible could be bequeathed to a daughter of religious leanings and a lyre to whichever child sang the best. But for landholdings and political power the process was rather more complicated.

We do not know exactly what the constitutional arrangement was in the Civitas of the Belgae at this time. Clearly Cynric occupied some post in the government that gave him great power. By the time Alfred the Great's scholars were drawing up the *Anglo-Saxon Chronicle* in the later ninth century they interpreted his role as being that of a king, holding similar powers and rights as did his descendent Alfred. Cynric was not a king – that being an English concept – and we do not know what position he held.

We do know how later Welsh princes managed their affairs, so it may be that Cynric followed similar customs. A prince held a constitutional position akin to that of an absolute ruler, though in practice his powers were limited by the influence of the Church, the nobles and traditional customs. That position as ruler of a state was held to be quite distinct from the personal wealth of the prince. On his death, the prince could pass on the position of prince to any of his male relatives, while dividing up his wealth among his sons and daughters. Given the vagaries of inheritance, poor financial judgement and pure luck this separation of constitutional position from wealth could mean that after a few generations the title and rank of prince was held by a relatively impoverished noble surrounded by much richer subjects. Such a man would be seriously hampered in trying to enforce his rule on wealthier cousins and weak government would result. Equally, a wealthy man might decide that he was better qualified to be prince than his weak cousin and plunge a state into civil war to get his way.

Typically a later Welsh dynastic family counted a title and wealth as being part of a shared inheritance over four generations. This would mean that any great great grandson of a prince had a claim to his title, and if a man were to die without children his lands and wealth would be shared out among anyone up to his second cousins on his father's side.

Thus Ceawlin was far from secure in his inheritance. If Cynric were to follow this agnatic system of inheritance, then his wealth might be divided up among a large number of male relatives, any one of whom would be in with a chance of inheriting the political position – whatever that was – that Cynric held. Events were soon to prove that Cynric had his eye on young Ceawlin as his political heir. And after his years of training, Ceawlin was ready for the task.

Chapter 5

Ceawlin Goes To War

Ceawlin marched to war as a young man in around AD 560. He would have made an impressive figure as he rode off out of Winchester, or wherever Cynric had his residence. As the scion of a ruling family, Ceawlin would have been given the very best war gear available.

The arms and armour that Ceawlin would have worn were works of art, not just functional gear. His helmet would have been of iron, but decorated with silver plates and with gilding. The silver and gold would have been embossed or engraved with a riot of imagery, both secular and religious. He would probably have had a full or partial faceplate and cheek pieces, features often gilded and engraved with exaggerated eyebrows, moustache and other facial features. The body armour would have been steel mail, no doubt regularly rolled in a barrel of sand and vinegar to keep it shining and bright. The armour would have been held in place by removable clasps and fittings of iron overlaid with more silver and gold, perhaps embellished with enamelling in the brightest of colours. His sword would have had a hilt similarly decorated in gold, silver and enamel, decorations which would also have appeared on his shield, belt buckles, scabbard and knife. A rich young man going to war was a wonderful sight to behold.

The purpose of all this display was not simply to show off, though no doubt that played a part. The elaborate and highly-skilled decorative work served to mark out the richest men in the army, but also served as badges of rank. In the turmoil, blood and fear of a battle it is important for men to be able to recognize their commanders instantly and without any possibility of confusion. While most men wore leather armour and plain iron helmets, a man bedecked in gold, silver and enamelling would have been instantly recognizable.

The ostentatious display of wealth by Ceawlin also played a role in maintaining the morale of the army. A general who went to war dressed in such astonishingly costly gear was giving his men a very clear message. He was intending and expecting to win a great victory. He would not be risking such an important and costly outfit if there were the slightest chance he might be captured or killed and his war gear stolen by an enemy. A leader who left his best armour behind was one who anticipated defeat or a hurried retreat, and that would have been disastrous for the spirits of his men.

The outfit was also intended to intimidate the enemy. Most battles were preceded by a short discussion between the rival commanders. These usually took the form of calls for surrender and offers of terms for an honourable retreat or capitulation. Fighting a battle was expensive in terms of men lost even to the victor and so some form of deal was often preferable. Sometimes that was not possible, of course, so the meeting would instead take the form of threats, insults and jeers. The ability to insult the enemy with skill was highly regarded. Commanders would write poems or songs that included references to the enemy commander's past, his parentage and his deeds. Such poems or songs were chanted to the enemy army, or to one's own in order to lower or raise morale in the vital minutes before the fighting began. Such words coming from a big man mounted on a fine charger and clad in the finest armour glittering with gold and silver would make a much greater impact than the same words coming from a fellow on a pony wearing battered leather armour.

The importance of morale in battles at this period is often overlooked, but it was crucial. For men to advance to within spitting distance of an enemy armed to the teeth is a daunting task. Warriors at this date risked the most hideous injuries from swords, spears and axes, all meted out at close quarters. Even the most professional of fighters would have wanted to know that they were in with a good chance of survival, let alone victory, if they were to form a shield wall and advance to the killing zone. This was why men sang, chanted, waved flags and hammered their swords on their shields. The noise served to raise spirits and to prepare men for the clash to come. The noise set up by an opposing army, their confident advance and the brandishing of banners and trophies could be highly intimidating. We know of more than one battle where an entire army simply turned and fled before a single blow was struck.

Morale was vital, and the outfit of a leader such as Ceawlin was all part of the mix.

The *Anglo-Saxon Chronicle* records Ceawlin's first campaign under the year 556 with the terse statement 'Cynric and Ceawlin fought with the Britons at Beranbyrg'. As ever with the older entries in the *Chronicle*, the precise date cannot be taken at face value. By the mid-sixth century, however, it is generally thought that the dates cannot be more than twenty years adrift, and are possibly more accurate than that. What is taken as reliable is the sequence of events, and the years between different events is probably not too inaccurate.

The place Beranbyrg is now known as Barbury, a hill on the northern flank of the Marlborough Downs a few miles south of Swindon. On top of the hill is one of the most impressive hillforts of Wiltshire, a structure known today as Barbury Castle.

The site was of crucial strategic importance in the mid-sixth century. It stood where the territory of the Dobunni, Atrebates and Belgae met in what is now northern Wiltshire. We do not know to which civitas it belonged, though its position on a north-facing escarpment looking north into Dobunnic territory would make it unlikely to belong to that civitas. It most likely fell under either the Atrebates or the Belgae. Since we know that the Germanic mercenaries of the Gewisse were based in Atrebatic territory and were allied to the Belgae, it would seem that one way or another the hillfort was held by men loyal to Cynric at this date. A battle fought there would therefore most likely be because of an incursion by the Dobunni.

This invasion may have followed on from Cynric's victory at Salisbury, fought just four years earlier according to the *Chronicle*. That battle had been fought against the civitas of the Durotriges, and as we have seen the *Chronicle* emphasized the scale of that victory. The post-Roman history of the Durotriges is very poorly known. Nothing is to be found in written records, so we are reliant on archaeology. That shows us the Durotriges suffered a violent time between about 400 and 600.

There are numerous fortified sites spread through Durotriges territory, from isolated farmsteads surrounded by a ditch and bank right the way up to massive fortified enclosures large enough to hold an entire army. We have already seen that armies coming apparently from Durotrigan territory had penetrated deep into Belgic territory early in the sixth century and that Belgic versus Durtotriges battles were frequent. There are some hints that the Durotriges had co-operated with the Dobunni in conquering the western parts of the Belgic civitas. Some areas of land south of Bath seem to have fallen under Durotriges rule, or at least influence, from around 440 onward.

However, the second half of the sixth century was quieter in the archaeological record. This was the period after Cynric's victory at Salisbury. The territory of the Durotriges re-enters the written record in 614 when a battle was fought at Bindon. This is now a small hamlet located in a narrow, steep-sided valley just east of the estuary of the River Axe. It was therefore, right on the eastern edge of Durotriges territory where it bordered that of the Dumnonians. In 614 the battle fought there was between an invading Dumnonian army and a defending army led by Cynegils, a great grandson of Cynric. In other words, by 614 the territories of the Durotriges had been incorporated into the lands ruled by Cynric's heirs. The name of the Durotriges survives in the form of Dorset; the two words mean pretty much the same thing 'The People of Duros'.

Any conclusion from this must be tentative, but at some date between the Battle of Salisbury in 552 and the Battle of Bindon in 614 the Durotriges had ceased to exist as an independent state and become part of the state ruled from Winchester. The most obvious time for this to have happened was in the wake of Cynric's great victory at Salisbury. If so, then the move would have doubled the lands ruled by Cynric, and removed a useful ally of the Dobunni. Either would have been enough to bring the Dobunni into the fray, invading the Belgic lands from the north in an effort to humble their newly powerful southern neighbour.

The fact that Ceawlin's first battle was fought at a hillfort would indicate that this was either a siege or a storming of the fortress. Barbury has never been properly excavated, but other hillforts in the area have and the results give us a good idea of how the post-Roman Britons would have gone about fortifying an ancient hillfort such as Barbury.

Barbury was first built around 600 BC. It covers an area of just over twelve acres and stands on an oval spur of high ground protected to north, south and west by steep slopes, of which those to the north at the most impressive. To the east a narrow neck of land leads to a plateau about a mile long and up to half a mile wide. A gateway enters the east side of the fort from this flattish neck of land and another enters from the west. The eastern gateway was surely the more vulnerable of the two, and has been substantially strengthened by the addition of an outwork. This takes the form of a semi-circular ditch and bank that projects out from the main walls. Anyone entering the fort through this gate was forced to turn left, exposing their unshielded right side to the men manning the ramparts.

Those main ramparts take the form of two massive ditches, each backed by a rampart. These are now overgrown with grass and smooth in outline, but originally would have been much more formidable. The inner face, up which any enemy would have to scramble, would have been embanked with chalk blocks to make the bottom eight feet or so sheer and vertical. The tops of the ramparts would have been surmounted by a wooden wall behind which defenders could hide in safety from arrows and javelins, and from which they could fight off an assault. The two gateways would have been protected by wooden towers and by massive gates. That on the east at least would have been a double gate so that any attackers getting past the first would have found themselves trapped in a brutal killing ground made up of a courtyard surrounded by wooden walls topped by hostile warriors. This would not have been an easy fortification to take.

Although no detailed excavations have taken place at Barbury, a few trial digs have been carried out over the years. These have turned up the burials of three men dating to somewhere between AD 550 to 620. All three men were equipped with military equipment of a Germanic type, though the artefacts were so badly damaged that precise dating and identification could not be made. They may have been casualties of the battle fought here by Cynric and Ceawlin, or they may have been men on garrison duty who died of some natural cause.

The short entry in the *Chronicle* records only that Cynric and Ceawlin fought at Barbury, it does not record whether they won or lost. This in itself is significant as the *Chronicle* writers were usually keen to emphasise the glorious victories of the ancestors of their patron Alfred the Great. If they do not report a victory, the chances are that the battle was a defeat.

The defeat at Barbury cannot have been catastrophic, however, for there is no sign in the archaeology of an extension of Dobunnic power into Belgic lands. Nor does the written record show any sign of a serious lessening of Belgic power. The next entry is for the year 560, four years after the battle at Barbury. This entry records 'Ceawlin received the kingdom'. It is usually assumed that Ceawlin began to rule when Cynric died, though that is not stated in the text.

As ruler of the Belgic lands, Ceawlin inherited something of a poisoned chalice. On the plus side his ancestors had secured the grip on power of his family. Whatever the constitutional niceties of the position of Cerdic when he 'undertook to rule' the civitas of the Belgae, there seem to have been no problems when the time came for Cynric to hand power over to Ceawlin. It should be assumed that by this date the legal basis by which the family was in power had been settled. The old *curia*, or council, of the Belgae that was elected by all adult free men and composed of the richer and more influential men was probably no longer in existence, though the rich and influential no doubt continued to dominate the society. Ceawlin's rule may not have been absolute, but he was quite clearly the ruler and was no longer a first among equals.

Another advantage Ceawlin could look to was the Gewisse. These 'reliable allies' seem to have been first employed by the Belgae a century or so before Ceawlin came to power. As Germanic mercenaries they had come to garrison the fortress town of Dorchester-upon-Thames, but had long since become settled along the upper Thames. Archaeological finds in the area show that they retained their Germanic culture and were not integrated into the local populace. Maybe this distinctive character kept them loyal to their paymaster Ceawlin rather than feeling a kinship to the Britons among whom they lived. In any case they were a potent source of military muscle.

Thirdly on the positive side of the balance sheet, Ceawlin had wider territories than had his ancestors. The western Belgic lands had been lost some generations back, but had been replaced by the lands of the Atrebates civitas. These would seem to have been added to the Belgic lands in the early-sixth century. More recently the lands of the Durotriges had been annexed by Cynric. Exactly how quiet the new acquisitions were we cannot know. There is no sign either in the meagre written sources nor in archaeology of much fighting after the Battle at Salisbury. Presumably Cynric had either come to some sort of accommodation with the local landowners and nobility that assured him of their loyalty, or he had enforced a secure military takeover. Whichever course he took it had worked and the rich lands now fell to Ceawlin.

But all was not rosy for the new ruler. His lands were surrounded on all sides by states that were emerging from the overlordship of the Wide Ruler. They were flexing their muscles, attempting to extend their lands and influence at a time of declining populations and prosperity. We have seen how the Belgae had annexed the civitas of the Durotriges and the Atrebates, while fighting a war against the Dobunni that had already lasted some generations. But there were other states whose influence Ceawlin would have to face up to.

To the west of his own lands lay Dumnonia. The history of the civitas of Dumnonia in the sixth century is poorly known from the written record, and the earliest accounts contradict each other. We know from Gildas that by his day the civitas had been taken over by a tyrant named Constantine, and by the 560s the area seems to have been ruled by a man named Gerren rac Denau (Garren from the South) who may have been a son of Constantine. Archaeology has revealed trading links to Spain and the Mediterranean, presumably in return for exports of tin. The principality seems to have been reasonably prosperous, extending east as far as the River Axe in the south and the Somerset Levels in the north.

To the east, on the far side of Chichester Harbour were the lands that for centuries had been the civitas of the Regni. In the later fifth century this area had been the base for Aelle the Saxon and later generations would know it as the Kingdom of the South Saxons. Today it is Sussex. The fact that the borders of this land have remained fairly constant over some 2,000 years would argue that there has been a continuity of control throughout that period. Unfortunately we have effectively no written sources for what was going on here when Ceawlin was in power.

Archaeological digs show that by around 550 people were being buried with Germanic jewellery and weaponry around Chichester and at various inland sites across the area. Contemporary with these burials are found those of people with obviously British pots and jewellery. The two types of burial are sometimes found in the same cemeteries, indicating that the two peoples were living side by side in apparent peace. The only Roman walled city of any size was Noviomagus, now Chichester, which seems to have been largely abandoned by this date. The walls, however, remained in good repair and dark earth shows that the city was inhabited on a temporary basis from time to time. The large villas of the area, such as those at Bignor and Fishbourne had been abandoned by around 460, though they may have continued in use as farm dwellings for some time after that.

The overall picture of this area in the second half of the sixth century is one of peaceful obscurity. This may be an illusion caused by lack of evidence, but at the least it would seem that the South Saxons were not a threat to Ceawlin. As we have already seen the civitas of the Regni, like that of the Atrebates and the eastern end of the Belgae were all carved out of what in pre-Roman times had been the tribal kingdom of the Atrebates. Perhaps the cultural affinity between the two areas led to some sort of political affinity.

Farther east beyond the South Saxons (or Regni) lay what had been the civitas of the Canti. By the time Ceawlin came to power this area had become the English Kingdom of Kent. There is some disagreement as to when and how this happened. The later English monarchs traced their ancestry back to Hengist in the 440s and declared that they had been ruling Kent ever since. However, it is difficult to trace English rule back much before King Octa who came to power in around 512. This date is surprisingly close to when Cerdic is said to have undertaken to rule the Belgae, and the establishment of some form of Kentish independence from the authority of the Wide Ruler may have had similar causes. In this case, however, it was a Germanic mercenary who grabbed power, not a local magnate.

Octa and most of his Germanic followers seem to have come from Jutland (now southern Denmark), but the archaeological record shows strong Frankish influences. It may well be that the Kingdom of Kent was friendly with the Frankish rulers on the other side of the Straits of Dover. This would have made sense for both political and economic reasons. Indeed, Octa's son (or possibly grandson) was King Eormenric, a name which is a Frankish one. He ruled from about 540 to about 560 or so. Eormenric was succeeded by his son Ethelbert, who was later to marry a Frankish princess named Bertha.

North of the Thames lay the extensive lands of the civitas of the Catuvellauni, which included London and some lands south of the river. When Ceawlin came to power this civitas seems to have remained united and strong. It seems to have been a powerful state, but written evidence is entirely lacking. Archaeological digs show that Germanic mercenaries had been stationed at various points around the borders of the Catuvellauni from at least around 430 onwards. As time passed these garrisons tended to become larger and more settled, but still distinct from the surrounding British villages.

To the east of the Catuvellauni was what is now East Anglia. The southern part of this area had been covered by the civitas of the Trinovantes. Again written evidence is lacking, but archaeology shows that there was a fairly large settlement of mercenaries based in or near the civitas capital of Camulodunum (now Colchester) by about 420. Within fifty years other mercenaries were stationed at Caesaromagus (Chelmsford), Saffron Walden and elsewhere. Again, the settlements of the Germanic warriors seem to have remained distinct from the native population. There have been some finds of Germanic equipment in otherwise British cemeteries, but it is unclear if this represents a blending of populations or if the locals began wearing Germanic style clothing.

North of the Trinovantes lay the civitas of the Iceni. As with the Trinovantes, there is no written evidence for the mid-sixth century. Archaeology shows that there was a fairly large mercenary garrison near Swaffham by around 425, and another at the civitas capital of Venta Icenorum (Norwich) by 450. Other Germanic settlements sprang up in the decades that followed, mostly around the borders of the civitas. Again, these seem to have remained separate from the British settlements, though the Germanic warriors were often living in or close to towns that had Roman walls.

Across the Wash lay the civitas of the Corieltauvi, a territory almost as large and prosperous as that of the Catuvellauni. This was centred around two Roman cities: Lindum (Lincoln) and Ratae Corieltaurum (Leicester). The garrisons of Germanic mercenaries seem to have arrived in this civitas later than elsewhere, starting in around 460, but otherwise there is a similar pattern of settlement. The mercenary bases are located on the coast, on the borders and they grow in size and number as the decades pass.

North of the Humber was the small civitas of the Parisii based on Derventio (Malton). There are no early Germanic settlements here, but some small ones had appeared by the 490s. Compared to settlements in lands further south, however, the Germanic mercenaries remained small in number.

North of the Parisii and west of the Pennines stretched the vast, sprawling and thinly populated civitas of the Brigantes. There are no archaeological finds of Germanic mercenaries here at all. This is probably due to the fact that this area lay largely within the control of the Roman military forces manning Hadrian's Wall. Mercenaries would have been unnecessary and probably unwanted. It would seem that the political structure of this sprawling land was breaking up.

Eboracum (York) was the centre of a small but prosperous state that probably covered the rich farming lands of the Vale of York. The smaller state of Elmet covered the area around the Wharfe and the Sheaf rivers. Even smaller was Craven, around the River Aire. North of the Tees sprawled Berneich, which seems to have extended up the east coast over Hadrian's Wall. West of the Pennines spread Rheged, which extended north from what is now Lancashire up to Hadrian's Wall. Dunutinga seems to have been a small state around Ennerdale.

The precise relationships between these states is unclear, nor is it obvious how independent they were of each other. The dynasties that were ruling these lands in the later sixth century traced their ancestry back to a period around the 460s to 520s, but this does not mean that they were ruling their states at this date. The families may have been able to recall grandfathers of the men who set themselves up as princes.

Also generally free of Germanic settlements were the lands of the Dobunni (occupying the lower Severn Valley) and the Cornovii (covering the area from what is now Birmingham to Liverpool). What is now Wales was by 560 made up of a number of small states. In the south the civitas of the Silures had divided into Gwent in the east and Glevissig in the west. The rulers of Gwent would later claim to be descended from Cerdic of the Belgae, indicating a family link between the two states. The fact that Gwent lay west of the Dobunni and the Belgae south of the Dobunni would indicate one very useful reason for this link. The civitas of the Demetae in the far southwest of what is now Wales would seem to have remained united and fairly strong.

Beyond the southern states that we have surveyed the situation was no less fragile. The reasons had much to do with the general situation in Britain as a whole. The old order was on the brink of collapse, though it is unlikely that many of those living at the time realized this. It was almost certainly Ceawlin who would push Britain past a tipping point, but the slide to that catastrophic change was already under way.

Gildas had identified Maelgwn as the Dragon of the Island, the Wide Ruler, but Maelgwn had died in about 547. Dates are, as ever, difficult to pin down but the relative course of events would seem to make it clear that Maelgwn had died between ten and thirty years before Ceawlin came to power in Winchester.

The death of Maelgwn meant that his own lands were inherited by his son Rhun ap Maelgwn, also known as Rhun Hir (Rhun the Tall). The outline, but not the detail, of Rhun's career is reasonably well known from poems, songs and other accounts that are recorded in later Welsh manuscripts, but which can be fairly well dated to the later sixth century. He is also mentioned in the Welsh Triads as both one of the three most handsome princes of Britain and one of the three men with the finest golden bands. Presumably he was a rich and good-looking man.

The most important of Rhun's various actions was a protracted and far-reaching war that he fought in the 560s. That war raged across much of northern Britain and seems to have involved nearly all the emerging states and civitates north of the River Trent. His career sheds a light on the situation across the area at the time.

The war was sparked in around 560 by Elidyr Mwynfawr (the Courteous), a prince of the royal family of Rheged. Elidyr was a son in law of Maelgwn, being married to his daughter Eurgain, and it may be that he hoped to claim some share of Maelgwn's inheritance in the name of his wife. Elidyr came by sea to Caernarfon to confront Rhun, and was killed at Llanbeblig. The details of the killing are lost but they must have been rather underhand as Elidyr's relatives were outraged and mustered their armies for war. Four great warriors Clydno Eiddin, Nudd the Generous, Mordaf the Generous and Rhydderch Hael marched into northern Wales. They burned Rhun's palace, pillaged the coastal lands and then went home.

Rhun at once mustered his own army and set out on an epic campaign. He crossed the Dee with a mighty force and began a methodical sweep north. The advance was slow and careful. Elidyr's son, Llywarch, who would later be a famous poet, had plenty of time to gather his treasures and flee into the hills. But Rhun was on no mere raid. His men spread out over the land to take possession. Messengers rode over the Pennines to York, Craven, Malton, Elmet and Berneich to propose treaties of friendship that were weighted heavily in Rhun's favour. The King of York sealed the treaty by marrying his daughter to Rhun.

Rhun moved on slowly, imposing peace on his terms on the nobles of Rheged. Eventually even Llywarch came down from the hills to submit and make peace. Still Rhun was not satisfied. He marched on north again to the Forth and the Clyde, imposing terms on all the minor rulers he met. According to one source, Rhun did not fight a single battle during this whole campaign for the sheer size of his army and the scale of its supply system convinced all rulers that they could neither defeat him in battle nor wait until his supplies gave out. On the upper Forth, Rhun met his half brother, King Bridei of the Picts. Then finally he turned for home. His men had been away so long that several found that their wives had thought them dead and remarried or begun affairs.

The actions of Rhun on his great campaign, and the way in which he subsequently treated the petty rulers of the north sounds very much as if he were imposing himself as an overlord on the area. He did not seek to annex any lands, not even those of Elidyr. It would seem he was establishing himself in the position held by his father, that of Wide Ruler or Dragon of the Island. A man able to raise tribute and men from other rulers, but not to rule their lands himself. But if this is what Rhun achieved, he failed in one significant respect.

It must be borne in mind that, depending on how the dates are interpreted, the great campaign fought by Rhun took place some ten to twenty years after the great plague that killed his father and so many hundreds of thousands of others. Whatever the actual spark that ignited the war, the underlying causes may have been related to the greatly changed economic and political situation in the plague years. If Rhun inherited a claim to be Wide Ruler from his father, he would have wanted to gather the tribute due to him. But the other rulers and states may have been struggling to keep their own finances and bureaucracies functioning as the staggering death toll of the plague took a grip. If they refused, or delayed, payments that Rhun felt were his due then the march of a vast army as far north as the Clyde and Forth would have been a useful way of reminding people what they owed.

Rhun's life and exploits took place exclusively in an area north of the Midlands. A line drawn from Aberystwyth to the Wash would mark the southern boundary of Rhun's influence. None of the sources from the south mention him at all. It is unlikely, therefore, that Rhun was able to make a reality of his claims to be Wide Ruler in the south.

Looking around at the Britain around him, it would seem that Ceawlin made a momentous decision. Rhun Hir was unable to make a reality of his father's claims to overlordship over all of what had been Roman Britain. The words of Gildas would have been ringing in Ceawlin's ears. What Britain needed, Gildas had declared and many more believed, was a righteous Christian warrior to restore the fortunes of God's chosen people by enforcing morals on society, waging war on the heathens and uniting the old Roman Britain under a single ruler. Ceawlin decided that he was the man for the job.

He declared himself to be the Wide Ruler, and set out to make his claims a reality.

Chapter 6

Power Bid

By making his bid for power, Ceawlin was seeking to establish himself as the supreme political authority in Britain. The move was set against the background of declining populations, prosperity and order that had followed the fall of Rome and then been accelerated by the devastating plague that swept Britain some twenty years before the Battle at Barbury.

As with so much about Britain in these years we have to grope toward an understanding of what the powers were that Ceawlin was seeking to acquire, and how he set about doing so. Clearly Ceawlin was seeking the position and powers of the Wide Ruler, successor to the Vicarius of Britain in Roman times. Whether he stated his ambitions openly at this stage is not known, though as we shall see it is likely that he did.

That raises two immediate questions. The first is how the then holder of the position felt about Ceawlin's presumption and the second is what process was supposed to be followed by men seeking that position.

As we have seen, Rhun the Tall would seem to have followed his father Maelgwn to the position of Wide Ruler. In about AD 560 he had fought a long and arduous campaign to impose his position across the northern parts of Britain. His failure even to try to exert influence over southern and eastern Britain might be explained by the presence there of increasingly large numbers of Germanic mercenaries. Those warriors were now settling in communities that were growing steadily and impressively. In most areas, the incomers remained separated from the local Britons, the only exceptions being in areas where the mercenary captains appear to have supplanted the local rulers. It would seem that in most areas the Germanic fighting men were kept at arm's length by their employers. No effort was made to convert them to Christianity nor to invite them to live among their employers. Nevertheless they remained a potent military fighting force. Perhaps Rhun was wise to steer clear of the German spear carriers and their employers.

It would seem that by around 565 Rhun the Tall had become overlord of the entire north, though the precise nature of the duties owed to him by other rulers is unknown. His death is usually placed in about 585, but the evidence for this is weak. His great-great-grandson Cadwallon ap Cadfan is known to have died in 634. Counting back the generations, allowing the usual thirty years for each generation, would put Rhun's death in about 550. However, Rhun is generally described as having been very old when he died and his son Beli had a very short reign in northern Wales. This would push Rhun's death forward by as much as forty years. However, the poems and chronicles record nothing for Rhun's reign after his great campaign to the north in around 560. It is possible that he died very soon after. Indeed, if he was an old man the rigours of a lengthy campaign may have hastened his death. It is perfectly reasonable to suggest that he died in the mid or late 560s.

If that death date for Rhun the Tall is anything like accurate, it would make sense of Ceawlin's actions. He inherited power in Winchester in 560, according to the *Anglo-Saxon Chronicle*, but it was not until eight years later that he launched his career of conquest. Perhaps it was the death of Rhun, the Wide Ruler, that prompted Ceawlin to believe that he could make a bid for that position.

Such a move could have had a family dimension. The sources are unclear, but it may be that Rhun and Ceawlin shared an ancestor. According to one source Rhun's great-grandfather had been Einion Yrth. Another source makes Einion Yrth to be the great-great-grandfather (or perhaps the great-great-great-great-grandfather) of Ceawlin. Under the elastic inheritance customs of the time, therefore, Ceawlin might have had a vague claim to the inheritance of Rhun Hir. That claim was at best dubious, but it would at least have given Ceawlin a legal excuse for his actions.

Which brings us on to the problem of how a man could achieve the position of Wide Ruler in the later half of the sixth century. In the days of Roman control the position of Vicarius of Britain was filled by a man appointed by the Emperor, on whose behalf he exercised his powers. When he relinquished control over Britain, Honorius had told the authorities of the civitates that they should choose their own senior officials until such time as he could appoint men properly.

We do not know how the British went about appointing a vicarius or the other officials, but there are hints to be found. In several sources we read that Vortigern acted with a Council. Sometimes Vortigern gave the Council orders, sometimes he asked its advice and sometimes he seems to have needed its permission to take certain actions. This Council would seem to have been composed of representatives of the various civitates who met periodically to attend to such business as needed the co-operation of the civitates.

One of the key tasks of the Council must surely have been the appointment of a Vicarius, and putting his replacement in position when he died or stood down. Although the Roman empire was, in many important respects, a top-down authoritarian regime backed by military muscle, it prided itself on its democratic credentials. Each emperor was, in constitutional theory, elected to office by the Roman Senate, though in practice they rarely went against the wishes of the army. At a more local level, the officials of civitas government were elected by the local free men.

These elections were far from being the orderly elections that we experience today. One of the perks of being a free man was to have a vote that could be sold to the highest bidder, producing a healthy bonus for the voter in question. Elections were very often a contest in wealth and influence rather than competitions of policies. Men voted for whoever paid them the most, or for the man who could give them lucrative government contracts or well paid government jobs. There was nothing wrong with this, in Roman eyes, and there were definite rules and conventions that governed such offers.

It would be sensible to assume that the election for the position of Vicarius, later Wide Ruler, would have been no different. The duties of a high official in a civitas involved a lot of effort and hard work. Having a vote to sell in the election of Vicarius would have been seen as a legitimate reward for that effort. The position of Vicarius would, at first, have been won by the richest and most influential man in Britain – or at least by whoever he nominated.

It can be imagined that at first it was the Vicarius or Wide Ruler who had the upper hand at these meetings. He was, in theory at least, acting with the authority of the Emperor in distant Rome and nobody would have wanted to incur the wrath of Rome for fear of what might happen when Honorius made good his promise and came back to Britain in full authority. But as the years passed and the Romans never came back, authority would have drained away from the Wide Ruler. With neither men nor money coming from Rome, the Wide Ruler would have been entirely dependent on taxes and men raised by the civitates for his actions. As time passed, Council meetings may have come to resemble market-stall bargaining more than an arm of government.

This shift in the balance of power between Council and Wide Ruler would inevitably have begun to have an effect on the elections. The heads of the civitates would have begun to realize that it was in their interests to have a weak and ineffective man as Wide Ruler. Such a man would be unlikely to be able to force a civitas to hand over much in the way of taxes, nor to insist that they send men to fight in a centrally organized army. Instead of electing the richest and most influential man, the electors would instead have had a strong motive to go for the exact opposite.

That such a process is likely can be deduced from other historic examples of an elective monarchy. In 1572 the Jagiellon dynasty that had built Poland up to be a large and powerful state became extinct. The nobles met to choose a new king, and decided that henceforth the ruler of Poland would hold office for life and could not pass on the crown to his heir. Whenever a King of Poland died the nobles would elect a new monarch. At first the nobles chose able and wealthy men to be king, but from the 1640s onward they preferred to chose progressively weaker and less powerful kings who would not impose high taxes or interfere with the private feuds of the nobles. Inevitably Poland went into decline. By 1795 Poland had ceased to exist, its lands being partitioned between Russia, Prussia and Austria. The decline of the elective Holy Roman Empire was more drawn out, but no less certain. In 1300 it was the most powerful state in Europe, by 1650 it was an empty title bringing no power and little prestige.

Maelgwn would have been elected in about 520 or 530. He may have been chosen because he was the ruler of a state tucked away in a remote corner of north Wales, and so unlikely to interfere in the business of the rich and wealthy civitates of lowland Britain. It was just this ineffectiveness that Gildas complained about.

The employment of increasingly large numbers of Germanic mercenaries by the lowland civitates would fit this situation. The rulers of those minor states – whether they were tyrants, princes or councils – were becoming increasingly independent of the central authority of the Wide Ruler. They would have wanted their own armed forces both to resist the Wide Ruler and to bicker with each other. Mercenaries were a ready source of cheap muscle for the central shield wall while the local nobles and their men carried out the more glamorous fighting on horseback and as light infantry.

If Ceawlin's bid for power was precipitated by the death of Rhun the Tall, then he had a tough task on his hands. He had to get himself appointed or elected by whatever system then prevailed. Secondly, and rather more daunting, he had the task of imposing his overlordship on to the recalcitrant civitates of Britain.

How and when Ceawlin got himself appointed to be the Wide Ruler we do not know. We know only that he achieved this ambition. The fact is recorded both in the *Anglo-Saxon Chronicle* and by Bede. His contemporaries were rather more interested in how Ceawlin went about enforcing his new found authority.

The short biography of Ceawlin, written in Welsh many years later, includes a peculiar story about his early years in power. As the tale has come down to us it is clearly distorted and incomplete – and as ever with material put down much later than the events they purport to describe we cannot be certain whether it is even approximately true.

The story runs as follows. The Pope – the manuscript does not say which one – was beset by a vast pagan army led by a King Burras which was plundering the papal lands, persecuting the Christians and spreading violence far and wide. King Burras had fixed to his helmet a flask of magical potion that could cure any wound and restore to life any warrior killed in battle. The potion gave him and his people an obvious advantage in battle. The Pope then had a vision in which he travelled far to the north over mountains and sea to reach a town called Hampton Port. There he met a young man clad in shining, golden armour. A voice declared that this man was the scourge of the pagans and was the man to help the pope. When the vision was over, the Pope set off north, crossing the Alps and the Channel to reach Hampton Port in southern Britain. There, just as in his vision, he met a young man clad in golden armour. The man's name turned out to be Collen, and he at once agreed to act as the champion of Christendom by leading the papal army into battle against King Burras and the pagans.

Hurrying south with his new commander, the Pope met Burras on the field of battle. Collen strode out to challenge Burras to single combat, with the loser and his army adopting the religious faith of the victor. Burras agreed, laughing and told Collen that he would surely wound the impudent man from Britain. 'And then let us see if your God can cure your wounds, as my gods can cure mine,' sneered Burras.

The two heroes fell to fighting and sure enough Burras slashed Collen across the hand with his sword. But Collen deftly flicked his sword so that the flask of magical potion was cut from Burras's helmet and fell into his hands. Rapidly opening the flask, Collen poured the potion on this hand and was at once cured. The two men again began fighting. This time it was Burras who was wounded, receiving a sword thrust under the arm that penetrated his lung. He collapsed to the ground begging Collen to use the ointment to cure him and promising to convert to Christianity. Collen did so and Burras was healed. The pagan army knelt to receive baptism and everyone ended up the best of friends.

Although the tale as we have it dates from some centuries after Ceawlin's time it has some interesting historical facts contained within it. By the time the manuscript was written, the name of 'Hampton Port' had fallen into disuse and the place was then known as South Hampton (now Southampton) to distinguish it from North Hampton (Northampton). This might indicate that the story originated some centuries earlier than the date it was written down.

It is also true that in the 560s the Pope was beset by pagan enemies. The pope at the time was John III, who held the throne of St Peter from 561 to 574. The pagans in question were the Lombards, a Germanic tribe led by their king Alboin, which poured over the Alps in 568 to conquer Italy as far south as the River Arno. The Lombards were held on the Arno, and converted to Christianity some fifty years later.

It remains somewhat unlikely that Ceawlin would have left his native home to lead a papal army into battle in Italy. And the details of the magical potion and mass baptism are typical of folklore and early Christian legends. Moreover, the story is remarkably similar to a much more widely known Welsh folktale about the Roman Emperor Magnus Maximus. As we have seen, this emperor reorganized the defences of Britain in the 380s and was remembered by several ruling dynasties in what is now Wales as the man who established their families in power. He is recalled in Welsh as Macsen Wledig and the folktale seeks to explain why he gave power to local Welsh families.

The story recounts how Macsen Wledig one night has a dream while asleep in Rome. He sees the most beautiful woman in the world sitting in a palace beside the sea with a large island off the coast. So smitten with love is Macsen Wledig that he sends scouts galloping through all the world to find the damsel. One man finds the girl in the palace of Conan Meriadeg at Caenarfon, with Anglesey off the coast. He hurries back to Rome and leads the emperor to the home of his beloved. Macsen Wledig marries the girl, Helen, and gives to her brothers power over the areas of Wales where their families would later rule. Meanwhile a usurper has made a bid for power in Rome and ousted Macsen Wledig. With the help of Conan's warriors Macsen returns to Rome and defeats his enemies.

It could be that the story of the dream of Macsen Wledig was borrowed to explain links between the pope and Ceawlin that were known to have existed, but the details of which had been lost. We can never know quite what the links between Ceawlin and the pope were, but comparisons can be drawn from other arrangements between rulers and popes during these centuries. The papacy had no armies of its own to command, instead relying on moral pressure to get what it wanted from Christian rulers and on the armies of loyal Christian rulers to get what it wanted from pagans. A Christian ruler going to war with pagans could obtain a sacred papal banner to carry with his army to show that he was engaged in holy war, though he usually had to grant privileges to the Church or otherwise pay a fee to the pope to get the banner. Some popes were remarkably cynical in their granting of holy banners, allowing one Christian state to war against another with papal support in return for bribes and payments.

Ceawlin was hoping to become Wide Ruler of Britain. He was a good Christian and some of the people he was aiming to subdue were pagans, so he was a prime candidate to get a papal banner. Moreover, we know from Gildas that many outwardly Christian rulers in Britain were using their powers to appoint bishops, tax Church lands and sell Church appointments all in contravention of ecclesiastical law. If Ceawlin promised to bring these rulers to the papal heel and stamp out such abuses then he might easily have been given papal blessing even for a war against fellow Christians. Remember that Ceawlin is reported to have been educated for some time at Orleans, a city at that time in frequent if sporadic contact with Rome and the papacy.

It may well be that the garbled tale of Collen, Burras and the pope is a confused memory of a very real contact between Winchester and Rome. Ceawlin may well have been made a papal champion in the struggle to quash secular control over Church property in Britain.

Gildas had made this demand a central plank of his cry for action. He had called out for a Christian champion who could return the British to the ways of God, end the civil wars, restore proper government along Roman lines and get rid of the pagans. As we have seen, it is at least possible and perhaps likely that Gildas was preaching his message in southern Britain when Ceawlin was a boy beginning his education. It would be pushing the evidence too far to suggest that Gildas was his teacher, but certainly his views would have been widespread at the time and much discussed.

It may well be that Ceawlin heard these views and aspirations, and he shared them. It is an open question whether he genuinely set out to fulfil the call of Gildas for a great Christian champion to save the British people or whether this was a convenient mask to put over his personal ambition to become the Wide Ruler of Britain. Either way, his first step was obvious.

The most powerful of the pagan Germanic-ruled states in Britain at this time was undoubtedly Kent. Not only was Kent a fertile land, it gained a fair degree of wealth from its control of much of the cross-Channel trade to the Low Countries and the Rhineland. This trade was much reduced from Roman times, but not inconsiderable. That trade gave Kent strong links and friendly relations with the Franks. The lands on the continent closest to Kent were at this time ruled by Chilperic I. Chilperic was a rather unsavoury ruler even for a Frank, murdering his wife and his brother among others. More to the point he was a heretic who was at odds with the papacy over the doctrine of the Trinity and who had confiscated huge tracts of Church land as part of that dispute.

By striking at Kent, Ceawlin would be demonstrating to his fellow Britons that he was willing to fight the pagan Germans, and show the pope that he could humble a key ally of the heretic Chilperic. The decision was made all the easier by the fact that Kent had a new king in the shape of the young and inexperienced King Aethelbert.

According to the *Anglo-Saxon Chronicle* the campaign took place in AD 568.

> Ceawlin and Cutha fought with Aethelbert and put them to flight into Kent, killing two ealdormen at Wibbandune, Oslaf and Cnebba.

From other sources we know that Cutha was a son of Cynric, and was therefore Ceawlin's uncle on his father's side. The two Kentish noblemen Oslaf and Cnebba are otherwise unknown but they must have been important at the time to be remembered long enough to be mentioned in the *Chronicle*.

The location of the battle is both important and problematic. If Ceawlin and Cuthwulf chased the army of Aethelbert back to Kent after the battle then it follows that the conflict took place outside of Kent. The King of the South Saxons at this date is not mentioned so it is unlikely that the battle took place in Sussex. That leaves Surrey as the most likely location. We know that a few decades later the Kings of Kent claimed to be also the rulers of Surrey, so perhaps Aethelbert had control over part or all of

Surrey at this time. If so, he did not keep it for long. The victory at Wibbandune quite clearly handed the area to Ceawlin.

The place name of Wibbandune is not recorded anywhere. A case can be made for the name being ancestral to the modern place name of Wimbledon, though some scholars think that Worplesdon is more likely. From a military point of view in the sixth century, Worplesdon would seem to have been an unlikely place for a battle. It is not close to a Roman road and is quite a long way from Kent. Wimbledon, however, is very close to Stane Street, the major Roman road from London to Chichester, and it is only about ten miles from Kent. Ten miles is a reasonable distance over which a post-battle pursuit could have been maintained at this time, so on balance Wimbledon is probably the more likely site of this battle.

If Ceawlin and Cutha were marching up Stane Street, as would seem likely, then their route from their power base at Winchester would have been along the Roman coast road through what are now Havant and Fishbourne to Chichester, then across the South Downs on the road to Pulborough and so north-east to cross the North Downs near Leatherhead and down the far side into the Thames Valley to be met by Aethelbert at Wimbledon. That raises the question of Ceawlin's relationship with the rulers of the South Saxons.

We do not know who ruled in Sussex from the time of Cissa's death to the accession of King Aethelwalh in around 650. The only account of the land in these years comes from a manuscript called *Flores Historiarum* (*Flowers of History*) written by Roger of Wendover in the 1230s. As the title suggests this is largely a collection of anecdotes from the past rather than a serious work of history. We have no idea what sources Roger of Wendover used for much of his work, though he claims to have scoured the monastic libraries of southern England for material. So, although the source for his information is obscure, Roger's account is quite clear.

Roger states that King Cissa of the South Saxons, son of King Aelle the Bretwalda, lived for ninety years but died without a male heir to inherit the kingdom. The lands of the South Saxons then passed to the dynasty of Cerdic. We know that the next known King of the South Saxons, Aethelwalh, came from a minor branch of the royal family based in Winchester. It may be that Cissa left a daughter, who was married to the first available member of the dynastic rulers of the Belgae. That is speculation, as is the date on which Cissa died. It could have been any time between around 550 and 570.

Whether Cissa was alive or dead by the time of the Battle of Wibbandune it is inescapable to conclude that the South Saxons and Belgae were on friendly terms at this point. The march route by way of the Sussex capital of Chichester may well have been to pick up troops to join the army marching against Kent.

Assuming that Ceawlin was able to call on the military forces of Sussex, it would mean that he was effectively the commander of four civitates. His own Belgic homeland would have been the core of his territories, but he also had control over the Durotriges added by Cynric after the Battle of Salisbury while the Atrebates were dominated by the Gewisse – those reliable allies on the upper Thames. None of these civitates were in themselves particularly large or powerful, but together they must have constituted a formidable force. No wonder Ceawlin aimed high.

His next move was to strike further to the northwest. The *Chronicle* records the campaign under the year 571.

> Cuthwulf fought the Britons at Bedcanforda and took four places Lygeanburg, Agelesburg, Benningtun and Egonesham. He died the same year.

It would seem from this entry that Ceawlin's uncle Cuthwulf was operating on his own. Presumably he was doing so with Ceawlin's permission and with armies drawn from the forces of the Belgae. Given the location of this battle it may well be that Cuthwulf was operating with the Gewisse. The places captured by Cuthwulf can be located. They were Limbury, Aylesbury, Benson and Eynsham. These places reach from Eynsham in the west on the Thames northwest of Oxford to Limbury, now a suburb of Luton. Bedcanforda is not so easy to pin down. It is often said to be Bedford, but this identification is uncertain.

All these places are in the southern parts of the civitas of the Catuvellauni. As we have seen, the Catuvellauni was the largest and most prosperous of all the civitates in Britain. Having dealt with Kent, a strike at this state would make sense for the ambitious Ceawlin. If he could subdue the single most powerful state on his borders then it would make it much more likely that he could browbeat the others into submission.

Assuming that the battle was fought at Bedford this would indicate a strike deep into Catuvellauni territory. If Ceawlin were fighting a simple war of aggression and conquest it would be natural for him to follow up Cuthwulf's victory by annexing all the lands of the Catuvellauni south of Bedford, and perhaps much else besides. This is not what was done. Instead four places considerably to the south of Bedford were taken. The reasons for this are not hard to find and lie in the four places named as having been taken over.

Eynsham stands where the River Evenlode enters the Thames northwest of Oxford. Just upstream of the confluence is a ford over the Thames, now replaced by a bridge, that was the only crossing of the river open in all weathers for many miles in each direction. Moreover only five miles to the north was the Roman road from Cirencester in the civitas of the Dobunni to Alchester in the civitas of the Catuvellauni. A garrison based at Eynsham could therefore block the main routes for the Catuvellauni into the lands of the Belgae and those of the Dobunni.

Benson stands on the north bank of the Thames just downstream of Dorchester-on-Thames, presumed base for the Gewisse. A base for Catuvellauni troops so close to their own must have been a long-standing annoyance to the Gewisse. Its capture would have been a relief. A few decades later Benson is recorded as being a royal vill, that is a personal possession of the ruler. This would imply that a garrison was stationed here.

Aylesbury stood astride the Roman road from Alchester to London, and guarded a ford over the River Thame. This was the site of a strong pre-Roman hillfort built on an outcrop of limestone that stands above the surrounding clays. It takes its name from Aegel, a solidly Germanic name indicating that at some time a force of Germanic mercenaries was stationed here. Due to the highly built up nature of the site excavations have been limited so we cannot prove that the hillfort was refortified in post-Roman times, though this seems likely.

Limbury is another fort blocking a Roman road, this time the route from Towcester south to St Albans and London. Again, a second important route is nearby. This second route is the Icknield Way that runs from Salisbury northeast to Norwich.

Each of the four places dominates an important road in use in the later sixth century. Three of the four (and perhaps the fourth) were fortified and so could have been used as a place for a military garrison. What Ceawlin seems to have done here is to strip the Catuvellauni of the border forts on their southern frontier and garrison them with his own men. This would have both stopped the Catuvellauni from launching a surprise attack, and put men loyal to Ceawlin into a position to strike hard and fast into Catuvellauni territory. It was a sensible move if Ceawlin's aim was not so much to conquer territory as to enforce his position as Wide Ruler.

But Ceawlin may have gone much further in neutralizing the most powerful civitas in Britain. At some unknown date between 500 and 650 the territory of the Catuvellauni fragmented in truly spectacular style. In place of one civitas there emerged around a dozen mini-states. The largest of these was London, and significantly the northern boundary of the London state ran through Aylesbury and Limbury. This region would later become known as the Kingdom of the Middle Saxons, or Middlesex.

Smaller states included the Cilternsaetna in the Chiltern Hills, the Hicca around Hitchen, the Gifla around the River Ivel, the Spalda at Spalding, the Witherigga based at Wittering, the Faerpinga around Charlbury (Oxfordshire) and the Gyrwe around Peterborough. There are others, but they cannot all be located precisely. We do not know when this fragmentation happened, but if it was forced on the Catuvellauni by Ceawlin it would have been a smart move. Instead of facing a single, powerful enemy he would be able to dominate a multitude of small, weak states that may well have spent more time bickering with each other than confronting the Belgae.

The position of the great city of London at this time is uncertain. Obviously London was a pale shadow of itself in Roman times. Much of the city seems to have been abandoned, but there were still houses that were inhabited, warehouses being used and pilings driven into the river at which ships could be moored. There seems to have been a resident population of some kind, and a relatively prosperous trading community. That the city was part of a much larger political unit would indicate that it was considered to be important in its own right. We do not know if Ceawlin incorporated London into his own state, but this seems unlikely. It is more reasonable to suggest that London was established as some sort of a client state. When London and the Middle Saxons re-emerges into the written record in 604 they were a client state of the East Saxons.

With the Catuvellauni dealt with in impressive fashion, Ceawlin turned northwest. As we have seen the Dobunni and the Belgae were old enemies. The animosity dated back perhaps to when the Romans broke up the Dobunni lands to form the civitas of the Dobunni in the north, the colony of Gloucester in the centre and hived off the southern lands to form part of the civitas of the Belgae. Sometime in the fifth century, the Dobunni had reunited their lands. They had annexed Gloucester peacefully, but had conquered the lands around Bath only after a war against the Belgae. Now Ceawlin was leading his armies to get back what he believed was rightfully his.

Although the terse description of this campaign in the *Anglo-Saxon Chronicle* makes no mention of the fact, it should be recalled the Ceawlin had cousins ruling in Gwent. The boundaries of Gwent at this time are uncertain, but it probably included the valleys of the Wye and the Usk, and may have extended some way farther west. This small state lay on the western borders of the Dobunni. It is thought that the ruler of Gwent at this time was Nynnio, a man about whom almost nothing is known except that he died sometime around the year 580. Both he and Ceawlin were great-great-grandsons of Cerdic and so would have been expected to keep in touch and to have a shared sense of inheritance. Even if Nynnio did not join Ceawlin in a war against the Dobunni, the very fact that he was there would have forced the Dobunni to keep an eye on him and, perhaps, to keep valuable troops watching the routes from the Wye Valley into the Severn Valley.

The *Anglo-Saxon Chronicle* places Ceawlin's campaign against the Dobunni in the year AD 577, six years after the Catuvellauni were defeated.

> Cuthwine and Ceawlin fought the Britons at the place called Deorham and killed three kings Coinmail, Condidan and

> Farinmail. They captured three cities Gleawanceaster, Cirenceaster and Bathanceaster.

The Cuthwine referred to here was Ceawlin's son. If the entry were to be taken at face value then Cuthwine was fighting at Deorham, which would mean he was fourteen or more years old. That would put his birth date at around 563. This has caused scholars endless debates over the years for the simple reason that Cuthwine was still alive and active in politics in 645, by which date he would have been over eighty years old. It has been suggested that this is highly unlikely, leading to the idea that Cuthwine was not at Deorham at all but that his name was later inserted to enhance his reputation. There is something to be said both for accepting that Cuthwine was there and for suggesting that he was not. On balance, there seems no reason to believe that a man could not live to be in his eighties at this date so long as he managed to escape death in battle and evade the many fatal diseases of the time.

This time we can identify all the places named with confidence. The battle took place at what is now Dyrham, a small village to the north of Bath. Just outside the village stands Hinton Hill which is crowned by a pre-Roman hillfort. The sides of Hinton Hill slope steeply away on three sides with only the eastern side easily accessible. The fort has never been excavated so we do not know if it was refortified or occupied in the post-Roman period, but this series of defences would be the most likely site for the Battle of Deorham. It is certainly a dramatic spot occupying a spur that projects west from the western face of the Cotswolds Hills and offers sweeping views across to the Severn Estuary.

Deorham was in the heart of the territory lost by the Belgae to the Dobunni a century or so before. Clearly Ceawlin was aiming not just to curb the power of the Dobunni and to impose his overlordship as Wide Ruler, but also to reunite the lost lands of the Belgae to his own civitas. The victory was a convincing one. As the *Chronicle* tells us, three of the leading men of the Dobunni were killed in the fighting. The *Chronicle* calls these men kings, but this is another example of the ninth-century scribes using a word familiar to their audience to describe a term that was not. It would seem most likely that the word '*kyningas*' was here being used to describe what historians term a sub-king. In the context of sixth-century Britain this would be a man in command of the armed garrison and local militia of a town.

The towns captured by Ceawlin are known. Gleawanceaster is now Glouceseter, Cirenceaster is now Cirencester and Bathanceaster is now Bath. Together these three cities were the great population centres of the civitas of the Dobunni. By the time Ceawlin captured them Bath was practically deserted, Gloucester almost empty and the populated area of Cirencester probably restricted to the amphitheatre which had been heavily fortified. All three probably acted as fortified organizational centres for the surrounding countryside rather than as towns. Cirencester had been the capital of the Dobunni civitas in Roman times and so was the greatest prize of the three.

It seems that Ceawlin followed the pattern set with his destruction of the Catuvellauni. It would seem that the lands of the Dobunni were divided up again just as they had been during Roman times. A number of smaller states appear in the record soon after the defeat of the Dobunni. The Husmerae lived around the River Stour, the Stoppingas occupied the valley of the River Alne, the Weorgoran were based around Worcester and the Hwicce were around Gloucester. No such small state is known from the southern lands of the Dobunni, so presumably those areas that had been part of the civitas of the Belgae in Roman times were reincorporated into the state ruled from Winchester. A man named Crida was installed at Cirencester, though in what capacity we do not know. It is noticeable that the only two civitates to be broken up in this way were the two that were defeated by Ceawlin. This is not conclusive proof that the fragmentation occurred as a result of his victories, but it does seem likely.

It was at about this time that archaeology reveals the first arrival of Germanic warrior burials in the northern areas of the Dobunni civitas. The main concentrations were around what is now Droitwich and Redditch. If, as seems likely, these were garrisons installed by Ceawlin then they were facing northeast against the frontier with the Corieltauvi. This large and prosperous civitas would thus seem to have been next on Ceawlin's list. Ceawlin had a firm grip on the territory southeast, south and southwest of the lands of the Corieltauvi.

The attitudes of the other states to the sudden and apparently unstoppable rise of Ceawlin's power is unknown. The Cornovii, Trinovantes and Iceni all shared a border with Ceawlin's lands. Perhaps they had submitted and accepted his impositions as Wide Ruler, perhaps they had sent messages of friendship while arming for war or maybe they were openly up in arms. We simply do not know.

What we do know is that Ceawlin was by 580 the most powerful man in southern Britain, and probably in all of Britain. He seemed unstoppable and invincible. But things were about to go disastrously for Ceawlin.

Chapter 7

Disaster at Adam's Grave

The first sign that something was wrong comes with an entry in the *Anglo-Saxon Chronicle* for the year AD 584. The entry is in two distinct sections, so we shall deal with the first section before moving on to the second. This reads:

> Ceawlin and Cutha fought the Britons at the place called Fethanleag. Cutha was killed. Ceawlin took many towns and countless spoils of war.

For the historian, there are two serious puzzles about this entry – quite apart from the usual unreliability of dates in this section of the *Chronicle*. The first of these is to determine who was the enemy that Ceawlin and Cutha were fighting. The *Chronicle* is the only source we have for this battle, and it names the enemy vaguely as being 'Britons'. At least we know that the enemy did not come from Sussex or Kent, but beyond that the word 'Britons' is little help.

The location of the battle might help us to identify the enemy, but unfortunately the name 'Fethanleag' is the second puzzle of this entry. There is no modern place name that is known to derive from this name. The closest that has been identified is a woodland called Fethelee near the village of Stoke Lyne in Oxfordshire. The site is not beyond dispute and is quite different from the battlefields that we have looked at so far. Battlefields that can be identified clearly tend to be located at good defensive positions. Typically these are river crossings or hillforts, though they may also be narrow valleys.

Stoke Lyne is very different. It stands in a wide, shallow valley through which flows a narrow stream that any fit person could wade across with ease. Nor are there any earthworks or other signs of fortifications. The nearest defensive position is Rainsborough Camp, a small pre-Roman hillfort some six miles to the north. A defensive position Stoke Lyne is not. The only hint that this may have been a suitable place for the Battle of Fethanleag is that a Roman road lies two miles to the southeast. This is the road that runs from Towcester to Alchester. Neither of these places was particularly large as Roman towns go, but both had impressive stone walls that were kept in good repair and so may have been of military importance into the sixth century.

Stoke Lyne lies in the northwestern section of territory of the Catuvellauni civitas, not far from the borders with the Corieltauvi to the northeast and the Cornovii to the northwest. If the location of Stoke Lyne is correct, the most obvious cause of this battle would have been an alliance between the Corieltauvi and the Cornovii against the rising power of Ceawlin. The army of the Cornovii may have advanced from their old capital at Viroconium Cornoviorum (Wroxeter) east to the Corieltauvi capital of Ratae Corieltauvorum (Leicester). The combined forces would then have headed south toward Alchester and the fords over the Thames.

The problem with this scenario is that we have no written sources at all for the Corieltauvi in the post-Roman age. Archaeology shows us that they hired substantial numbers of Germanic mercenaries, who were stationed primarily around their southern and southwestern borders where they faced the Catuvellauni and Cornovii. Our knowledge of the Cornovii is rather better, and the records do seem to indicate that they were involved in some sort of war at this time.

The civitas of the Cornovii would later emerge into early medieval history as the state of Powys. We are reliant on histories of the ruling dynasty of Powys for our knowledge of what was happening in the area during the 560s. According to these later, and possibly not entirely reliable, sources the royal house of Powys originated with Vortigern. His son Catigern was killed fighting Hengist and Horsa at the Battle of Aylesford, but not before he had fathered Cadell who seems to have been a major landowner in the civitas of the Cornovii in the mid-fifth century. Cadell's lands were inherited by his brother (or perhaps son)

Rhyddfedd Frych who seems to have been the first of the family to style himself Prince. This Welsh title is derived from the Roman title *Princeps*, which means something akin to 'first among equals' and was used to refer to a man who ruled with the advice or support of a council. At some point the Welsh princes became more absolute in their powers, but it is not clear when this happened. Rhyddfedd was succeeded by his son Cyngen Glodrydd who, in around 540, was succeeded by his son Brochwel Ysgithrog.

Brochwel had two sons. One, Tysilio, entered the Church and was made Bishop of the Cornovii by his father. This was just the type of improper appointment against which Gildas raged. The other son was Cynan Garwyn who followed his father Brochwel on to the throne of the Cornovii (or Powys) at some date around 580 or 590. It is thus unclear if Brochwel or Cynan would have been in power among the Cornovii at the time of the Battle of Fethanleag.

The later sources portray Brochwel as having led a fairly peaceful reign during which he devoted most of his time to hunting and founding Christian churches. Cynan, however, is remembered in rather different terms. His reign was marked by a war against Gwent and by other unspecified combats. Gwent, it will be remembered, was at this date ruled by cousins of Ceawlin and seems to have been allied to him. Cynan also seems to have moved his court from the old civitas capital of Wroxeter to a more heavily fortified place called Pengwern. We do not know for certain where this place was, though Whittington in Shropshire has been suggested. The move to a fortified residence would imply that warfare was a threat in a way that it had not been before.

A campaign by Cynan of the Cornovii against Gwent may well have been staged as part of a wider war against Ceawlin. Perhaps his blow was the western counterpart of a campaign by the Corieltauvi that ended at Fethanleag.

While the Cornovii or Corieltauvi are the most likely opponents of Ceawlin and Cutha at Fethanleag, it is not certain that they were the enemy. Perhaps some elements of the Catuvellauni were in rebellion, after all Stoke Lyne is in what was Catuvellauni territory.

Whoever the enemy was, the battle was another victory for

Ceawlin. As the *Chronicle* entry notes, 'Ceawlin took many towns and countless spoils of war'. If the enemy were the Corieltauvi his looting would have been done around what is now Leicester. The fact that the *Chronicle* does not name the many towns that he captured – unlike the earlier entries for the battles of Bedford and Dyrham – would indicate that he did not hang on to them for long. The reason for that is probably linked to the death of Cutha, Ceawlin's uncle, in the battle.

The *Chronicle* entry that records this battle at Fethanleag and its aftermath ends with a sentence that presaged disaster for Ceawling. The entry finishes 'And Ceawlin turned from there in anger to return to his own place'. It would seem that there was trouble back in the Belgic heartlands that not only required Ceawlin's urgent attention, but caused him great anger.

According to the *Chronicle* it was to be another seven years before the cause of that anger became apparent. Under the year 591 the Chronicle records that 'Ceol reigned for six years'. So far as we know, Ceawlin was still the ruler in 591. The *Chronicle* does not use its usual phrase to indicate that a man inherited a kingdom from his father or some other relative. Instead of saying 'feng to rice', or 'received the kingdom', it states merely '*ricsode*' or 'reigned'. Clearly the ninth-century scholars were using a different term to get across to their ninth-century readership that something other than the usual succession from one ruler to the next had taken place. Quite what the distinction was, we do not now know for certain but it is likely that some sort of usurpation or rebellion was indicated.

This Ceol was the son of Cutha, Ceawlin's uncle who had been killed at the Battle of Fethanleag. Ceol was not recorded as having been at the battle, so presumably he was elsewhere – perhaps back at home looking after the family estates while his father was off at the wars. It will be recalled that soon after the battle, and apparently before he could secure his grip on the captured towns, Ceawlin had been forced to turn back in anger. Perhaps the cause of that anger was something that Ceol had said or done. Certainly Ceol was now causing a lot of trouble.

We do not know the reasons why Ceol turned against Ceawlin. It may have been that he felt that he deserved a greater share of the family inheritance than he was given. The customs and rules of sharing family wealth at this time were complex and we do not fully understand them. Perhaps Ceol had been given a share based on the family wealth as it had been at the time of the death of Cynric, the grandfather he shared with Ceawlin, but now wanted a larger slice of Ceawlin's wealth. Ceawlin, who had done the hard work of building up his lands and fortune may well have looked askance at the claim.

However, the fact that Ceol was apparently causing trouble within a few weeks of the death of his father might indicate that there was a more immediate cause than some squabble over family inheritance rights. The timings on this event are difficult to reconstruct with accuracy, but would seem to have been something like the following.

Cutha and Ceawlin set off on campaign in the spring or summer of 584. It may have been a campaign of aggression to enforce Ceawlin's claim to be the Wide Ruler on to the Corieltauvi, or it may have been a response to an attack from the Corieltauvi – possibly with the Cornovii striking into Gwent at the same time. Given the likely time needed to muster an army and the speed of movement of a force on the road at this date it would have been a month or so later that the Battle of Fethanleag was fought. In that battle Cutha was killed and the Corieltauvi defeated.

Ceawlin would have spent a day or two making his post-battle arrangements. These would have included care for his wounded; sorting the prisoners into those to be sold into slavery, those rather richer men to be ransomed and the key leaders (if any) who would be kept prisoner for political reasons; and he would also have sent news of the battle back home to Winchester. Ceawlin would have then reorganized his army for the victorious follow up to the victory in battle. This would have entailed sending out groups of mounted men to sweep over the countryside of the Corieltauvi. The task of these men was to extract surrender from as many towns, strongholds and villages as possible. Most of the warriors stationed in the southern part of the Corieltauvi civitas would have been in the defeated army and it would take some time before they could rally somewhere and the leaders of the Corieltauvi could summon men from other areas, or raise local armed levies, to form a new army. In the meantime Ceawlin had things all his own way.

Arriving at a village, Ceawlin's riding parties would usually find the place deserted. They might do a quick search for anything of value but would soon be riding on. When they came to a town, they would find the old Roman walls hiding the farmers and villagers of the surrounding lands. No doubt the walls would be manned by armed farmers with a few soldiers or warriors who had been too old or ill to march with the main army. Ceawlin's riders would then open talks with those sheltering behind the town walls. Depending on how complete the battlefield victory had been, and how strong the walls were, Ceawlin's men might offer the defenders as little as their lives in return for prompt surrender, or they might be prepared to strike a bargain to avoid the need for a lengthy and perhaps bloody siege or assault. The defenders would be asked to recognize Ceawlin as the Wide Ruler, to hand over treasure or food, and probably to give hostages as well. Once a deal had been made, a rider would be sent back to Ceawlin to announce the details, while the main force rode on to the next town.

Ceawlin would have been following up with the bulk of his army. These men would actually occupy the surrendered towns and strongholds, while Ceawlin took the formal surrenders. If a town or stronghold refused to come to terms, Ceawlin would come up with his army to attack the place. The defenders would be gambling that their Corieltauvi lords could raise a new army and march to their rescue in time. If they lost and Ceawlin took the place by storm he would be quite entitled to kill or enslave everyone he found. The stakes were high.

Sooner or later, Ceawlin would have known, he would have been faced by a fresh Corieltauvi army. Then he would negotiate the terms of peace. Ceawlin would have wanted to impose a clear recognition of his status as Wide Ruler, extract tribute and secure hostages. But if the new army was large and well positioned, he might have been forced to accept a lesser offer from his enemies.

For Ceawlin it was a race against time. He and his men had to secure the surrender of as many places as possible before the process was brought to a halt. Inevitably this all took time. We do not know how long the process might have taken, but a similar campaign by England's King Edward III in France nine centuries later managed an average of four miles a day. It is almost forty-five miles from Stoke Lyne to Leicester, so it may have taken about eleven days for Ceawlin to advance as far as the first major city in Corieltauvi territory. If his army was spreading out widely to the flanks, as it probably was, or if he faced the need to assault a walled town then the march may have taken considerably longer.

At some point in this process, Ceawlin received news from home that caused his great anger. It is perhaps sixty miles from Stoke Lyne to Winchester. A messenger on a fast horse could cover that distance in a couple of days, quicker if he had a change of horses to speed him on his way. It would seem that it was the news of the Battle of Fethanleag that stirred up the trouble at home. A fast rider would have then set out to bring the news to Ceawlin. Conceivably that news could have reached Ceawlin as quickly as four days after the battle. It is more likely that whatever trouble had been sparked at home would have taken time to fester, so Ceawlin may have heard the news a week or so later.

Whenever he got the news from home, Ceawlin would not have had time to complete his follow up to his great victory. Instead of being able to secure the fruits of victory in terms of plunder, loot, ransoms and new territory, he was forced to turn around and go home. No wonder he was so angry.

But what could it have been about a great military victory that caused such trouble? The only possible answer is that it was the news of the death of Cutha that was the problem. At this distance in time it is impossible to know exactly what the problem was. Perhaps the manner of Cutha's death meant that some blame attached to Ceawlin. Maybe Cutha got into difficulties and Ceawlin did not go to his aid. Or perhaps the body of Cutha had not been treated with due respect. We do not know, but certainly something was wrong.

The problem was evidently serious enough for Ceawlin to have to call off his campaign and go home. Presumably Ceol had been loudest in leading the complaints, and his calls had gained enough support to put him into a strong position or Ceawlin would have ignored his moans and carried on with the campaign. Perhaps there was some justice in Ceol's accusations, whatever they were. At any rate, Ceawlin had to go home to deal with the situation.

Clearly the settlement that Ceawlin made on his return was not final. Ceawlin remained as ruler, but Ceol was unhappy and the people of the Belgae must have been divided in their opinions. In 591 they had to make a choice.

While the absolute dating accuracy of the *Chronicle* might be in some doubt, its grasp of the order in which things happened is not. We can accept that some years passed between the death of Cutha at Fethanleag and the revolt of his son Ceol against Ceawlin. We can also accept that the *Chronicle* is correct in saying that Ceol announced that he was the rightful ruler and that up to a year passed before the issue came to battle. The *Chronicle* records the battle between Ceol and Ceawlin as being in 592, the year after Ceol claimed the throne.

For a revolt such as this to succeed needed military muscle. There would have been two sources of fighting men open to Ceol. He could either loudly proclaim his grievances, and seduce Belgic nobles and warriors away from their loyalty to Ceawlin, or he could hire mercenaries. Probably he tried both. We have no way of knowing how successful he was at raising men from either source of recruits, but of one thing we can be almost certain – he had the Gewisse on his side. We know that this powerful force of mercenaries subsequently stayed loyal to Ceol's branch of the family and that by the 650s the Gewisse and the Belgae were together blended into a single new people. Given what was about to happen across Britain as a whole, it would seem that the support of the Gewisse, and perhaps other Germanic mercenaries, was to be crucial to Ceol.

The *Chronicle* records the outcome of the conflict between Ceol and Ceawlin under the year 592: 'There was great slaughter at Woddesbeorge, and Ceawlin was driven out.' The place name Woddesbeorge translates as Woden's Barrow, and is now known as Adam's Grave, at Alton Priors in Wiltshire. Ceawlin's military career had thus come full circle, for Adam's Grave is barely seven miles south of Barbury where he fought his first battle back in 556. The two battlefields have much in common. Barbury stands on a steep-sided spur of high ground on the northern flank of the Marlborough Downs, while Adam's Grave stands on another steep-sided spur of high ground on the southern flank of those same hills. And like Barbury, Adam's Grave is protected on three sides by precipitous slopes that fall away some 300 feet to the valley below. Barbury has an impressive hillfort on its crown. Although Adam's Grave lacks this feature, there is a deep ditch and bank built across the neck of land that connects the spur to the top of the downs. Its date is unknown, but it has all the hallmarks of a hurriedly-constructed temporary field defensive work. Both places are suited to infantry battles, perhaps giving the advantage to the Germanic warriors over the horsemen of the wealthy Britons.

But although the battlefields have much in common, this time Ceawlin was on the losing side. As the *Chronicle* states he was 'driven out'. The English sources then lose interest in Ceawlin, transferring their attentions to the men who replaced him as rulers in the lands of the Belgae and the fate of the other lands in lowland Britain. The only other mention of him in the *Chronicle* comes in 593, the year after the Battle of Adam's Grave when it is recorded that 'Ceawlin, Cwichelm and Crida died'.

It is presumed that the Crida mentioned here was the same Crida who was given lands around Cirencester after the Battle of Dyrham and who had remained loyal to Ceawlin. Who Cwichelm was we do not know. The name is not common and seems to have been used only among the Belgae. The short, dismissive nature of this entry makes it clear that the people whom Ceawlin had once ruled had lost touch with their one-time leader. Presumably news got back at some time that Ceawlin and his fellow exiles had died, and so the news was recorded in some form. Perhaps the scholars who compiled the *Chronicle* so many years later knew the year in which he died, or perhaps they just guessed.

But if the English sources lose touch with Ceawlin after he was driven out, the Welsh sources do not. Under the old Welsh version of his name, Collen, he is recorded as leaving his homeland and heading northwest. He may have stopped for a while in Gwent but, if so, this is not recorded. He next appears paddling a coracle up the River Dee and heading into the lands of Gwynedd. By this date the lands of northern Wales were ruled by Beli, son of Rhun Hir, or perhaps by his son Iago. This dynasty were probably remote cousins of Ceawlin. Certainly, three brothers of Ceawlin's great grandfather had moved to live in Gwynedd where they founded churches and were later remembered as saints. Now it was Ceawlin's turn to come to Gwynedd.

According to the story recorded later in Wales, Ceawlin had dreamed that he would find a safe place only when he came across a lone horse grazing beside a river which allowed him to mount it bareback and ride it to the top of a nearby hill. A few miles upstream of the fortress of Ruabon Ceawlin found just such a horse. He mounted it and the steed carried him up to the top of a small hill, from which Ceawlin could see spread out to the south a stretch of fertile and flat land that could be easily farmed. A local man told him the place was called Rhysfa Maes Cadfarch.

If Ceawlin did paddle up the Dee in a coracle he must have brought with him a good-sized hoard of gold, or perhaps he could tap into family links to get some money. He bought the land and settled down here. On the hill he built a church, surrounded by a rampart and wall that could easily be defended by armed men if an enemy approached. Interestingly, up on the mountain on the opposite bank of the River Dee stood a mighty, but abandoned pre-Roman hillfort named after Bran, the mythological figure who we met earlier as the nephew of Gwyn ap Nudd, ruler of the fairies that Ceawlin was said to have encountered at Glastonbury.

The supernatural was not yet finished with Ceawlin. According to the Welsh tale a hideous and aggressively violent giantess lived in the nearby mountain valley of Bwlch. Taking out his sword once more, Ceawlin climbed up to the valley to be confronted by the giantess wielding a mighty club in her right hand. Ceawlin managed to slice off his opponent's right arm, but she simply picked up the severed limb in her left and used that as a weapon instead. Only after a lengthy battle was he able to kill her. He then went back to his fortified church, laid his sword on the altar and turned to a life of sacred meditation.

In deciding to become a cleric as an effort to seek safety from vengeful relatives, Ceawlin was perhaps remembering his meeting with Clodoald. Better known as St Cloud, Clodoald had narrowly escaped being murdered as a child and had found safety by becoming a monk. Perhaps Ceawlin decided to seek safety in the same fashion and went to Gwynedd to find a remote spot where he could live out what was left of his life in safety. Even so he took care to fortify his church and so presumably had some fighting men with him.

Having found his safe retreat, Ceawlin lived for some years in peace and holy prayers. He died some years later on 21 May at some date around about 615. In Welsh, Ceawlin was known as Collen, and a fortified church was known as a Llan. So the place that had been called Rhysfa Maes Cadfarch became known instead as the 'fortified church of Collen', or Llancollen. Today it is Llangollen. Ceawlin's grave lies just west of the present church, erected some 700 years after he died to replace the fortified chapel he had built. The local Welsh remembered him as a holy man, well educated in the scriptures and learned in theology. After his death they made him a saint. So Ceawlin the Wide Ruler, the warrior king, became St Collen.

But while Ceawlin had retreated to find peace and prayer, a very different future awaited the lands he had left behind. The next twenty years were to be ones of unprecedented violence, savagery and change.

PART III

England and the English

Chapter 1

Britain Divided

It has long been known that something happened between AD 570 and 590 that destroyed the old order, swept away all that had happened before and created England. In essence one nation was destroyed and another created in the space of a single generation. It was an astonishing event.

The only significant event in that time period that we know of was the overthrow of Ceawlin, the Wide Ruler who had brought nearly all of Britain under his sway. Of course the ousting of a single ruler, no matter how great, could not of itself destroy a nation unless it provided the tipping point that pushed over the edge a situation that was already highly unstable. By the 580s, Britain was just such an unstable society.

Ever since direct rule from Rome had ended in 410, Britain had been in a long, slow decline. The gradual disintegration had affected almost every aspect of human existence. The size of the population had at least halved as plague and famine stalked the land, economic prosperity had collapsed as trade to Europe almost ceased and people were thrown back on subsistence farming, agriculture had become harder as the climate got cooler and wetter and material culture had degenerated as fewer people with less money were able to afford brick houses, mosaic floors or surfaced roads. The disintegration had progressed in fits and starts, with some years or decades being close to catastrophic and then followed by years of stability or slight improvements. Generally, however, life had got a lot worse in Britain for those who survived. This was not a good time to be alive.

In one respect, however, Britain's decline had been less noticeable. That was in the sphere of government. In a late-Roman context, the Christian church can be included in the broad category of governmental bureaucracy as it was staffed by the same types of educated gentry and was run on broadly similar lines. These men clung to their Roman heritage in a world that was slowly falling apart around them. They read and spoke good Latin as well as speaking their native Brythonic tongue. They were producing reports, letters and accounts that they sent to each other and discussed, again often in writing, at some length.

Crucially, they kept a tight hold on the business of power and politics. There may have been a change in some areas from the sort of democracy practised in late antiquity to a more authoritarian rule, but it was still the same types of men from the same families who were in charge. Ceawlin was far more of an autocratic ruler in Winchester than had ever existed before Cerdic, but he was still a Christian Briton able to read and write, versed in the classics and ruling over a civitas shaped on Roman borders. Elsewhere bishops preached in cathedrals, exacting their dues from the populace to spend on charitable works and on fine ecclesiastical buildings. Above all the position of Wide Ruler preserved the office of the Vicarius of Britain. Nowhere – except perhaps in parts of what is now Wales – had the Britons reverted to their pre-Roman heritage. Just as African leaders today call themselves 'President' or 'Prime Minister' after the offices of the British Empire, the British clung to the titles and offices of the empire that had ruled them for so long.

But behind his facade of normality a serious rot had set in. The prosperity and large population that had underpinned the structure of government had gone. Just as important, Rome had gone as well so that the locals no longer had any reason to fear retribution from higher authority. The habits of obedience, regularity and respect for office survived for decades but sooner or later a generation was going to grow up wondering why everyone behaved in a certain way when there was no longer any reason to do so.

Thus far, the situation in Britain could have been mirrored across wide swathes of what had been the Roman Empire. But there was one crucial and, as it turned out, fatal difference. Across most of the Empire the higher positions had largely been taken over by outsiders. In places barbarian rulers had usurped power openly and declared themselves to be independent rulers, either using their own titles of King or Khan, or appropriating Roman titles such as Duke or Count. In other places locals were officially in power, but it was barbarians who pulled all the strings.

In Britain that had not happened. Aside from the relatively small areas of Kent and Sussex, Britain was still very much in the hands of the locals. All the civitates were firmly in the grip of the families that had run them for generations. Such newcomers as had settled in Britain – and as the years passed there were increasing numbers of them – were kept firmly in their place. Germanic warriors were useful for fighting battles and on campaign, but they did not command armies and never held political power.

As with most aspects of these years, the evidence is not present in large quantities, but it is clear that there was a degree of antagonism between the native Britons and the incoming Germans. Gildas was writing from an area under British political control, but he knew the Saxons well and was scathing about them. He calls them wolves, dogs and savage beasts. He talks of their lies and tricks and ferocity. He says that they were universally hated by God and by men, that they betrayed hospitality and that they were led by devils. Gildas may have spent much of his book criticizing British rulers, but his invective never came even close to the terms he used about the Saxons.

We know that the Britons made no attempt at all to convert the new arrivals to the Christian faith. This is important because elsewhere the conversion of the barbarians to the true faith was viewed as a key tactic in taming them and integrating them into the society that they had conquered. In Britain the Angles, Saxons and Jutes had not conquered and so there was no perceived need to convert them. Indeed, their status as hired barbarian soldiers was emphasized by their different religion.

The animosity may have been exacerbated by the division of tasks on the battlefield. The British rulers seem to have sneered at the men who formed their shield walls in battles. The more glamorous side of war that was celebrated in poems and epics by the British was that of commanders and cavalry, the 'poor bloody infantry' rarely rate a mention. Most armies in history have had a tension between the infantry slogging away in murderous close combat and the cavalry dashing about in flashy uniforms. When the two came from different races, spoke different languages and worshipped different gods the tension may have been magnified.

The Germanic settlers may have resented the greater wealth and more refined lifestyles of their employers. Across the former Empire, barbarians succeeded in acquiring at least some measure of the finer things in life from the Roman nobility, but not in Britain. Archaeology shows us that in most areas the German settlers formed their own communities distinct and separate from British villages and villas even if they stood less than an hour's walk apart. A hint of the feelings of the incomers may be found in the word '*ungerad*' used to describe the British. The meaning of the word is not entirely clear, but it seems to have a meaning akin to 'rude' or 'foolish'.

What seems to have been happening in the later-fifth and early-sixth centuries was that the two ethnic groups were becoming progressively isolated from each other and mutually resentful. The British would have resented their reliance on hired barbarian soldiers, and sought to bolster their culture by retaining Roman titles, Roman religion and Roman manners while seeking to keep the Germanic soldiers in their place.

The Germans would have felt excluded from the luxurious civilization that they wanted to join, deprived of the opportunities for promotion and advancement that they saw existing in Europe and resentful of their conditions. Undoubtedly the Saxons, Jutes and Angles in Britain began to feel that they had a lot more in common with each other than they did with their employers. It may be anticipating things to say that an English national identity had formed by 550, but clearly that was the way things were moving. The Jutes seem to have lost their distinctive culture by around 500, merging into either a Saxon or an Anglian identity. Those cultural identities in turn began to merge and meld, though as late as 700 it was possible to tell a Saxon from an Angle.

The scanty written evidence that survives would indicate that by that date the Germanic language being used in Britain by 550 had already branched off from its parent north German. Quite how uniform this pre-English language was we do not know, but clearly language was as important in differentiating the ethnic English from the ethnic British as was religion and weaponry.

It is clear that Germanic identity in Britain was going in a different direction from on the continent. In Gaul the Franks had invaded, taken over and in so doing changed the name of the land to France. But they had taken over as a ruling elite that was small compared to the peoples that they had conquered. Secure in power and outnumbered, the Franks held their Germanic culture to be of little account. They could rule more effectively if they learned the language of their underlings and could see the diplomatic and political advantages of adopting their hosts' culture and religion. In Britain, the Germanic warrior settlements were being pushed the other way. They saw an advantage in emphasizing their own culture. Archaeologists are accustomed to finding Germanic style brooches, buckles and pots in quantity. It is almost as if the people were ostentatious about the material signs of their ethnicity. That this was not a feature of the Angles and Saxons is clear from the fact that Saxons who settled around Calais or Calvados lost their identity as quickly as did the Franks. It was something about Britain that made the Germans proud, even arrogant, about their ancestry and culture.

One question regarding this Germanic migration that created the English nation that is a great source of disagreement and contention is the size of the population move involved. In the historic accounts in the *Anglo-Saxon Chronicle*, Gildas and Nennius talk in terms of a few hundred warriors – a thousand at most. Even with women, children, craftsmen and assorted hangers-on, such as singers and pagan priests, these accounts indicate that the influx of Germanic settlers would have been less than 10,000. Archaeology gives a rather different picture. The numbers of people living in Germanic style may have been up to half the population in Kent and Sussex.

Although such large numbers of Germans might be expected in areas ruled by Germans, it would seem from the archaeology that in some other areas concentrations of incomers almost as great were to be found. The area between the Wash and the Humber had some large Germanic settlements, so did the areas around the Ouse and the Thames. Absolute numbers cannot be calculated but those civitates that relied on Germans for their military muscle might by AD 550 have had as much as twenty per cent of their population drawn from the incomers. And that twenty per cent was the most important from a military point of view.

Recent genetic studies have produced a broadly similar picture. The detail is still rather vague because large numbers of people have moved about within England since the invention of the railways. Researchers have therefore sought out modern residents with long-term family roots in the area where they live today. The results are unavoidably controversial and may be open to reinterpretation as better evidence and techniques of genetic study become available. However, the current picture from genetics is that in a few pockets as much as seventy-five per cent of the male lineage is of Germanic stock, falling to an average of perhaps thirty per cent across southern and eastern Britain as a whole. Further inland and to the west there was a marked decline in the level of male lineages coming from northern Germany. Female lineages showed a similar pattern, with higher Germanic counts in the south and east, and lower percentages to the west and north. However, the proportion of female lineages from Germanic sources was generally much lower, ranging from about five per cent to thirty per cent.

These genetic studies broadly support the archaeological evidence. Where archaeology shows larger concentrations of people living a Germanic lifestyle, the genetic evidence shows higher percentages of Germanic genes in the modern population. It has been suggested that the clear difference in male and female genetic indicators is due to the generally violent nature of the Germanic immigration. Men of fighting age would have been killed in battle, or slaughtered afterwards, while women and children would have tended to be kept on as slaves by the new landowners. The image of bloodshed should not be thought to apply to all areas nor to entire male populations. After all some seventy per cent of male lineages seems to have survived intact.

It must be remarked, however, that those male survivors eventually adopted the culture, religion and language of the incomers. Across all of what is now England the Roman and British cultures ceased to exist and were replaced with English culture. On the continent quite the opposite happened with the smaller population of incomers adopting the culture of the more numerous natives. The way in which the minority of Germanic immigrants was able to impose their culture on the bulk of the British population is key to the birth of England.

The timing of the immigration is almost as controversial as its size. Written sources talk of an '*Adventus Saxonum*' – the 'Arrival of the Saxons' – as if it were a single event. Even these sources accept that there were several episodes during which the Germanic mercenaries arrived, spreading them out between the 440s and 500s. In fact we know that Germanic warriors were employed in Britain before the Romans lost control, and that new bands of mercenaries were hired at intervals for generations. There was probably also some unofficial immigration as families and friends came over to join those already in Britain. There seems to have been an increase in immigration between the later-fifth and early-sixth centuries that might coincide with the power of Aelle of Sussex. There seems then to have been a slackening of incoming numbers, though another increase has been detected by some from around 550 on. Certainly the Germans were enjoying a natural increase in population once they were in Britain. A high birthrate can be deduced and there are some who argue that the Germans did not suffer as badly as the Britons from the great Plague of Justinian. Whatever the reasons, the Germanic population was increasing as that of the Britons declined across lowland Britain.

So long as the political and government structure remained intact and unshaken the situation could persist despite the growing ethnic tensions between the British and the English. But in the 570s a fresh economic crisis struck. From 525 to 550 the Byzantine Empire, that continuation of the Roman Empire based in Constantinople, had been gradually expanding. Italy, North Africa and parts of Spain had been reconquered from barbarian ruler or rebellious governors. The process reached its height under Justinian and the Byzantines appeared on the brink of reuniting the Mediterranean heartland of the Roman Empire. Then the plague struck and the imperial finances were drastically undermined. The next emperor, Justin II, managed to hold his own, but in 574 he went insane and was replaced by Tiberius II. To secure himself in power Tiberius II spent money in Constantinople and starved the army of funds. A fresh wave of barbarian invasions struck and soon the Empire was again driven out of the western Mediterranean.

This new collapse of Roman power had a more devastating impact on the economy of the Mediterranean than had the earlier more drawn-out decline. Suddenly, apparently almost overnight, archaeological traces of trade between Britain and the Mediterranean end. It was replaced by a much reduced trade to France and to Spain. Those who had gained wealth and prestige from that trade would have been much reduced in both, and the big losers must have been the British rulers of the civitates in Britain. By contrast the less prosperous trade of the Germanics across the North Sea to their homelands was unaffected, and so increased massively in comparison to their newly impoverished neighbours. It was a shift in the balance of economic power that cannot have gone unnoticed by those living in Britain at the time.

And yet even then nothing dramatic happened. The spark was still missing. The reason why that spark was provided by the fall of Ceawlin is not too difficult to find.

Ceawlin had been a great warrior, a skilled military commander and famous Christian, yet he had been crushed and driven out. The news of his defeat and exile must have swept across Britain. Everyone would have been agog to know the details of what had happened, who had taken which side and how the great battle at Woden's Barrow had been fought. It would seem that it was this news that set Britain aflame and changed everything.

At this distance in time it is impossible to know the details for certain, but we do know some of the story and can deduce more. It is enough to put together a credible picture of what happened and why it had the impact that it did. The Battle of Woden's Barrow was fought between Ceawlin, the then ruler of the Belgae, and his nephew Ceol. Both these men had British names, but Ceol's branch of the family was later to have very close links to the Germanic settlers. We know that his grandson Cenwalh married a woman with the very Saxon name of Seaxburh. Writing in the 720s, Bede stated definitively that the ruling dynasty descended from Ceol as the same as that ruling the Gewisse. Indeed, he described the two dynasties and peoples as being one entity: the West Saxons.

It can be assumed, therefore, that within two generations of Ceol his family had married into that of the leaders of the Gewisse and had produced a new dynastic family. It may be that these links went back to Ceol. His son was Cynegils, but no records remain of whom Cynegils was married to nor who his mother was. Perhaps Ceol or Cynegils had married into the Gewisse. At any rate we know that the Gewisse did not always fight under the direct control of Ceawlin, but under the command of other members of his family. Since we do not know what it was about the death of Cutha that caused his son Ceol to rise in rebellion we cannot be certain, but it does seem very much as if the Gewisse backed Ceol against Ceawlin.

Turning to the battlefield of Woden's Barrow itself, one thing is immediately apparent. This was no place for a cavalry action. The slopes that drop down from the Marlborough Downs into the Vale of Pewsey are precipitous. On three sides of Woden's Barrow the slopes are astonishingly steep, up to 1:3 in places. I have tried to walk up these slopes and found myself reduced to crawling on hands and feet over the slippery turf in places. Such an ascent would be suicidal carrying spear, sword and shield while an enemy rained down missiles from above. On horseback the ascent is simply impossible.

The only approach to the barrow that would allow an attacker to wield his weapons is from the north where a neck of level ground about 250-yards wide extends from the Marlborough Downs. That flat ground is cut by an earthwork of unknown date which makes for an effective defence. The earthwork may be older than Ceawlin's time, but it would have been improved and restored for the battle. It would seem that one side in the battle was barricaded on to the tongue of high ground, while the other attacked from the hills to the north.

Fighting a way across a defended earthwork on a restricted frontage is a job for infantry, not for horsemen. We do not know if Ceol was attacking or defending, but it seems likely that he was assaulting the position. The *Anglo-Saxon Chronicle* describes the action not as a battle, strife or conflict but as a 'great slaughter'. Such a massacre would be much more likely if an attacking force got into a defended position from which the garrison had no escape than if the defender drove off an attack. But whether it was as an attacker or a defender that Ceol won this battle, he would have been totally reliant on the infantry for his victory. And that, it would seem, meant the Gewisse.

If it was the Germanic warriors of the Gewisse who crushed the mighty Wide Ruler Ceawlin and put Ceol into power, this would have represented a massive shift in power between the Britons and the immigrants. In previous battles we hear only of army commanders with British or Roman names, and the few scraps of poetry that survive celebrate the exploits of men fighting on horseback. Inescapably the picture that emerges is of armies led by Britons and with elite units composed of mounted British men. It would have been those cavalry units that delivered the battle-winning charge in a battle, and which had exploited the victory in a pursuit. But now it was the infantry that had won a spectacular victory. And the infantry had been the Germanic warriors.

Suddenly it was no longer the established aristocrats with their refined educations, Christian religion and writing skills who were top dog. Now the illiterate, pagan, barbarian warriors were the power in the land. The events at Woden's Barrow seem to have marked a real shift in Britain. It was not so much that anything had really changed as a result of the battle, it was more that people's perceptions had changed. The British nobility had been in decline for generations, but they had masked that decline with pomp, glamour and a facade of real power. Now their lack of real power was clear for all to see.

Those who saw it most clearly were the leaders of the various bands of Germanic warriors employed by the civitates of southern and eastern Britain. It was as if a blindfold had suddenly been ripped from their eyes, allowing them to see things that before had been hidden. They reacted suddenly, swiftly and violently. Wealth, power and glory were theirs for the taking. And they grabbed it with both hands.

Chapter 2

The Savage Swords

We can follow the events that followed hard on the heels of the Battle of Woden's Barrow from later accounts in English sources. The sources in Welsh documents are patchy and incomplete for reasons that we shall soon discover. The English scribes who wrote down their accounts of what happened were doing so a century or more after the event.

Their accounts are clear enough, but their grasp on dates is poor. We cannot be certain if the events described were spread out over a dozen or so years, or if they all took place in one savage summer of swordplay. A modern analogy could be drawn with the fall of the Communist regimes of Eastern Europe in the summer and autumn of 1989. The economies of those regimes had been tottering for years, but the weakness of the Communist system had been masked by brutal repression of critics and dissidents. Then a single event set off a sudden collapse across the continent.

That single event in 1989 came when the Polish communist government allowed non-communist candidates to stand in a limited number of seats in the election to the *Sejm* (parliament) on 4 June 1989. Everyone expected a protest vote of some kind, but an overall Communist victory was confidently expected by everyone – even by the independent candidates. When the results came in the independents had won ninety-nine out of the hundred seats they had been allowed to contest. In itself this was no great earthquake for the Communists had reserved enough seats for themselves to give a Communist majority in the *Sejm*. What it did was to show how astonishingly unpopular the regime really was. Soon the Polish Communist Party was losing members and supporters so fast that a total collapse took place in August and in September a non-Communist government took office.

The flood of people deserting Communist structures spread to Hungary where, in October, the Communist Party ceased to exist and another non-Communist government came into office. East Germany was then paralysed by strikes and protest marches that led to the opening of the borders with the West on 9 November. The Communist government fell and the following year East Germany was re-united with West Germany. On 20 November 500,000 Czechs poured on to the streets of Prague and a national strike crippled the state. On 28 November the Czech Communist government likewise collapsed. The unrest moved to Bulgaria where massive street protests of hundreds of thousands of people and a wave of strikes forced the Communist government to first announce the end of communist policies and then to resign. In Romania the repressive crackdown on demonstrations was at first successful, but on 22 December the dam broke and massed marches swept the Communists from power. Romania's dictator Nicolai Ceausescu was hurriedly tried and shot, the only Communist leader to be killed. In Albania the Communists managed a more staged withdrawal that saw them retain some power until 1992. Yugoslavia, however, collapsed into civil war as ethnic tensions erupted into violence once the Communist clampdown was broken. In the mighty Soviet Union itself the Communists likewise fell from power and the constituent parts of the empire broke up into a dozen independent states.

What the events of 1989 in Eastern Europe demonstrates is that a single event can alter perceptions so dramatically that massive political and constitutional changes can occur within months. It would seem that this is exactly what happened in late-sixth-century Britain. The defeat of Ceawlin was surely the only event likely to have set off such a chain of events. This may not be entirely certain, but what can be said with certainty is that what followed was violent and swift.

The civitas of the Iceni occupied most of what is now Norfolk and Suffolk, with parts of adjacent counties. Germanic warriors had been stationed here since at least 410, probably earlier. Whether these early immigrants had been hired by the civitas government or by Vortigern the Wide Ruler we do not know. We do know that the numbers of immigrants increased steadily and that by the 580s this was one area where the newcomers had a particularly high population.

The later dynasty ruling the English Kingdom of East Anglia, which covered the lands of the civitas of the Iceni, traced their family back to a man named Wehha. This Wehha died in around AD 575 and was remembered as a great warrior. Other than that the only thing known about him is a list of ancestors that makes him the son of Wilhelm, son of Hryp, who was the son of Hrothmund, son of Trygil, son of Tyttman, son of Caesar, son of Woden. Wilhelm, Hryp, Hrothmund, Trygil and Tyttman are Anglian names, while Woden was the main warrior god of the north Germans. It is usually assumed that the first five names come from a genuine ancestor list, while Woden was added to give the family an impressive divine origin and Caesar was inserted to show a spurious Roman origin to the family's power.

It was not Wehha who established the dynasty in power. That feat was performed by his son Wuffa, after whom the dynasty was later named the Wuffingas. The name Wuffa means 'Little Wolf', a reasonable enough name for a warrior chieftain and mercenary leader. The date on which Wuffa grabbed power can only be guessed at from the fact that his grandson died in 624. A date coinciding with Ceawlin's defeat is certainly in order.

The only fact that we know about Wuffa's seizure of power is that it was total. There are no surviving records of events in the civitas of the Iceni after the withdrawal of Roman rule in 410. While other civitates to the west and north left records in the form of genealogies of noblemen, unreliable biographies of real saints and poems praising warriors and nobles, the Iceni left nothing. Almost two centuries of history, culture and events were wiped out without a trace. Whether the Iceni had become a dictatorship or retained some form of democracy they would have produced sizeable amounts of bureaucratic paperwork regarding taxation and expenditure. Title deeds to lands and estates would have been written up and witnessed. The bishops of Norwich would have compiled lists of clergy, issued pastoral instructions and kept track of Church lands and investments. Minstrels would have sung the praises of nobles and warriors. All this must have gone on for generations in the civitas of the Iceni as it did elsewhere, but not a trace remains today. Wuffa destroyed it all.

It would seem that there were no survivors of the old ruling caste. Wuffa's coup was launched using the spears of his Germanic warriors, and it was the ruling elite that were his targets. We have already seen how some degree of animosity had been building up between the Germanic infantry and the much less numerous British elite cavalry. That ethnic friction seems to have boiled over into a bloodletting that was awesome in its scale. The records of British states further west have no trace of survivors from the nobility of the civitas of the Iceni escaping west. Wuffa must have killed them all. Nor did any praise poems survive to be found in the Welsh Triads or other poetic works. The minstrels and historians must have been butchered as well. Perhaps a few men did survive to be kept as slaves by the triumphant Wuffa, and he may had kept a few of the womenfolk to be slaves or concubines. But Wuffa's triumph was total.

Wuffa's coup did not represent just a change in the ruling elite. That is what had happened in Gaul, Spain and elsewhere. The result had been that the Germanic invaders had taken over and preserved the functioning post-Roman bureaucracy, using it to extract taxes and revenues from their new conquests. That did not happen in the civitas of the Iceni. Wuffa was an Angle with an Anglian culture and an Anglian religion, and he meant to keep both.

The new style of English rule by kings did not need the complex written bureaucracy of the Roman-style state. Nor did the pagan religion possess a written Bible. Wuffa did not need to send off accounts and reports to Rome for he was the king and supreme ruler of his lands. The chief landowners and leading warriors in the new Kingdom of the East Angles were few enough in number for Wuffa to know them all by name, and for them to know him. This was an oral culture that placed emphasis on memory, oaths taken in public and shared experiences. The abilities to read and write were not needed by Wuffa, so they were lost. The old books were thrown out, used as kindling to light fires or left to rot.

Christianity was not wanted either. That was the religion of the despised previous rulers. It had been shown to be a failure, crushed by the triumphant paganism of Wuffa's spearmen. Nobody wanted to worship a God who failed his followers so spectacularly. If Christianity was not stamped out as a foreign faith whose priests were potential traitors, it withered away and died of its own accord.

This attitude by Wuffa and his nobles was reinforced by the relatively high number of Germanic immigrants. The Angles were not a tiny minority in the lands they now ruled, but a sizeable chunk of the population. Unlike the Franks, they did not need to learn the language and culture of the people they ruled if they were to be accepted in the long term. The boot was on the other foot here. It was the conquered who would have to learn the language and the culture of their new masters if they were to thrive in the new political situation. The state and its servants spoke English, so a farmer wanting to argue about his taxes had to speak English too. We know that in some areas at least the English lords favoured farmers who were English over those who were British. A Briton would find it advantageous to wear English-style clothes, use English tools and worship English gods. Before long his descendents would be English.

Archeology can trace the change in culture of the inhabitants of East Anglia from British to English. Within fifty years of Wuffa's take over, British-style burials had ceased to take place. English style jewellery and pottery was ubiquitous on farms and other living sites. By the time the Kingdom of East Anglia emerges into the written record in the 650s its population was exclusively English. So thorough had this cultural shift been that nobody claimed descent from the Romans or the Britons. Everyone in East Anglia was English and, so far as they knew or were willing to admit, their ancestors had always been English as well.

We can deduce the speed of the linguistic take over by adopting what has been termed the 'three generation model'. For the later sixth century we think that men married, on average, at about the age of twenty-five at which age they were likely to have inherited or acquired a patch of land to farm or some other means of supporting a wife and children. It is thought that most men were dead by the age of fifty, though a good number lived to sixty and very few into their nineties. Women tended to marry and die younger.

It can be assumed that anyone aged over about fifty at the time of Wuffa's coup – let us call them First Generation Subjects – would be highly unlikely to want to learn a new language or adopt a new culture. They would have remained monoglot speakers of Brythonic to the day of their death and continued to wear British clothes and worship Christ. Their children, ambitious youngsters aged between twenty and thirty – Second Generation Subjects – on the other hand, would have realized the advantages of adopting some English culture, particularly language and religion. They would probably have become quickly bilingual and been at least tolerant of paganism if they did not adopt it themselves. Those born after the coup – Third Generation Subjects – would have grown up with English as their first language and in a predominantly English culture. Their only Brythonic would have been a basic vocabulary to communicate with grandpa in the corner.

Assuming Wuffa took power in around 595, the progression of the generations of his subjects would have been roughly as follows.

> First Generation Subjects would have been born about 555, married about 580 and died around 615.
>
> Second Generation Subjects would have been born around 570, married about 595 and died around 630.
>
> Third Generation Subjects would have been born about 595, married about 620 and died about 655.

It can be seen that among the subjects of Wuffa and his descendents, a working knowledge of the Brythonic language would have become extinct by 615, and along with it died Christianity, fashions and culture. By the 650s the population would have been uniformly English in culture and ethnicity.

It was not only in the civitas of the Iceni that a violent and total takeover by the English took place. To the south of the Iceni lay the civitas of the Trinovantes with its capital at the great walled city of Camulodunum (Colchester). This is one of the few areas where the populations of Britons and Germanic immigrants are found intermingled in the archaeological record. It was a Saxon named Sledda who overthrew the British rulers of the Trinovantes. He died in 604, but the date of his coup is unknown.

Sledda is said to have been the son of a warrior named Aescwine who is recorded as having brought a large force of soldiers across the North Sea in 527. That seems a rather long time gap for a father-son inheritance so it may be that Sledda was a grandson of Aescwine, or perhaps there was no blood relationship and he was merely the leader of the local Germanic warriors who had first been brought over by Aescwine.

As with Wuffa, Sledda seems to have organized a particularly brutal and wide-ranging coup. We have no written sources, legends, poems or other accounts of Trinovantean history at all. It is as if they were simply wiped off the face of the map. Presumably the entire ruling elite was despatched. The Kingdom of the East Saxons, as the civitas of the Trinovantes became, was thoroughly converted to English speech and culture remarkably quickly, but counted as English by 610. In 616 Christian missionaries were driven out by force and the area remained solidly pagan for another fifty years.

The civitas of the Corieltauvi seems to have been subjected to two English power grabs. The northern half of the civitas was centred around the Roman city of Lindum (Lincoln) and by 625 it was the English Kingdom of Lindsey. This state was later swallowed by the larger Kingdom of Mercia and all that we have is a list of ancestors of the later kings.

This ancestor list goes back to the pagan god Woden and assorted legendary figures, but the earliest historical figure seems to have been Wintra. This mercenary leader was stationed in the Roman fort of Adabum, which stood on Ermine Street where it crossed the Humber Estuary by ferry on its way from London to York. North of the estuary was a different civitas, that of the Parisii. Perhaps Wintra was there to guard the border crossing point. The modern villages of Winterton and Winterham were named in his honour. We have no firm date for Wintra, but he may have lived around the 440s.

Wintra is followed in the ancestor list of Lindsey by Cretta, Cuelgils and Caedbaed. Nothing is known of these men, but they all have British names. They may represent genuine ancestors who felt it wise to adopt British names while the British were the power in the land. On the other hand, they might be the British rulers of the Corieltauvi whose names were later hijacked by the English usurpers to give their rule some mask of legitimacy. Nor would it be the first time that an invader or usurper had married the daughter of the man he ousted to give his own son a legitimate claim to power. After Caedbaed comes Bubba, a solidly Anglian name, in turn followed by the equally English names of Beda, Biscop, Eanferth, Eatta and Aldfrith, who died in around 796. It would seem that it was either Bubba or Beda who grabbed power in Lincoln and its surrounding lands.

As in the civitas of the Iceni, the takeover at Lincoln was total and apparently violent. Again, no survivors from the ruling elite of the civitas got away alive, nor was any trace left of their names, history or achievements. The British culture was utterly eradicated. When a Christian missionary arrived for a brief visit in 625 he found a population all of whom spoke English and all of whom were pagans.

The southern half of the civitas of the Corieltauvi was centred on Ratae Corieltauvorum (Leicester). It later grew into the powerful Kingdom of Mercia, and has an early history that parallels that of Lindsey. Like the ancestor list of Lindsey, that of Mercia has as its earliest historic figure a man with an Anglian name. This is Icel, after whom the dynasty of the Iclingas was named. We know that he was a son of Eomer who ruled Angeln in the early fifth century. Icel came to Britain with a large force of mercenaries and their families. A cluster of places named after Icel are found in eastern Cambridgeshire, indicating that the Corieltauvi may have hired him to watch the border with the civitas of the Iceni, as Wintra guarded that with the Parisii. Icel's ancestors are remembered as being Eomer, son of Angeltheow, son of Offa, son of Wermund, son of Wihtlaeg, son of Woden. Again the dynasty originated with the pagan god Woden, but the other names seem to be those of genuine rulers or nobles living in and around Angeln.

Like Wintra, Icel is followed in the ancester list by three British names – Cnebba, Cynewald and Cretta, then by the English names of Pybba, Penda, Eowa and Paeda. Presumably the British names were included for the same reasons as those in the ancestor list of Lindsey. We know that Pybba died in about 620 and a later source says that he began his rule in 596. Thus it would seem that it was Pybba who led the English spearmen to grab power in the southern lands of the Corieltauvi. Again the takeover was utterly complete with no survivors from the previous ruling elite. When Christian missionaries arrived in the 650s, this was a totally English and exclusively pagan land.

The civitas of the Parissi suffered the same fate, and at about the same time. Germanic warriors had been stationed here since around the 450s and do not seem to have been present in such large numbers as south of the Humber. But that did not save the rulers of the Parisii. At a date around 597 (or perhaps 581 in another source) a man with the Germanic name of Aelle grabbed power in the civitas. Little is known about Aelle, but his ancestor list is tells us that he was the son of Yffe, the son of Uxfrea, the son of Wilgisl, the son of Westerfalca, the son of Saefugl, the son of Saebald, the son of Segegeat, the son of Swebdag, the son of Sigegar, the son of Waedaeg, the son of Woden. These are all Germanic names, most of them Saxon. Waedaeg is recorded in some sources as having been a ruler in Saxony on the continent some time in the third century, though some scholars believe he was a mythological ancestor figure with no basis in reality. Woden, of course, was the warrior god of the English and may be presumed to have been included to give Aelle a divine ancestry.

Once again the takeover seems to have been brutal and swift. No sources survive of Parisii history after the Roman withdrawal, so it is fairly safe to conclude that Aelle wiped out the ruling elite of the area. The kingdom he founded was named Deira, apparently after the main town of Derventio (now Malton). The Kingdom of Deira was thoroughly English by around 620, but may not have been as decisively paganized as the kingdoms farther south. Aelle's grandson Edwin would convert to Christianity in 627 along with most of his nobles. From the account of the conversion of the king given by Bede there are hints that some at least of the population of Deira was already Christian, or at least familiar with Christian teachings.

As we have seen the civitas of the Catuvellauni was the largest and probably the most prosperous in Roman Britain. At some point it was fragmented into a number of smaller states. This book has argued that the one man with the motive to do this was

Ceawlin after he had defeated the Catuvellauni and sought to reduce their power to rise against him. Such a collection of small states would have made easy prey for warrior chiefs seeking to gain independent power for themselves. Unfortunately the process is poorly understood.

The city of London and the area to its north was later known as the land of the Middle Saxons. The land south of London was Surrey, the 'southern region' – presumably of the Middle Saxons. It seems, but cannot be proved, that this key region was secured for Ceawlin by garrisons of Belgic troops. In the mayhem that followed Ceawlin's fall the land of the Middle Saxons seems to have passed to Sledda and the East Saxons. Perhaps the local garrison commander chose to throw in his lot with Sledda and was given some form of local autonomy in return. The sources for the early history of the Middle Saxons are poor but do seem to hint at some sort of sub-king being in place at some point.

North of the Middle Saxons lay the lands later known as those of the Middle Angles, which stretched north to the Wash. These Middle Angles emerge into history in 653 when St Cedd arrived to try to convert them to Christianity. By this date the whole area was pagan, spoke English and was as English in culture as it was possible to be. The Middle Angles were a part of the Kingdom of Mercia, but seem to have had some sort of local power. Whether they had ever been an independent kingdom ruled by early English rulers who overthrew the weak post-Catuvellaunian states is unknown.

The situation regarding the South Angles is even more poorly known. They seem to have occupied the area around Towcester and St Albans, but almost nothing is known about them.

The Dobunni of the lower Severn had been divided by Ceawlin. Ceawlin had installed a number of Germanic garrisons in the northern section of the lands of the Dobunni. These seem to have grabbed power and set themselves up as an English kingdom called the Hwicce. The name Hwicce means 'holy cauldron' and may refer to a local Celtic goddess the Mater Dobunnica who is usually shown carrying a bucket-like object. If so, then the local English rulers may have been seeking to soothe their subjects by adopting a local deity. This would make sense as the English here were greatly outnumbered by the native Britons and it is not entirely clear how quickly the area lost its British identity and adopted that of the English. By 628 the sub-kings of the Hwicce had fallen under control of Mercia. Thereafter the pace of change may have been rapid.

By the year 600, therefore, all the civitates that had employed Germanic mercenaries had been overthrown. The British culture had been exterminated and the entire region become solidly English in speech, culture and religion. It was a truly cataclysmic change that changed Britain forever and in more drastic fashion than perhaps any other event in known history.

It has been suggested that there may have been a guiding hand behind this rapid and dramatic chain of events. At some date around the year 595 the title of Bretwalda – the English form of Wide Ruler – was claimed by Ethelbert, King of Kent. This was the Ethelbert who had been defeated by Ceawlin and Cutha at Wibbandune in 568, now a much older and a wiser man. In the meantime he had married Bertha, a princess from the Frankish ruling dynasty, and secured a grip on trade across the Channel to the realms of his Frankish in laws. He had grown richer and more powerful, but his kingdom was still fairly small and apparently weak in military terms.

It has always been a bit of a puzzle how he got himself to be recognized as Bretwalda. The answer may lie in the way in which the English took over so much of Britain so quickly. If Ethelbert, perhaps at Frankish urging, backed the rebels with money or men he would very easily have earned their respect and allegiance. That allegiance may not have had any great practical result in terms of money or resources, but it would have been enough to get him hailed as the Wide Ruler, or Bretwalda.

Thereafter no Briton ever claimed the title of Wide Ruler. Geoffrey of Monmouth may be unreliable on details, but at this point his lament for what was lost sounds genuine enough.

> Thereafter did the Britons lose the crown of the kingdom and the sovereignty of the island, nor made they any endeavour to recover their former dignity. On the contrary, they did many a time and oft lay waste that part of the country which did still remain unto them, subject now not unto one ruler only but unto tyrants.

The title of Bretwalda was then held exclusively by English kings. They seem to have viewed the title as bringing with it a superior position over other rulers that indicated prestige rather than power, glory rather than goods and fame rather than taxes. So far as we can tell the successive Bretwaldas made little attempt to force lesser rulers to pay tribute, though they did frequently seek to interfere with dynastic marriages, land grants and other internal matters.

But there was one British civitas that had employed Germanic mercenaries that was not swept away by the welter of rebellion and bloodshed. That was the civitas of the Belgae, Ceawlin's homeland. As we have seen it was an internal civil war in the Belgae that probably sparked the rash of English takeovers across lowland Britain. But in the lands of the Belgae, the Germanic soldiers had gained something of an upper hand as a result of the civil war. The new ruler may have been Ceol, but he had won power with the support of the Gewisse. As we have seen this probably led to a marriage alliance either by Ceol himself or his son Cynegils. Before long the rulers of the Belgae had English names such as Ine and Ethelheard.

The lands became pagan and adopted an English culture. The civitas of the Belgae, with the addition of the civitates of the Atrebates and Durotriges, became the Kingdom of the West Saxons. The change here from British to English may have been less violent than elsewhere, but it was no less complete. The newly English Kingdom of Wessex gradually pushed into lands that had been the civitas of Dumnonia. Somerset was captured by 650 and much of Devon soon after. By 750 Dumnonia had been driven back to the River Tamar and covered only what is now Cornwall. There the British remained in control both politically and culturally. Cornwall became a part of Wessex in around 850, but the Cornish language survived as the preferred tongue of the area to the 1690s, but died out around 1800. Efforts are now being made to revive the Cornish language.

Ceawlin had set out to make himself Wide Ruler of a Christian, British, literate state covering all of formerly Roman Britain. He had instead begun a chain of events that by 600 had turned the bulk of that land into a collection of pagan, English, illiterate kingdoms with an overall monarch using the title of Wide Ruler in its English form of Bretwalda. A new nation had been created: the English.

The English may have been created by the year 600, but England had not. The civitates that had not hired Germanic mercenaries remained British in culture and speech, but many of them would not survive long. The area north of the Dee and Humber was remembered by the later Welsh as Hen Ogledd – the Old North. British control here lasted for some years and when the English finally took over there were enough survivors of the nobles of Hen Ogledd to preserve something of their history in later Welsh annals and poetry.

Bryneich was a state stretching from Hadrian's Wall on the Tyne north up the east side of the Pennines to somewhwere near modern Dunbar. The *Anglo-Saxon Chronicle* records that in 547 an Anglian ruler named Ida had been in possession of Bamburgh, and probably Lindisfarne, but his power did not extend beyond these two border fortresses. In about 575 or perhaps a little earlier, the rulers of Hen Ogledd united under Urien, Prince of Rheged, to attack the Anglians, then led by Adda, son of Ida. The campaign was a brilliant success and soon the Anglians were isolated on Lindisfarne and facing surrender caused by starvation. But then Morgant Bwlch, ruler of Bryneich, murdered Urien fearing that he would seek to annex Bryneich as soon as Adda was defeated. The murder led to the gradual destruction of the Old North as the various rulers were never again able to unite against the English.

By 600 Bryneich had fallen to Adda's nephew Aethelric. Aethelric was by this date also ruling York, which for a time had been a small British state, and was also firmly in control of the Craven. Only Elmet, roughly modern West Yorkshire, remained under British control east of the Pennines. In 617 the last ruler of Elmet, Ceredig ap Gwallog, was ousted by King Edwin of Deira who then took over the area and began the process of turning the local Britons into English.

The lands west of the Pennines fell under the state of Rheged. This was ruled by a powerful dynasty, of which Urien was only the most famous, from Cynfarch Oer in the 550s to Owain mab Urien who may have died around 630. In 638 King Oswiu of Bernicia married Riemmelth of Rheged and their son Egfrith inherited both lands. He also conquered Deira and thus created the mighty Kingdom of Northumbria that covered all of what is now northern England. The Brythonic language survived in what had been Rheged for generations and does not seem to have died out until the tenth century. Christianity remained the faith of the people of Rheged throughout and the early English culture was never really adopted.

Thus did post-Roman Britain become England.

Conclusion

The Heirs of Ceawlin

It all happened a very long time ago, so one might ask if the train of events described in this book is all that important. I hope that I have established that they are of crucial importance to the development of modern Britain, and indeed of the world in general.

If the Germanic settlers had not taken over the rich and productive lands of southern and eastern Britain in the way they did in the later sixth century then the people of Britain would today be speaking a language descended from Brythonic Celtic, as do the Welsh and Bretons. Instead we speak English. And with the language came a host of other English cultural traits that have since come to define the English.

Those first English scorned to learn the language of the peoples that they conquered, instead forcing the more numerous Britons to speak English. The disinclination of the English to learn a foreign language has never wavered. Any white-skinned tourist struggling to order a beer on the Costa del Sol is continuing the culture he has inherited from his forbears more than a millennium ago. If they want to sell meals or souvenirs to English tourists, then waiters and shopkeepers around the world have to learn enough English to seal the deal. Some things do not change.

The early English did not share the complex inheritance laws of the Britons. Instead they favoured leaving their lands and wealth to the eldest son to keep the family estates intact. This primogeniture ensured both that such estates remained intact, but also that there was a constant stream of well-educated and ambitious younger sons sent out into the world to carve a career for themselves. On such foundations did the English go out to hammer the French at Crécy and Agincourt, colonize lands far overseas and instill a sense of get-up-and-go that is still with us.

There have also been long-lasting political and constitutional implications for the events that followed on from the fall of Ceawlin. It will be remembered that the Roman Emperor Honorius told the British civitates to choose their own Vicarius until such time as legitimate Roman authority could be restored. This they did. Ceawlin was the last of the Britons to hold the position of Wide Ruler that descended from the office of Vicarius. The Vicarius had had power over all of mainland Britain south of Hadrian's Wall, and later Wide Rulers had sought to enforce their influence over the same territory.

After Ceawlin, the title passed to the English in the form of Bretwalda. They too sought to exercise a vague but still very real overlordship over Britain south of the Wall. The list of men using the title of Bretwalda after Ceawlin is usually given as follows, though there is some disagreement over one or two of these rulers.

Ethelbert King of Kent (590–616)

Raedwald King of East Anglia (c600–24)

Edwin King of Deira (616–33)

Oswald King of Northumbria (633–42)

Oswiu King of Northumbria (642–70)

Wulfhere King of Mercia (658–675)

Ethelred King of Mercia (675–704, died 716)

Ethelbald King of Mercia (716–757)

Offa King of Mercia (757–796)

Cœnwulf King of Mercia (796–821)

Egbert King of Wessex (829–39)

The last-named of these Bretwaldas allowed the title to lapse and in its place adopted a new title, that of King of the English. Undoubtedly he understood this title to mean the same as Bretwalda and he claimed overlordship of the various rulers in Wales as well as those in England. The Kings of Wessex continued to use the title King of the English thereafter. Indeed, it was this title that Alfred the Great used to justify his wars of aggression against the Viking settlers who had taken over other English kingdoms. His heirs and successors would slowly make the claim to overlordship into a very real rule over a centralized and united Kingdom of England by about AD 950.

But the claim to overlordship of the Welsh princes had not been forgotten. In 973 King Edgar of England held a lavish ceremony at Chester to which he summoned the Princes of Wales and the rulers of Strathclyde and the Scots. At this ceremony he restated the claims to be the overall lord of Britain and demonstrated his power in a very real way. He had eight of the princes row him in his royal barge up and down the Dee outside the walls of Chester, while he steered the vessel. It demonstrated in very clear terms that although the lesser princes were powerful in their own right, it was Edgar who had overall control.

Later English monarchs retained this sense of superiority over the Welsh rulers. The princes were generally left to rule their lands as they saw fit, but the English kings reserved the right to interfere whenever they felt like it. English kings arranged marriages and inheritances in Wales, and were not above sending in armies to kill any Welsh ruler who had incurred the displeasure of the King of England. All this they considered theirs by right. It was not until the Norman kings took over in England that the relationships between Kings of England and Welsh princes changed. The Normans interpreted their overlordship in a strict and defined way. They saw the Welsh princes as no better than nobles of England, not as rulers in their own lands. In 1284 King Edward I imposed the Statue of Rhuddlan which set in stone his interpretation of the overlordship, that Wales was part of England and would henceforth be run as such. Not until devolution in 1997 were the institutional ties between England and Wales loosened again.

Meanwhile, relations between England and the Scots followed a different trajectory. The title of Bretwalda implied no overlordship north of Hadrian's Wall. Such English rule as extended north of the old Wall on the east coast came from the English conquest of Bryneich, not from any ancient constitutional arrangement. It was not until a King of Scotland inherited the throne of England through his English grandmother in 1603 that the mainland of Great Britain was united under one ruler.

Like Scotland, Ireland had never been subject to the Vicarius of Britain, and was likewise never any part of the realms of the Wide Ruler. English rule in Ireland came later and for complex dynastic reasons, as well as a perceived need by the Kings of England to control a potentially hostile neighbour.

But it is not only the relationships between the nations of Britain that can be traced back to the actions of Honorius. The legal right to rule over lands passed down from Honorius to later emperors until 476 when the regalia of the Western Roman Empire was sent to Constantinople to be united with that of the Eastern Roman Empire. In strictly legal terms all the lands of the western Empire – Italy, France, Spain, North Africa – were then ruled by their local barbarian kings exercising power by permission of the Emperor in Constantinople. The Eastern Emperors always intended to win back real power over the West at some point and from time to time they launched major campaigns that in part succeeded.

It was for this reason that the Empress Irene reacted with such fury when Pope Leo III crowned the Frankish ruler Charlemagne as Emperor of Rome in the year 800. Legally, Leo had no power to bestow the title and Charlemagne had no business accepting it. The title of Emperor and the legal right to rule lay exclusively with the Empress in Constantinople. The rift between eastern and western Christendom that was caused by the existence of usurper emperors in the west was never healed.

In 1453 Constantinople fell to the armies of Sultan Mehmet II of the Ottoman Turks. Emperor Constantine XI died fighting as the Turks surged into his imperial city. Mehmet then claimed the title of Emperor for himself, citing not only his possession of Constantinople but also the fact that his mother had been a granddaughter of a former Emperor. The title continued to be held by the Ottoman sultans until the forced abdication of Abdulmecid II in 1924. The legal rights of the ancient Roman Emperors then finally came to an end.

Except, of course, in Britain. There the devolved powers of the Vicarius had been handed on to the Wide Rulers, then to the Bretwaldas and so to the Kings of England. In the person of Queen Elizabeth II that legal power remains today in the hands of the latest in an unbroken line of holders of legitimate power that stretches right back to the Roman Emperors. Today Britain is being absorbed slowly into a new multinational empire, the European Union. It is perhaps ironic that the EU looks back for inspiration to the Empire founded by Charlemagne – for in legal terms Charlemagne was nothing better than a jumped-up barbarian usurper.

Bibliography – Further Reading

Most of the major sources – Gildas, Nennius, the *Anglo-Saxon Chronicle* – are available in a number of different modern translations with varying amounts of glossing and explanation. Some of the more obscure source material, such as the *Welsh Triads*, are not generally available but can be found. In addition the following make for good general reading on this obscure period in British history.

In Search Of The Dark Ages by Michael Wood, ISBN 978-0563522768, is a useful collection of mini-biographies that covers the early English period, though most of it is concerned with dates after Ceawlin.

Battles of the Dark Ages by Peter Marren, ISBN 978-1844158843 is a great read about warfare in this period, though again it is mostly concerned with later battles that are better documented than those of Ceawlin's day.

Britannia – The Failed State by Stuart Laycock, ISBN 978-0752446141, is an interesting and rather controversial look at the collapse of post-Roman Britain that draws on modern comparisons to the break-up of Yugoslavia and the Soviet Union in the later twentieth century.

More controversial still is *The Age Of Arthur* by John Morris, ISBN 978-0297176015. In his day Morris was the pre-eminent expert on post-Roman Britain and this monumental work represents the culmination of his scholarship. However, he is now considered to be terribly old-fashioned and out of date. This is not to say he is wrong, merely that fashions have moved on.

Arthur and the Fall of Roman Britain by Edwin Pace, ISBN 978-0955420146, is a good account of the years before Ceawlin, as is *The Reign of Arthur* by Christopher Gidlow, ISBN 978-0750934190. There are many other books dealing with the time of Arthur on the market.

Index